UNITED STATES

NATIONAL BANK NOTES

AND THEIR SEALS

by Dewitt G. Prather

Visited Longwood College
Dec. 1st, 1987

Dewitt G. Prather

UNITED STATES
NATIONAL BANK NOTES
AND THEIR SEALS

...

by

DEWITT G. PRATHER

Edited by
J. S. Prather
& Angela Prather

International Standard Book Number: 0-9616836-0-0
Library of Congress Catalog Card Number: 86-90441

Typography:
Angela Prather

First Printing:

Multi-Print, Inc.
Hampton, Va.

IN DEDICATION

This book is respectfully dedicated to my friend and partner, Richard Dreger, for his dedication to numismatics, for his determination in attaining the finest notes possible, for his faith and trust in me, and for his generosity in calling it "The Prather Collection." Cooperating with me and at the same time allowing me the thrill of discovering the rarities — working together, and pooling our resources, we were able to acquire many of the great rarities, which, singly, neither of us would have been able to procure.

This endeavor has been in progress for several years, and is still ongoing. Indeed, I am proud and honored to be associated with Mr. Dreger who is now the owner of "The Prather Collection" of United States National Bank Notes.

Syngraphically,

Dewitt G. Prather
SOPMC #862

ACKNOWLEDGEMENTS

First of all, my grateful appreciation goes to the several dealers and collectors who over the years have encouraged me to write this book: Arthur Kagin, Aubrey E. Bebee, Paul Kagin, Abe Kosoff, L.S. Werner, "Bill" Donlon, Amon Carter, Jr., W.A. Philpott, Jr. and others.

A special word of thanks is due to many people who have helped me or otherwise contributed to this book:

William Anton, Jr.
Richard Dreger
Frank Hannah
Gene Hessler
John T. Hickman
Ronald Horstmann
Frank Howard
Peter Huntoon
Paul H. Johansen
Don C. Kelly
George A. Nicholson
Dean Oakes
Morey Perlmutter
Robert V. Polito
Fred Schwan
Austin M. Sheheen

et. al, my sincere appreciation for their great help and expertise.

To Packaging Art & Design, Charlotte, NC; Lee Kolbe and his two sons, Mitchell (for 29) and Scott (for 3) for drawing and watercoloring in full color a total of 32 seals (PLATES IX - XVI), present-day seals and those from banknotes, to completely represent seals and changes.

Lem Whitsett, Mickey Brigman, George Saunders, and others at Pictorial Engraving, Inc., East Trade Street, Charlotte, NC, for their brilliant work with the reproduction and printing of the color plates.

Frank Howard for providing a chart, compliments of the Shiloh Gold Exchange: "Types of United States National Bank Notes: The Three Charter Periods and Time Spans of the Major Designs"

To my wife and daughter-in-law, thanks are due for their patience in putting up with me and for all the help given.

Special thanks goes to my son, without whose help there would very likely be no book. For his knowledge, help, and guidance in doing most all of the work in preparing the manuscript and taking his time to put it all on his computer, I owe him a huge debt of gratitude.

To my daughter Angela, in printing for ten years, I extend my heartfelt thanks. As a result of her experience she rendered much advice as final editor, as well as typesetter. Giving unstintingly of her time, aside from her regular work, and with the help and cooperation of her employer and fellow employees at Homes & Land Publishing Corporation in Tallahassee, Florida, the graphics, artwork, and page layouts for this book all came together. Working together at close range for several weeks in Tallahassee I came truly to appreciate how much work had to be done. For her dedication and zeal, I owe a great debt of thanks.

Thanks go as well to Sally Warner and Margo Nagy for their cooperation and can-do attitudes in proofreading and further correcting our errors. Without their help, our task would have been much more difficult.

Renee Carpenter-Vivas, Leonard Bowen, Sylvia Finkell and Richard Pinson gave their assistance in paste-up, artwork, electonic page makeup and camera work at Homes & Land Publishing Corporation. Not least, great thanks go to Lee Rodgers, for invaluable support, assistance and weekend time.

And to Homes & Land Publishing Corporation, Tallahassee, Florida: for the use of computers and state-of-the-art equipment, enabling us to electronically compose and preview each page before typesetting, we are greatly indebted. With the understanding cooperation of the management at Homes & Land, the book has materialized.

All facts in this book come from other books, which are credited as far as possible, or from 25 or 30 years of personal conversations and experience. Obviously, some statements herein may be proven false in time, and the number of rare notes will change from time to time. Please forgive any and all errors in this book — especially on any signatures which may have been misread. Corrections and further information are welcome.

STATE ARMS OF THE UNION —
A FEW WORDS ABOUT THE COLOR PLATES

This past June (1985) at the Memphis Paper Money show I was talking to a friend, from whom I had bought several rare National Bank Notes. I was relating to him the difficulty I was having getting some color into my book: how the National Geographic Society refused twice to let me use their artwork in the July 1946 issue of their magazine; also how Fleetwood had likewise turned me down. I even offered to pay what I consider a sizable sum just to rent their color separations on the recent series "Seals of the 50 States" on first-day covers. My friend told me he had something at home I might be able to use.

Soon after my returning home, a registered package arrived with a note saying if I could not use "the book", please register it for $1000. and return it; if I could use it, to keep it until August 1st, then register it for the same amount and return. He said nothing about selling it to me. Quickly, I called my copyright lawyer, told him about it and that the title page said "Copyright 1876 ...." My lawyer said that even if the copyright had been renewed the copyright would have expired long ago and that I could use it in any way desired.

I was ecstatic! The art work was superb! Everyone I showed it to was also excited. A commercial-art-oriented businessman friend said that if I did not buy it, he would like to buy it. That did it; I just had to have it, so I bought the rare book of 8 pages.

Next, I spent two or three weeks finding a graphic arts engraving firm willing to do the color separations and negative work. Finally I found one, Pictorial Engraving, Inc., of Charlotte, North Carolina, who offered to try two items from the "book" to show me what they could do.

These beautiful state arms were engraved long ago, when that kind of craftsmanship was more affordable. The cost of producing such art work today would be prohibitive.

The book contained, between completely severed brown cloth covers, a flyleaf, and, as shown, a handsome title page showing a large fierce-looking eagle and seven more pages showing 45 *STATE ARMS OF THE UNION*. The paper has aged and is quite brittle, and I will preserve it with care.

The real beauty of the arms (and later, seals) is the exquisite art work, especially the *gold* portions. They look as though the artist has laid on the beautiful gold with his brush. Over half the arms have fancy gold frames surrounding them. Two state arms have much gold work on them (as do South Carolina and Colorado). All are highlighted as with tints like varnish. One of the graphics workmen counted the different colors on one and said there were ten colors that he counted; they used the standard four colors (negatives) to reproduce it, adding a gold ink. The technique is a difficult one. They talked of having to remove the gold color and then add it again at the end, and told me that an employee spent three weeks on this "cut-work" alone.

Sadly, all printed pictures, both colored and black and white, lose something in reproduction. I am so well pleased, however, that I think the engravers achieved 95% or more of the quality of the original. Their company has won an award for this work in an annual contest sponsored by a professional organization to which they belong.

This "signature" of eight plates was done using special inks and using the offset method. The colors were printed and applied in the following order: 1-gold (which was run through the press twice), 2-blue (cyan), 3-red (magenta), 4-black and 5-yellow. Like other metallic reproduction the light must fall just right to reflect the true gold color.

Inasmuch as the first set of plates (I through VIII) show only 45 "State Arms of the Union" (and the last of these are generally territorial seals) and one of the District of Columbia's seals, I felt it necessary to add a second signature (Plates IX through XVI). In the first set of plates, the following "arms" are missing: the Dakotas (South Dakota is represented only by the [then-shared] arms of Dakota Territory, which, altered, became North Dakota's state seal), Washington, plus the later states like Oklahoma, Arizona, Alaska and Hawaii. Also, the arms shown for Wyoming, Utah and Idaho, though shown, are all more like the territorial seals, and mostly very different from the later state seals. There were eight states plus the District of Columbia which showed a second or changed seal on "brownback" notes (Second Charter Period National Bank Notes, Series 1882, first part).

To represent all the states and to show all the seals that appeared on the National Bank Notes, I asked an artist to draw and watercolor for me 32 more seals. A few states' seals as shown here are near duplicates of the arms. Several were drawn from the actual pictures of the seals as found on the notes. These seals are also shown in the order that the states came into the Union, as are most of those included in the rare book.

COLOR PLATES

PLATE I: Title page. Note the 1876 copyright date, realizing that some of the states, even those represented, were still territories at that time. The book was issued to help commemorate the Centennial Celebration of Philadelphia, 1876.

PLATE II: *Top Row:* Massachusetts,[1] possibly shown first because of the book's Boston issue. (Massachusetts was the 6th state to enter the Union); New York (the eleventh state to enter), more closely resembles New York's first seal found on National Bank Notes; Pennsylvania (the Union's second state). *Bottom Row:* Rhode Island, (13th); New Hampshire, (9th state); Connecticut, (5th state); New Jersey, (3rd state).

PLATE III: *Top Row:* Virginia, (10th state); Maryland, (8th state). This is the second and present-day seal of Maryland; Delaware, (1st state). *Bottom Row:* North Carolina, (12th state). This is the second seal of North Carolina, presently in use; South Carolina, (8th state); Georgia, (4th state).

PLATE IV: *Top Row:* Vermont,[2] (14th state). This version is most like the second seal used on bank notes; Kentucky, (15th); Tennessee, (16th). *Bottom Row:* Ohio, (17th). This seal is similar to the second seal found on bank notes; Louisiana, (18th); Indiana, (19th).

PLATE V: *Top Row:* Mississippi, (20th); Illinois, (21st); Alabama, (22nd), shows the second seal on bank notes; Maine, (23rd). *Bottom Row:* Missouri, (24th); Arkansas, (25th); Michigan, (26th).

PLATE VI: *Top Row:* Florida, (27th); Iowa, (29th state), shows the present-day seal. The first seal on Iowa bank notes was not the state seal, but a different large eagle; Texas, (28th state). *Bottom Row:* Wisconsin, (30th). This looks like a cross between the two Wisconsin seals, but much more like the first; California, (31st); Minnesota, (32nd).

PLATE VII: *Top Row:* Oregon, (33rd); Kansas, (34th); West Virginia, (35th). *Bottom Row:* Nevada, (36th); Nebraska, (37th), shows the present-day seal. NOTE: ALL Nebraska bank notes, however, show the *territorial* seal; Colorado, (38th).

PLATE VIII: *Top Row: New Mexico, (47th state); Utah, (45th state). This shows the first, or territorial seal; Dakota, (39th and 40th states). The arms here shown is like the territorial seal; Montana, (41st state); Wyoming, (44th). This shows the territorial seal; District of Columbia, (District created, 1800; Seal adopted, 1871); the arms show the first seal of the District that appeared on the notes.*

NOTE: See text for further information on the seals.

PLATE IX: **Pennsylvania** seal (as contrasted with complete arms, on Plate II) does not show the two horses supporting the seal. State #2.

Maryland — This is the first seal used on Maryland notes. All of the first charter and part of the brownback notes used this seal. (Drawn from the bank note.) State #7.

South Carolina — Shows the obverse of their state seal. (Taken from the South Carolina notes — all seals on notes are the same). State #8.

New Hampshire — Taken from the bank note picture, this shows the workmen in the actual building of the *USS Raleigh*. Many modern versions show no workmen and the ship from different angles. State #9.

PLATE X: **New York** — This shows the second seal as found on the latter part of the brownback notes. Note that most all these second seals are similar to the state's present seal, referred to in this book as the "official" seal. State #11.

North Carolina — This is the first seal, taken from the earlier bank notes. State #12.

Vermont — This is the first seal shown on bank notes. The second seal used on bank notes is shown with the arms on Plate IV, with the elk's head as the crest. State #14.

Vermont — This is the "official" seal in use today, and is not shown on the notes. Because this is so different from the others, I show it here.

PLATE XI: **Ohio** — This is the first seal of Ohio as shown on nationals. The second or present-day seal shows 17 arrows on the *left* side of the sheath of wheat. State #17.

Mississippi — This is taken from the picture on the note. Somewhat different from the arms. State #20.

Illinois — Also taken from the note, and somewhat different from the arms. State #21.

Alabama — This is the first and present-day seal of Alabama. See text for further comments. State #22.

PLATE XII: **Arkansas** — This is taken from the bank note picture, shows the seal supported by two large eagles. State #25.

Florida — As shown on bank notes. The hills (or mountains) have now been eliminated. State #27.

Texas — The star and wreath on the Texas seal are all similar. State #28.

Iowa — First seal on Iowa notes. This is not a state seal. See comments in text. State #29.

PLATE XIII: **Wisconsin** — The second (present day) seal of Wisconsin, signifying development and fulfillment. State #30.

Oregon — Drawn from the banknote picture (refer to arms, PLATE VII, for minor differences). State #33.

Kansas — Drawn from the banknote picture (refer to arms, PLATE VII, for minor differences). State #34.

Nevada — Drawn from the banknote picture (refer to arms, PLATE VII, for minor differences). State #36.

PLATE XIV: **Nebraska** — This is the territorial seal of Nebraska, used through the entire banknote issuing period. It is altogether different from the state seal, which was not used on national bank notes. State #37.

North Dakota — This is the state seal of North Dakota (also see notes under seals). State #39.

South Dakota — This is the state seal of South Dakota (also see notes under seals). State #40.

Washington — This is the state seal of Washington — not pictured with the arms. State #42.

PLATE XV: **Idaho** — State seal of Idaho — very different from the territorial seal, which is similar to arms. State #43.

Wyoming — State seal of Wyoming, altogether different from the territorial seal (again, similar to arms). State #44.

PLATE XVI: **Utah** — State seal of Utah, adapted from the territorial seal. State #45.

Oklahoma — State seal of the 46th state — not shown on bank notes.

Arizona — State seal of the 48th state — not shown on bank notes.

Alaska — State seal of the 49th state — not shown on bank notes.

Hawaii — State seal of the 50th state — not shown on bank notes.

District of Columbia — This is the second, or present-day seal of the District.

[1] States #1 through #13 do not appear here in the order in which they entered the Union, an order which is followed throughout this book, and which is cross-referenced in several places as well. States 29 and 28 are in reverse order, and, as mentioned later, several of the latter states are not represented with the arms at all.

SPECIAL NOTICE

All materials in this book are copyrighted, and none may be reproduced without the express permission of the author. The notes pictured herein are reproduced at less than 75% of the original size, and may not be reproduced in any form — neither the seal nor any other part — without written permission of the owner of said note or notes.

The *State Arms of the Union*, (PLATES I through VIII), the original 110 years old, was reproduced at great expense to me, and now, incorporated into this book, are copyrighted.

For the original artwork for the second set of seals (PLATES IX through XVI) an artist was commissioned by the author expressly for this book, and likewise may not be reproduced without express written permission and consent.

FOREWORD

Historically speaking, the national bank note issues of the various towns and cities of the states and territories far outshine all the other major issues of old large-size United States currency.

From an artistic and aesthetic viewpoint, the national bank notes must rank very high among U.S. paper money, if indeed not at the top, especially when one considers the beautiful paintings reproduced on the back of each First Charter note. The reproductions of (and *changes* in) the state seals on the backs of the notes, as well as some of the territorial seals, have added to the fascination that has become my chief numismatic interest within the last 20 some years.

There are relatively major changes in the seals of eight states and the District of Columbia, most of which occurred between the years of 1890 and 1900. Also consider how some states used their territorial seals with certain adaptations for their new state seal. Nebraska used the territorial seal on all notes, never using the state seal. In some territories that had territorial seals, the banknote companies, or, later, the bureau, did not use the seals on the early (or any) territorial bank notes. Montana, Washington & Wyoming Territorial notes showed no seals. Territorial notes on Oklahoma (46th state to enter the Union), New Mexico (47th to enter), Arizona (48th), Alaska (49th) and Hawaii (50th), showed no seals because they entered the Union after the first part of the Second Charter Period (the time of the brownbacks, last notes to display the seals) was over.

The questions arising from the mysteries and inconsistencies, the uncertainties, and indeed the confusion resulting from the above circumstances have led me (in fact, driven me) to collect national bank notes and to make a study of the seals. In addition to these factors, the work of my predecessor, Dr. Frank A. Limpert's *United States National Bank Notes* (1953), now simply falls short of the mark. I say "simply," because many of the very rare notes had not been located at that time.

But now, some thirty more years have lapsed into history and all but two of the rarities have surfaced. One that has not is the Mississippi First Charter note. If and when it does come to light, it will have the Mississippi State Seal thereon, as does the "brownback." The second missing note is the Juneau, Alaska brownback. I feel certain that this will show no seal.

At the time of the Declaration of Independence all nations used their Coats of Arms or seals to authenticate documents. On that day, July 4, 1776, the Continental Congress appointed a committee "to bring in a seal." Seals used by states are heraldic in origin; sixteen qualify as armorial by having a shield as the main device. About half of our state seals have landscape designs: mountains, prairies, bodies of water; others have ships, wagons and trains; some have the rising sun indicating hope for the future; others have the setting sun over the western ranges to signify development.

To celebrate all the varied points of interest, and to show proof of similarities, exceptions and changes, I write this book.

Types of United States National Bank Notes

THE THREE CHARTER PERIODS AND TIME SPANS OF THE MAJOR DESIGNS

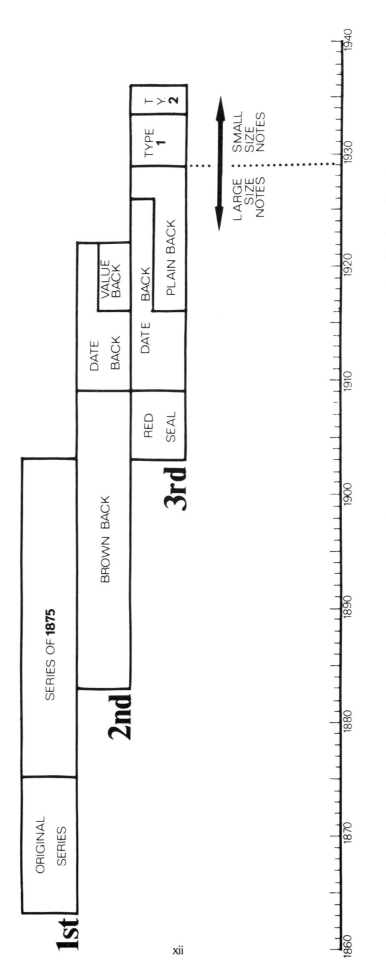

Overlapping of the Three Charter Periods and Time Spans of the Major Designs

COMPLIMENTS OF SHILOH GOLD EXCHANGE

225 THIRD STREET
P.O. BOX 886
MACON, GEORGIA 31202

GA. RESIDENTS:
912-743-8951/743-8952

OUT OF STATE TOLL FREE
1-800-841-8913

xii

TABLE OF CONTENTS

ALPHABETICAL CROSS-REFERENCE
OF COLOR PLATES, STATE NOTES AND SEALS

NOTES

The Arms of the
THIRTEEN ORIGINAL STATES

are in accordance with
the paintings deposited in
Independence Hall Philadelphia.
by the States.
For the other Arms the material
was supplied by the Executive
authorities of the various
STATES.

The Arms of the
STATES OF THE UNION
have been prepared
with the assistence of
MR. H. MITCHELL,
the well known Heraldic
Designer and Seal Engraver of
BOSTON.

ARMS OF THE UNITED STATES.

PLATE I

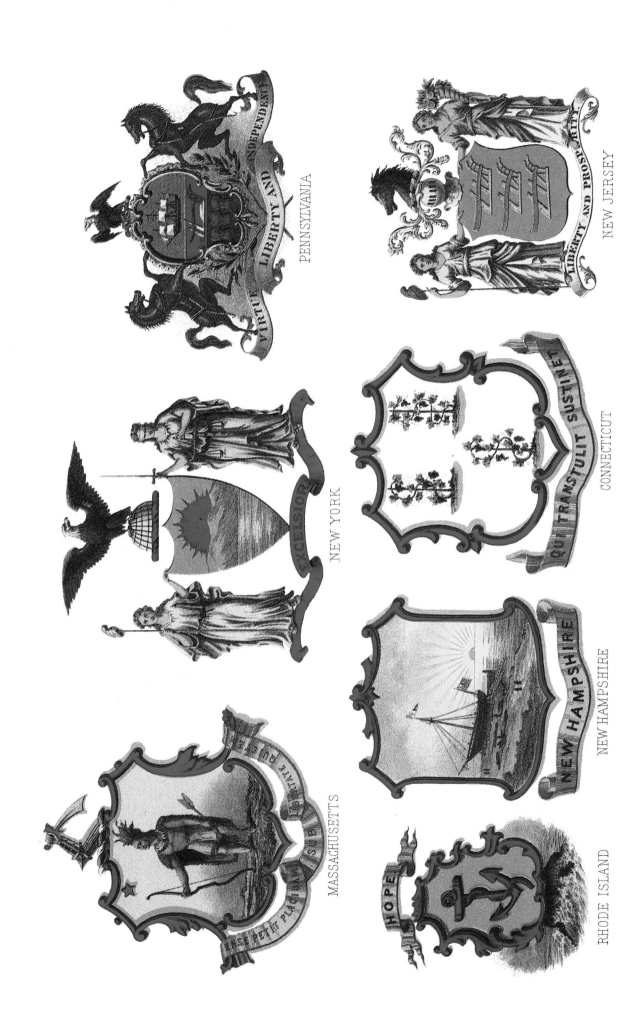

PENNSYLVANIA

NEW JERSEY

NEW YORK

CONNECTICUT

MASSACHUSETTS

NEW HAMPSHIRE

RHODE ISLAND

PLATE II

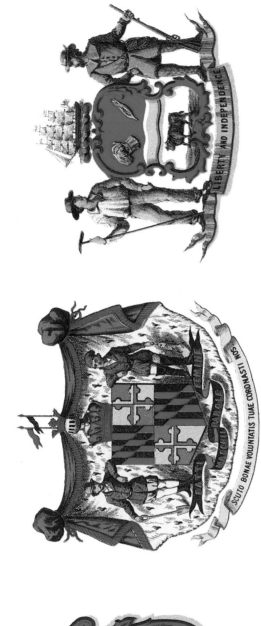

DELAWARE

GEORGIA

MARYLAND

SOUTH CAROLINA

PLATE III

VIRGINIA

NORTH CAROLINA

TENNESSEE

INDIANA

KENTUCKY

LOUISIANA

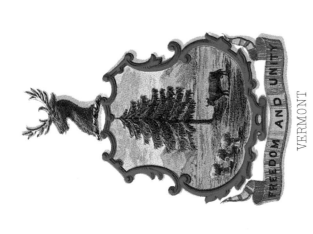

VERMONT

OHIO

PLATE IV

MAINE

MICHIGAN

ALABAMA

ILLINOIS

ARKANSAS

MISSISSIPPI

MISSOURI

PLATE V

STATE ARMS OF

TEXAS.

TEXAS

L'ÉTOILE DU NORD

MINNESOTA

EUREKA

CALIFORNIA

OUR LIBERTIES WE PRIZE AND OUR RIGHTS WE WILL MAINTAIN

IOWA

IN GOD WE TRUST

FLORIDA

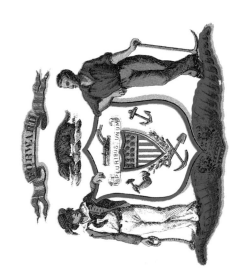

FORWARD

E PLURIBUS UNUM

WISCONSIN

PLATE VI

WEST VIRGINIA

MONTANI SEMPER LIBERI.

COLORADO

NIL SINE NUMINE

COLORADO

AD ASTRA PER ASPERA

KANSAS.

KANSAS

EQUALITY BEFORE THE LAW

NEBRASKA

OREGON

NEVADA

THE UNION.

ALL FOR OUR COUNTRY

NEVADA

PLATE VII

DAKOTA

DISTRICT OF COLUMBIA

UTAH

WYOMING

MONTANA

NEW MEXICO

IDAHO

PLATE VIII

PLATE IX

PLATE X

MISSISSIPPI

ALABAMA GREAT SEAL

OHIO

ILLINOIS

STATE SOVEREIGN NATIONAL UNION

PLATE XI

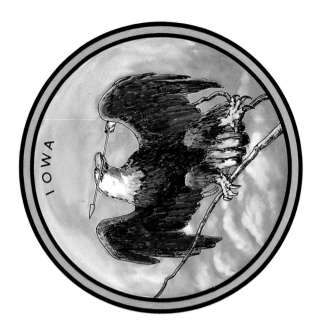

PLATE XII

PLATE XIII

PLATE XIV

PLATE XV

PLATE XVI

UNITED STATES

NATIONAL BANK NOTES

AND THEIR SEALS

BY

DEWITT G. PRATHER

CHAPTER ONE
COLLECTING — REMEMBRANCES

Fun and profit — collecting can be both. All collectibles run in cycles. In times of economic prosperity, collectibles swing up in price, along with everything else. During economic depression, the value of collectibles takes a nosedive. The same fluctuations have been true of coins and rare paper money, especially when they have been held for an extended period. The general upward economic trend over the last 20 years has certainly contributed to my interest in collecting. Fun-wise, the years have been no less rewarding.

As a young man I lived in Waynesboro, Pennsylvania. I knew very little of numismatics. One Sunday afternoon in May 1944, my next door neighbor called me to his house. He was the cashier of one of the two banks in town and had been collecting gold coins and National Bank Notes for some years. With the banking holiday in 1933 F.D. Roosevelt called in the gold. My neighbor was in a good position and added quite a bit to his collection by having access to the gold which was redeemed. We sat at his dining room table for four hours looking at his gold coins which were all in manila 2 x 2 envelopes. I was bitten by the bug and started collecting United States coins by type — minor coinage — half-cents, Indian-head cents, etc., up through the dollar. My neighbor received coin catalogs. He would glance at them and then hand them over to me. I started collecting purely as a hobby, having no idea of ever gaining a profit from it.

Over the next few years I collected a virtually complete type set of coins, some proof sets, and commemorative half-dollars. The type set lacked only the 1793 half-cent, the 1793 cent, the 1796 second type half-dollar, and the flying eagle Gobrecht dollar of 1836-1838 or 1839. One of the last coins I needed to complete my type set was the 1796 quarter-dollar. Although I knew that I should try to get the best condition possible, my means were very limited. The 1796 quarter that I bought was only listed as Good to Very Good. In addition it had the initial "M" scratched in the field in front of the face. I paid $34.75 plus a few cents postage for this coin. When I sold my collection in 1963, the 1796 quarter was worth more than $500. I had been collecting for twenty years when I sold the collection. I had $4,000 invested in this collection and realized $11,000 out of it. At that time I paid capital gains tax on the profit, but since then I have learned to put all my profits back into coins and paper money.

In the late Forties and early Fifties I visited New York City several times, spending time in the shops of some of the larger dealers. I usually bought a few pieces of the "common" old large-sized paper money, mostly one-dollar notes. Two incidents during my visits to the city are memorable. In 1946 I walked into Stack's, then on West 46th Street, and asked to look at a 1795 (first year) half-eagle. Ben Stack pulled out a tray and placed it on the counter for me to see. There were eleven 1795 pieces, all too steep for me then. I could have had my pick for around $200 or less. None were in holders. Then Mr. Stack reached into his pocket and showed me an Ephriam Brasher doubloon, also without a holder. Of course my mouth watered at all these goodies. Next I visited the store of Abe Kosoff, one of our hobby's greats, who was then in partnership with Abner Kreisberg. Abe showed me a "year set" of U.S. quarters in a National folder, beginning with the 1796 issue (first year of issue) and, I think, including most of the years. I have long ago forgotten the price, but I have never forgotten how I feasted my eyes on them or the wishful thinking that followed.

The large-sized United States currency has always greatly appealed to me. It is colorful, the art work is beautiful, and *the lathe work!* The currency we carry in our wallets today has some of this work (steel engraving) but it is so commonplace we scarcely ever notice it. But have you ever taken the time to examine under magnification the face border of an 1886 Silver Certificate (actually picturing 5 silver dollars) and study the fine lines in the intricate lathe work there? The backs of the Series 1890 Treasury Notes (also called "Coin" Notes — stating "Pay to the bearer in coin...") were especially ornate.

Another factor in my fascination with paper money is the individuality of each note. One can look at a roll of *uncirculated* coins, as they come from the mint, and find them virtually identical. Not so with paper money. Even with our present currency, there exist no two pieces that are exactly alike. The serial numbers, plate letters, block numbers, and tiny letters on the back insure that each piece is unique.

Early Silver Certificates and Coin Notes, among others, had vignettes of many famous Americans: presidents, secretaries of state or war, chief justices, admirals, and generals, etc. Civil War greats (Southerners notably excluded) such as James Birdseye McPherson, who fell at Gettysburg, also appear. There are so many elements of interest both historical and artful, but the notes that interested me most were the National Bank Notes, especially those of the First Charter Period and the first issue of the Second Charter Period, which are normally called "brownbacks" by collectors. On their backs, inside the green borders, the First Charter Period notes show reproductions in black and white which were copied from the large wall-sized paintings in the rotunda of the United States Capitol Building. The pictures on the backs of the $500 and $1000 notes are shown in Friedberg's catalogs of United States Paper Money.

Boasting is not my nature, but I must say it is difficult to conceal my pride and joy in being able to assemble this collection. Collectors will understand. The amazing part, I think, is that I am a man of very modest means; I had good parents, good health, a large family, and very little schooling. This is my legacy — not a money inheritance. Yet with conservative and thrifty habits, this collection has been assembled. Please do not take this to mean that I am a self-made man. Like most men I must give my good wife credit as a wonderful helpmate. She has raised a son and a daughter and kept a home these nearly fifty years, yet worked outside as well most of the time. Of late she is more sympathetic with my hobby; at first she had little patience or interest in my spending "good money" for what she termed "you can't spend it." I suspect, like most numismatic-minded husbands' wives, she was kept in the dark for the most part about such purchases, though eventually most of us are found out. That day of reckoning behind me, with her slow acquiescence and mixed sense of pity and condescension, she eventually forgave my foolishness(?) and all is serene again. To the man, this joy approaches ecstasy. Now when I sometimes make a profit and tease her about her earlier statements, she will say, "Why didn't you buy two of them?"

COLLECTING AREAS

Most collectors of National Bank Notes collect by categories. Some collect notes with unusual place names or bank names. The town names are especially varied, such as towns that liked their chosen names so well that they used them twice, as in Walla Walla and Paw Paw. Consider John T. Hickman's poem in the back of this volume. Other collectors concentrated on trades, Indian names, boy's or girl's names, short titles, long titles, different formats or layouts. (Note: It is said that when a bank applied for a charter [deposited bonds with the U.S. Treasury] they were sent several title "layouts." Each bank could select one of their liking to fit the name of the particular bank. Some of them had a small template area, usually in the lower part of the bank's title, that came to be called a monument or "tombstone.") By far the majority of collectors choose to collect notes of the particular state, city, town, birthplace, county, or area such as New England, the Northwest, etc.

I, among others, was interested in collecting ALL the states. I was born in Georgia, raised and educated (such as it was) in Charlotte, North Carolina, home of the Charlotte Mint and some old gold mines. I lived for about three years in Harrisburg, Pennsylvania on the Susquehanna River (— the bottom is black with fine coal that washes down from the coal mines). I fathered a family for nearly twenty years in Waynesboro, in the heart of Pennsylvania's fruit growing region. Waynesboro is 25 miles west of Gettysburg. (I remember the first time I saw the battlefield and North Carolina's monument — it really ... "got" me.) I moved back to Charlotte at Christmas, 1955 and have lived here now for 30 years, traveling frequently. My moving around has made me feel a bit more cosmopolitan. This was not the only reason I decided to try to collect all of the various states, but it was certainly a factor.

Certainly high on the list of reasons for my interest in collecting the seals of all the states, studying them, and comparing their differences was the beauty of the notes. The backs, showing replicas of famous paintings, and on the brownbacks, the large charter numbers in green; the faces, showing the place names, formats (layouts) with the bank title, dates on the notes, U.S. Treasury seals, and the signatures of bank officials all added to my interest. Practically all of these notes were hand signed since the use of stamps for the signatures did not start until later. Facsimiles of these signatures were printed on the notes for later issues. We also have notes signed by the assistant cashier, usually indicated by a small "a" after the name, as well as notes signed by vice presidents for the president — these shown as "V. pres," "vice," or simply "V."

Some banks did not issue any notes. Others issued only one or two denominations. Still others, such as the First National Bank of Tallahassee, Florida (charter number 4132) issued one or two high denominations, possibly because the bank officials did not want to sign a lot of notes. The variations in National Bank Notes are almost inexhaustible.

I am thrilled when I see a seal on a rare note for the first time. I remember the two brownback notes I purchased from venerable dealer Bill Donlon. One was on Delaware, which is rather rare, but the other one, from a state missing completely in the collection at that time, was Idaho. This was the first time for me to see the *state* seal of Idaho on a brownback note. This experience however takes a back seat to the thrill of acquiring the first Idaho *Territory* note known to collectors. When I purchased that note (1974), it was a record price for a piece of paper money. This was a Series 1875 First Charter period note of five dollars on The First National Bank of Idaho, Boise City, Idaho Territory. What a thrill! I felt like jumping up and down and shouting!

I was overwhelmed when I successfully bid at auction for the only known Nevada First Charter note. Long considered the most valuable note in the collection, it was a joy to feast my eyes on this note with its beautiful Nevada seal which has 37 stars around it. (This is presumably an error, for Nevada was the 36th state to enter the Union.)

But perhaps the greatest thrill of all was seeing for the first time Amon Carter's very rare twenty-dollar bill on The First National Bank of Ogden, "State of Utah," but which shows the territorial seal. As great as that thrill was, it paled when we finally acquired the note.

4

CHAPTER TWO
A SHORT HISTORY OF U.S. CURRENCY

With the coming of the Civil War in 1861, the United States Government realized that drastic measures would be required to keep the nation financially sound through the war. Prior to this time the money system in this country was a hodge-podge. Even our hard currency, our coins, most of which were legal tender, including the Spanish Milled dollar, had difficulties, and certain coins were sometimes discounted. At times, even our United States half-cents and large cents, in volume, were rejected for the dead weight involved.

But if the coinage was in trouble, imagine the problems the paper currency had! The paper money was backed (but not in full) by the troubled coinage. The average citizens were accustomed to handling copper, nickel, silver, and gold in their daily transactions; it is no wonder they were not ready or willing to accept paper as money. Even so, the fledgling United States Government finally established the "Bank of the United States" which issued paper money. Various issues were made mostly in the 1830's and 1840's. But from that time until the war years most paper money was issued by private banks. Today we call this currency "broken bank bills" or "obsolete currency." There is quite a lot of this currency around and many collectors specialize in this branch of numismatics. Possibly these issues account for the usage of the common term "rag pickers." Today, we paper money collectors like to call ourselves syngraphists, a modern term denoting the collection of all kinds of paper, past and present. Bonds, stock certificates, fractional currency, encased postage stamps, die proofs, and vignettes of all kinds, old checks, almost everything, old and new, even baseball cards and comic books are of interest and value. In recent years, due chiefly to inflation, this odd list of material is becoming ever more popular.

With the government issue of "Demand" Notes in 1861, and especially with the first Legal Tender issues of 1862 and 1863, the private banks were ordered to stop issuing paper money and forced out of business. Hence, the "Broken Bank Bills" or "Obsolete Currency."

The Demand Notes of 1861, in only fives and tens, and less frequently, in twenties, were payable in certain cities, such as New York, Boston, and Philadelphia, and to a lesser extent in Cincinnati and St. Louis. A full run of denominations of Legal Tender Series 1862 and 1863 commenced. The Demand Notes and the Legal Tender backs were printed principally in green (banker's green or bank note green), therefore these notes all came to be called "greenbacks." More Legal Tenders followed in 1869; a few denominations only were included in the issues of 1874, 1875, and 1878; a longer issue of more denominations

came out in the Series of 1880. The year 1907 saw a run of five-dollar denomination only. Series of 1901 and 1923 issued tens only, and one-dollar notes only were issued in 1917 and 1923, and twos in the 1917 series.

Then came the Compound Interest Treasury Notes, which were issued in tens and twenties as well as fifties and hundreds, which are rare. These notes all had a table of redemption values printed on the back for each six months and running for three years (depending on when the note was surrendered). Next were the one year Interest-Bearing Notes, followed by two year and three year Interest-Bearing Notes. The latter were issued in larger denominations (up to $1,000) with coupons attached on one end which the holder could detach each six months to collect his interest. The sixth six-month interest was paid with the surrender of the note itself. This writer at one time owned a fifty-dollar note with all five coupons still attached.

Let me state here parenthetically that each and all of these issues of currency began with an Act of Congress referred to as "Act of August 15th, 1870" or whatever date. As time progressed, these issues overlapped and ran concurrently.

Next to be issued were the two issues of ten-dollar Refunding Certificates of 1879. These were payable to order at 4% interest, each with a limited value of $23.30 when the note was finally redeemed. Gold Certificates also began to be issued in 1863, in denominations of ten to ten thousand dollars, but none of the larger denominations are known to collectors. The largest volume of Gold Certificates that can be remembered by many old timers consisted of the 1907 and 1922 issues in tens and twenties of 1882, 1905, 1906, and 1922 as well as some of the fifties of 1882, 1913, and 1922. There were also hundreds issued in 1882 and 1922.

Here, please let me interject a personal experience. As a boy of 16 or 17 (about 1927 or 1928) with jobs delivering newspapers and Western Union telegrams in the city on a bicycle, I saved my money and accumulated forty dollars. I exchanged my money for Gold Certificates, as required by law, took it to the American Trust Co. (now a part of the giant North Carolina National Bank of Charlotte) and asked the teller to see some gold coins. He opened a cloth bag and poured out on the counter probably 300 to 400 dollars in gold coins. I picked out one 2½, one 5, one 10 and one 20-dollar gold piece, totalling $37.50. At home I hid them in the bottom of my trunk until some time later, my father needed to borrow the money. There went my first gold coins.

Beginning in 1878 the Silver Certificates started running concurrently with all the other issues. Some were countersigned by the Assistant Treasurer of the U.S. at New York

City or Washington, D.C. and also in San Francisco, CA on the fifty- and hundred-dollar denominations. These rare issues of 1878 and 1880 have large black (gray-black) block letters and are very distinctive, interesting, and beautiful.

One of the most beautiful and ornate classes of large type paper money was the Treasury Notes called Coin Notes, Series of 1890 and the Series of 1891 with the more open backs. An explanation may be in order. Back in those days, as well as today, there were counterfeiters. This problem became most severe with the introduction of the Treasury Notes of 1890. The fancy backs were difficult to counterfeit, but the wealth of small detail made it even harder to detect a counterfeit note. So in 1891, in an effort to fight counterfeiting, the government changed the backs to what we call "open backs."

With an act of February 1863 as amended in 1864, the National Bank Act became law. Beginning in November 1863, national banks began organizing and in late November 1863, the First National Bank of Philadelphia received Charter #1. From 1863 to 1935 over 14,000 banks were chartered. A charter was good for twenty years, at which time that bank could apply again and was then said to be rechartered. The First Charter Period started in late 1863; notes were issued in the Original Series up to 1875 and most of these showed no charter numbers. Beginning in 1875 the act was amended requiring notes to show the charter number twice. These notes are marked by a red "surcharge" placed vertically on the left center face ("Series 1875"), and by including the scalloped treasury seal instead of the darker red, smaller, round seal with small rays, which is found on the Original Series. These two series comprise the First Charter Period.

The Second Charter Period began on July 12, 1882 with a new design for all the backs. The denominations to be issued were reduced to only the fives, tens, twenties, fifties, and hundreds. Only the five-dollar note received a new face design: President James A. Garfield had recently been assassinated; therefore, it was decided to place his portrait on the left end. The backs on all five denominations were altered to show the charter numbers in large green numerals in a larger green lathe-work design. Around the large, central, flat oval and over the top of this oval in several lines of print was stated the obligation of the government to pay the face amount on the note. Likewise on the underside of this flattened oval were several lines stating the penalty for counterfeiting the note. These we call the "obligation" and "penalty" and they appear on most, if not all, United States currency. On the Series 1882 (first part of issue), this obligation and penalty and other areas, particularly the ends, including the left and right ovals, the predominant color is brown. This is how these notes earned the nickname "brownbacks."

The *right* upright oval on both First Charter and brownbacks shows a United States eagle. The oval on the left, in most cases, has the seal of the state (or territory) in which the town and bank on the note is located. These seals, and the differences between the seals or lack of a seal on the banknotes, are the subject of this book.

On the backs of First Charter Notes are reproductions of the famous paintings found in the rotunda of the Capitol in Washington. They are as follows:

One dollar — *Landing of The Pilgrims* at Plymouth Rock in 1620
Two dollars — *Sir Walter Raleigh, 1585,* showing products of the American colonies to the Court of England
Five dollars — *Landing of Columbus, 1492*
Ten dollars — *DeSoto Discovering the Mississippi*
Twenty dollars — *Baptism of Pocahontas*
Fifty dollars — *Embarkation of the Pilgrims*
One hundred dollars — Signing of the *Declaration of Independence*
Five hundred dollars — *Surrender of General Burgoyne* to General Horatio Gates at Saratoga, October 17, 1777
One thousand dollars — *Washington Resigning his Commission*

After the brownbacks, the next issues (still Series of 1882), second and third issue of the Second Charter Period are the "date-backs" and "value-backs." The date-backs have a similar front (all the way to the Third Charter Period Series 1902) but the backs are changed. There are no more seals and eagles in the ovals as before on each end, and the centers are open. But in the center the dates "1882" and "1902" appear, separated by a design. The left oval on both of these issues shows (on fives only) a bust of George Washington, and in the right oval, the Capitol. (The other denominations have other combinations of pictures within the ovals.) On the last part of the Second Charter Period, in rather large letters, is the value of the note, spelled out, e.g., "FIVE DOLLARS," etc. These we call "value-backs."

The Aldrich-Vreeland Act shortened the length of the brownback issuing period from forty years (1882 to 1922) to 26 years (1882 to 1908) and seems to have limited the number of notes released. This act was prompted to relieve panics and the issues were designated emergency monies. The act changed the wording on the prior National Bank Notes which had read, "This note is secured by bonds of the United States deposited with the U.S. Treasurer at Washington" to "This note is secured by bonds of the United States or other securities."

The central concept of the National Banking Act was the principle of the banks depositing bonds with the treasurer by which the bank could then order sheets of currency up to 90% of the value of those bonds.

The Third Charter Period began in 1902. It was divided into three parts:

"a": The design was changed, face and back. The design is much more open or plain. The treasury seal is red, and these notes are called "red seals." As a whole these are scarce, and some are rare.

"b": These notes have a blue seal on the face, and on the backs, above, on each side, the dates 1902 on the left and 1908 on the right. This gives them also the name "date-backs" (Series of 1902).

"c": The largest issue was printed without the dates, and therefore these are called "plain-backs."

From 1929 to 1935 the small-sized notes were issued.

But of all these notes, the most interesting, exciting, and beautiful notes are the First Charter and the brownback notes, because they usually show the seal of the state or territory of issue. These seals portray so much of the history and character of the political divisions of our beloved country! Some of the key visual elements on these notes follow, along with a brief explanation.

PRINTING: In the early days National Bank Note production was farmed out to private concerns; active in the field were the American Bank Note, National Bank Note, and Continental Bank Note Companies, all in New York City. They used different kinds of paper and usually finished the notes in their own plants before shipping them to the Bureau. The Bureau of Engraving and Printing added the treasury seals and serial numbers. Sometimes one company printed one side and another company printed the other side. The Columbian Bank Note Company of Washington usually printed the black portion of the five dollar bills. Finally in 1877 the Bureau took over the entire operation.

DATES: All notes have a full date, usually on the upper or lower right hand side of the bank title and city. Sometimes it is the charter or recharter date, but it can also be earlier or later; neither is it necessarily the issue date. There are so many inconsistencies with these dates that they have little meaning.

TREASURY SIGNATURES: The signatures of the treasury officials are misleading. The set of officers which was serving when a plate was engraved had very often been changed by the time the note was printed and sent to a bank.

CHARTER NUMBERS: After 1875 all notes bore the bank's charter number boldly, twice. Since the charters were designated singly and consecutively in order, it is an easy matter to determine the year in which a charter was granted.

SERIAL NUMBERS: Both federal and bank serial numbers were added to each sheet. Since no numbers could be duplicated, the federal treasury numbers got larger and larger. However, they were limited to six numerics by the addition of prefixes and suffixes, usually capital letters. As circulation grew, the suffixes came to include several symbols. An examination of the pictures of the notes will more quickly explain their appearance than any wordy description. (In the listing of data from the notes beginning in Chapter 6, when these suffix symbols appear, they are most often indicated by a dash. Parentheses, when so used, are shown.)

PLATE LETTERS: Each sheet had the same serial number. Check or Plate letters were added so that each note was different. Even though cut apart, the sheet could be put back together. Usually the four subject sheets were "A," "B," "C" or "D," when all notes were of the same denomination. But when a second denomination was printed on the sheet, the letters could be repeated. For example, a sheet of three one-dollar notes and one two-dollar note, would have letters "A," "B," "C" and "A."

REGIONAL LETTERS: When thousands of these notes were sent in for redemption, it became quite a chore to sort the notes. Therefore large letters were placed on notes to facilitate sorting from 1902 to 1924. These letters appeared twice on the face of each note: toward the top right and at the lower left, just following or above the charter number. The letters were "N" for North, "E" for East, "S" for South, "M" for banks in the Midwest, "W" for West, and "P" for Pacific area banks.

NOTE: A chart, "Years of Issue of Charter Numbers," from Robert Friedberg's *Paper Money of the United States* appears in the appendices.

CHAPTER THREE
COLLECTING STATE AND TERRITORIAL SEALS

Seals, coats of arms, are a part of history beginning with the feudal lords in medieval times, even before the knights appeared. Each castle or manor, to survive as an entity, had to swear fealty to its lord. As the number of fiefdoms grew, it became necessary to have a banner to indicate to which fiefdom, earldom, or dukedom one belonged. Thus heraldry was born. In France and England, heraldry probably reached its greatest development. Signet rings have been used since early times to sign letters, and the ancient Egyptians were probably the first to use scarab rings to sign and seal official messages, even in hieroglyphics. So, it is not too difficult to understand why countries, states, and many governing bodies adopt seals. (NOTE: The term "coat of arms" or coats of arms preceded the seal, even to the beginning of heraldry. The knights and warriors wore plates of armor. Since their coats sometimes covered both horse and rider, they needed some identity outside, hence the "arms", then "coat of arms", and then "coats of arms.")

Our territories and state seals vary widely in detail. Some have coats of arms and then use only a portion of this for a seal. Some changed in progressive steps that we call the evolution of the seal.

I began collecting my seals and notes some 25 years ago. I noticed that the then-newly-elected president, John F. Kennedy, lined up his delegates and supporters for his inaugural parade in the order in which their states came into the Union. Number one was Delaware, number two Pennsylvania, number three New Jersey, etc. So, for historical accuracy and detail I have lined up my collection of seals and National Bank Notes the same way, placing the District of Columbia at the end.

For the 1961 ANA convention in Atlanta, I prepared eight large boards, 21 inches high by six feet long. In conjunction with seals of each state I also showed the relative shape and size of each state (except Alaska), this on three-inch silver disks (round), the outline of the states in gold foil, along with the nickname of each state, the state bird, flower, tree, state motto, capitol, flag, etc. These boards were displayed at the ANA Convention in Atlanta (1961), again in Washington, D.C. (1971), and in conjunction with our local Charlotte Coin Club Show at NCNB in Charlotte, N.C. Also, I collected and showed the crown-sized (one ounce) silver (.999 fine) proof finish "States of the Union" medals. These also show the seals.

I won third place in U.S. currency competition at the Atlanta ANA Convention in 1961. The judges said I had too much on the eight boards, mounted on easels. I admit they were crowded, showing one to three notes of each state (plus D.C.) with all the other symbols. But for the real student, I feel that all of the data is necessary, both perti-

nent to the seals and pictures of the actual notes. I still have the boards and some pictures of the boards. Also I had a serialized article on the seals that appeared in *Coin World*, beginning December 15, 1961 and running through February 16, 1962. But now the seal collection is complete and the collection of National Bank Notes lacks only the Nevada brownback of known notes with seals to complete it.

Doctor Frank A. Limpert of Royal Oak, Michigan was the forerunner in the study of the seals on National Bank Notes. I have his autographed books and his permission to use any of his data. So I follow in his footsteps.

A population of 60,000 was necessary for a territory to reach statehood. Usually upon becoming a territory or a state, a committee was formed, or the governor or another individual was designated "to bring in a seal."

As for the seals as shown on National Bank Notes, the seals sometimes had to be altered a little to get all the main features into the oval reserved for the seal. The seals, as part of the overall design of the notes, were done by artists at the Bureau of Engraving and Printing. Leibler, Fenton & Burt are some names associated with design and engraving on National Bank Notes.

THE OFFICIAL SEALS

Almost as difficult to secure as the notes themselves are "official" present state seals. Collecting these state seals afforded me a challenge, pleasure, and quite an experience.

As a family, in 1965, we took a trip out west. We went up and down the country to visit all of the state capitals, going inside each capitol building, going to the governor's office or, in most cases, to the office of the secretary of state. In 1968 we made a longer 11,000 mile trip all the way to the Northwest until we had actually gone inside all 48 capitol buildings. We had to re-visit Frankfort, Kentucky, having first gone on a Sunday when we could not get into the building. In May 1974 my wife and I flew to Hawaii. In Honolulu, in the old Iolonai Palace, we visited the only throne room in the United States. We also visited the new capitol building, which is built in a manner to simulate the area surrounding a volcano.

Then in 1975 we got together with a friend and his wife who had also been to 49 states, though not to all the capitols. The four of us took off to Alaska in his motor home. The "ALCAN" highway is much improved today, a goodly portion of its 1300 miles now paved, however, in 1975, only the first sixty miles were paved with macadam to a point just beyond Fort St. John. The object was to drive 35 to 40 mph (or as fast as possible) and to miss as many pot-holes as possible, which were cup size to platter size. By taking a state ferry from Skagway to Aukey Bay and taking the motor home off the ferry, it is only about ten miles to Juneau. We arrived on a Saturday. The front door of the State House was locked, so not to be discouraged after our long trip, I went around to the back and gained entrance. (This building was previously called the District House, for it was also used as the seat of government during the time when Alaska was officially designated as a district.)

Obtaining the "official" state seals was not easy. In fact, if I had not had some help, I doubt that I would have completed this collection. Some of the state statutes strictly forbid the issuance of the seal "...except upon an official document...." Delaware, the first state, was the most difficult of all. In Albany, New York in the State Department, they opened a handbook to the center, cut out the page with a picture of the seal on it and gave it to me. They were afraid someone would take the official seal and use it illegally to defraud. Hawaii, Connecticut, and Virginia were also impossible for me to secure, but a new-found friend, the secretary of state of one of the western states who owed me not a dime, was kind enough to help. Because of his position and through his organization, he obtained the missing seals for me. But Delaware turned him down. Later, he wrote and asked if I wanted him to try once more. Naturally I said "Yes," and he again wrote to Secretary of State Bunting at Dover, Delaware, forwarding a copy of the statute laws of his State, and requesting a certified copy of the statute laws of the State of Delaware in return. This time Secretary Bunting took an official letterhead, addressed the letter to my friend stating that he was sending a set of the statute laws of the State of Delaware, signed the letter, and affixed the "official" seal of the state to the letter. My friend forwarded it to me. It is not always *what* you know, but often *who* you know. So I now have the complete set. They are available for inspection and study. Please contact me personally or through the society (Member #862, SOPMC).

The "official" seals are usually on a gold saw-toothed wafer which is placed in the seal press where the impression is made. A few states still retain (as antiques) their old seals (New Jersey, for example) and, with a lever, apply the pressure by hand. A bold impression must be made and each protected to keep it from being obliterated. A few cases come to mind.

The name of General Francis Elias Spinner (signed F.E. Spinner), who was later appointed the first Treasurer of the United States, probably appears on more notes, bonds, letters, documents, etc., than perhaps any other one person's name. Mr. Spinner had a daughter named Josephine who later married a man by the name of Schumaker, who in some way was connected with an early Jacksonville, Florida bank. Josephine collected the early seals, mostly on the western states and territories. Accompanying some of these seals were short letters autographed by the territo-

rial governors. One which I remember was written by Governor Lyman H. Low of California, teasing Josephine about her boyfriend. In 1954 Doctor Frank E. Limpert, now deceased, sent me "The Spinner Album" for thirty days and offered it for sale at $1,000. Since I was putting all the money I could afford into the notes themselves, and thinking also that perhaps I would get another chance at it, I returned it to Dr. Limpert. After Dr. Limpert's death at near 90, his widow or estate sold it to the well-known dealer, Mr. Aubrey E. Bebee. I remember that the album contained about half of the states and most of the territories' seals plus some of the autographed letters. So, historically, it is a very valuable item. Some of the seals were silver colored, (e.g. Nevada, which was larger than usual) and some of the details were already obliterated.

Another set, also incomplete, was formed in the late 1880's. It recently sold at auction, but I think that the details of many of these were hard to distinguish.

Gold wafer seals, usually saw-toothed, are used by all states except Maine, which uses blue, Massachusetts, which uses light green, Virginia, which uses dark blue, and New Jersey, which uses a white background with lettering and details in various colors, although they also use a light blue seal or a gold wafer. Gold wafers for seals are used by the District of Columbia. (They told me the seal had no color and gave me a white impression on an index card, but all around I could see both red and gold ones being issued).

The seals are round and vary in size from two to three inches or more in diameter, averaging about two and one-half inches. Connecticut is the only state which actually uses an upright oval. The seals show varied patterns, and each one has something pertinent to its history or development. Five states have both obverse and reverse sides which are placed mostly on very important documents, usually back to back, sandwich style. Virginia's dark blue seal has a light blue ribbon running through twice, looped back at top. When the ribbon is placed in, glued, and the two parts pressed together, parts of the detail are obliterated. Maryland, Pennsylvania, Georgia and West Virginia also have an obverse and reverse. The seal I have from Georgia, which came from an important document given to me by a secretary in the Governor's office, is the only one that has a wax disk between, with a doubled purple ribbon encased in the wax. Normally, where obverse and reverse seals are designated, the obverse is used exclusively on National Bank Notes. The exception here is Maryland, which uses the *reverse* officially, and it is shown on the later brownback notes.

Indeed, the history of this country's development can be traced through the issuance of the National Bank Notes. The Northeastern states had a greater density of population than other regions: more business, therefore, more banks. The cities of New York, Boston, Philadelphia, and Baltimore issued many notes and included the higher denominations during the First Charter Period, followed closely by Chicago, Cleveland, Washington, and others.

The South was set back by the Civil War, some say fifty years; therefore, there were fewer notes issued. Those that were issued, for the most part, were heavily circulated, consequently they are difficult to find in acceptable condition. The same thing holds true for the West. Indeed, one can almost feel the hardships borne by the pioneers, in settling and developing the West, with plagues, drouths, Indian uprisings and attacks, and many other hardships. The motto of Kansas comes to my mind: *Ad Astra per Aspera,* "To the stars through difficulty." In another example, the seal of Minnesota shows that a farmer, even while plowing, has his gun nearby.

By looking at these notes and all the place names, romance also comes to mind. Many years ago "Mr. Phil" (Mr. William A. Philpott, Jr.) put together a group of national notes with interesting and unusual place names. Given boy and girl names and Indian names, it was not too difficult to do. With towns named Sleepy-eye, Wahoo, Deadwood, and Intercourse, the list becomes endless. Indeed, some syngraphists collect and organize their collections by subjects such as mining, cattle, lumber, citizens, merchants, traders, drovers, stock growers, even shoe and leather.

Even the territories had seals, but the notes of certain territories did not have a seal. In these cases another eagle was placed in the left oval (backs of First Charter Period notes and Second Charter Period brownbacks only — date-backs and value-backs show no seals.) An upright eagle (we call these different eagle positions "stances") appeared in the right oval of the one, twenty, fifty, one-hundred, five-hundred and one-thousand dollar denominations. All the five and ten dollar denominations showed a "squat" or wings half-way open as in a landing or take-off position. Beginning with the Series of 1882 (this includes the brownback notes) the National Bank Notes were issued only in the five, ten, twenty, fifty and one-hundred dollar denominations. Of course, not all denominations were issued in all fifty states in the Union plus the District of Columbia, or by all banks.

Sometime after July 11, 1882, but before the end of the period in which brownback notes were issued, the Bureau issued a composite picture of the seals, reproduced at the beginning of Chapter 6. This composite, circa 1900, shows the final versions of the seals (8 states and the District of Columbia), which were changed for various reasons between 1890 and 1900. All but three of the seals are overlapped by their neighbors. Inside the square center are two shields. The smaller, superimposed on the larger, is a United States shield with red and white stripes and, across the top in a blue field, there are 45 stars to match the 45 seals shown. Around the outside edge of the larger shield are the seals of the original thirteen colonies. The remaining 32 seals are around the outside of the square. All states whose notes showed seals are represented in this picture, with the exception of the District of Columbia.

There are seals from many sources, the chief source of single seals would, of course, be the individual states. The secretary of state of each state is usually the keeper of the seal, but occasionally I have found the governor's office is responsible. In my drive to obtain the "official" seals as mentioned before I have had varying degrees of success. In some states there was no problem at all. In a few I got no results when there, but upon arriving back home and writing, my request was granted. In the case of ten or twelve of the states, it was impossible to obtain the seal because of the laws.

There are also many examples of multiple seals. Most of these are used in advertising. These are rarely available however, in exactly the size, uniformity or completeness one desires. A friend in the Society of Paper Money Collectors sent me an example of a Dwight & Company circular. This company apparently used it to advertise their name at the Centennial exposition held in Philadelphia in 1876. I understand that Dwight & Company were customs house brokers. The circular pictures eighteen presidents, Washington through Grant. Also there are 38 state seals, Delaware through Colorado, which came into the Union by 1876. Upon examination, quite a few of these seals show differences, most of them minor. In the evolution of the seals these must be older versions.

THE WILLIAM WINDOM BOOK OF SEALS

William Windom was an American financier born in Belmont, Ohio on May 10, 1827. He began practicing law in Mount Vernon, Ohio in 1850. In 1852 he was made prosecuting attorney of Knox County, Ohio. He held this position for three years, and then moved to Minnesota. Windom was sent to Congress from that state in 1859 and was reelected to serve four successive terms. He was appointed to the United States Senate in 1870 to fill the unexpired term of the deceased Daniel S. Norton. He was also elected for the terms ending in 1878 and 1883. He resigned, however, in 1881 to accept the treasury portfolio in President Garfield's cabinet, and upon his departure from the cabinet after that president's death, he returned to the Senate where he served the remainder of his term. He became secretary of the treasury in President Harrison's cabinet in 1889, and died in New York City, January 29, 1891.

At the 1981 annual paper money show held in Memphis I was fortunate to find a rare book. We believe it to be unique. It is 6" x 8", leather bound, with gold leaf edges, a fly-leaf between each page, and 2 or 3 blank pages, randomly placed. On the front, stamped in gold is "William Windom." On the inside flyleaf are some pencilled notes. The book contains 46 die proofs of the seals as found on the First Charter Period notes, the first (or earliest) through Utah territorial seal, plus the District of Columbia. It contains the North Dakota and South Dakota state seals, the Idaho and Wyoming territorial seals, as well as that Utah territorial seal. In addition there is also the following: An upright eagle as found in the right oval of the one, two, twenty, fifty, one-hundred, five-hundred, and one-thousand dollar notes; and an oval containing a squat eagle as found in the right hand oval on the five and ten dollar notes.

We believe that in order to honor William Windom, or as a memorial to his memory, someone in the Treasury Department went to the Bureau of Engraving and Printing and had this book put together. Its blank pages would indicate that it was put together hurriedly, but I cannot explain why these pages were left blank in the particular order in which they were. We believe it was then presented to his widow.

On the inside front cover of the book I have taken the liberty of placing a United States Silver Certificate, two-dollar note, Series 1891. This note portrays a picture of William Windom as a central vignette commemorating his past service to his country.

It was a big thrill to see this book and being a student and collector of the seals I just had to have it. Further information anyone can supply on the William Windom Book of Seals will be more than welcomed.

CHAPTER FOUR
PERSONAL NOTES AND STORIES

In a life-long endeavor such as this, many experiences and incidental happenings occur. The interesting people we meet, and the friendships that develop are the real substance of this hobby. In retrospect, we call our most memorable experiences "stories." Several of my priceless memories follow.

THE STORY OF THE ANA CONVENTIONS

The American Numismatic Association conventions have proven to be a major catalyst in my hobby experience. The first ANA convention I attended was in 1953 in Cleveland, which will be discussed in more detail later.

Living in south-central Pennsylvania from 1936 through 1955 placed my family not far from the larger cities. Often our vacations would include these cities and the ANA convention. Since these conventions were so important to me, I feel it would be useful to list the ones I attended. This list also makes mention of specific events which will be recounted later in this chapter.

1957, Philadelphia PA: I met Amon Carter.
1961, Atlanta, GA: By this time I had decided that nationals with the seals were the way for me to go. This is when I took my eight boards and exhibited my collection, winning third place.
1962, Detroit, MI, Cadillac Hotel: Here I first met "Mr. Phil," William A. Philpott, Jr.
1964, Cleveland, OH, Carew Tower
1965, Houston, TX: Here Amon Carter loaned me 24 rare notes overnight to copy information.
1967, Miami, FL: See the Tallahassee story.
1968, San Diego, CA: See the Tuscon story.
1969, Philadelphia, PA.
1970, St. Louis, MO: See the Winnemucca story.
1971, Washington, D.C., Sheraton Hotel: Here I last exhibited my collection.
1972, New Orleans, LA, Jung Hotel.
1973, Boston, MA: Sold 20 or 30 duplicate notes and, as usual, made some mistakes. I sold one note and bought it back the next morning — at a higher price.
1974, Miami Beach, FL: I almost sold my collection. WOW! Sure am glad that I didn't.
1975, Los Angeles, CA, Marriott Hotel: We were on our way home from our camping trip to Alaska with another couple.
1976, New York, NY, Americana Hotel: Attended Stack's sale.
1977, Atlanta, GA: Bought the Tallahassee $100 brownback for the second time.
1978, Houston, TX: This is the last ANA convention I have attended as of this writing.

By this time the Memphis Paper Money show had been organized. I did not attend the first show and realized later that I had made a mistake. Since that time I have made an annual trip to Memphis with a friend, missing only one year.

AN EARLY EXPERIENCE

The year was 1953. Also living in Waynesboro, Pennsylvania was a veterinary doctor who wanted to go with us to Cleveland. We went as far as Canton, Ohio where my wife's aunt lived. Of course, "Doc" was welcome. We all enjoyed Aunt Cora's hospitality, bed and breakfast. Then it was on to Cleveland and the ANA convention at the Carew Towers Hotel. "Doc," in his profession, plied his trade at a lot of farms around Waynesboro. He would go into the farmhouses and sniff out the good ladies' antiques. Being a pretty good horse-trader, he had a three-story brick home on the edge of town in which he and his wife carried on an antique business as a sideline. This rascal knew that I had three early gold eagles, the 1795, the 1799, and the 1801, for which I had paid a total of some $265. "Doc" pleaded with me to sell him my three eagles. Before we reached home I reluctantly sold him my gold pieces for $300. I sure hate for someone to beg from me! Needless to say, I'm still kicking myself everytime I think about it, God rest "Doc's" soul.

IN ANTICIPATION OF FINDING AN UNKNOWN NOTE

The fact that the first three banks in Mississippi all issued First Charter notes and that they are still unknown makes me real anxious to be the first to find one. So we went to Vicksburg to the First National Bank where we met an official who showed us what real Southern hospitality is. He took us personally to visit a merchant in town who was interested in coins, antiques, etc., but he could not help me. The banker pleaded with my wife and me to go to his club to dinner; he called his wife and arranged everything. After sightseeing we came back and went to dinner. I found no Mississippi First Charter Period note, but we sure found some gracious living.

Next, was Jackson where we had less luck than Vicksburg. We then went to Columbus where we talked to several people as well as a couple of bankers. We learned that there was a former history professor who had been interested in Mississippi broken bank notes and had evidently formed a sizeable collection. He had left his family and town, but we found his ex-wife at her place of work. She wanted us to come by her home at lunch time. We did, but stayed just a few minutes. She said her ex-husband had gathered all his notes and taken them with him. He had left a small frame with a North Carolina broken bank note of less than a dollar value. Of course, I was not interested in that, but she told me that one time he had come home from one of his note-buying forays and was ecstatic...just beside himself. I put two and two together and decided that he had found a rare Mississippi First Charter Period note. Inquiring where I might find him, she told me that the last she had heard he was somewhere up in our area; High Point or Greensboro, N.C. A few weeks later we went to High Point and searched in the city directory with no luck. There are about five colleges in the Greensboro area, so I thought perhaps he was teaching at one of them. No luck. Giving up, we started home. About five miles down I-85 is a very large antique establishment. We decided to stop and look around. There was a man in there with whom I happened to strike up a conversation. It turned out that he was a police officer, moonlighting there. He asked me who I was looking for. I told him, and he pulled out his billfold and handed me a business card. He said that he knew the man, that he was a member of his church. The man was now a locksmith. We turned around and went back into the city. I found him in his shop, but he said he had no Mississippi First Charter Period note and he had left his collection in a safe deposit box in a Birmingham, Alabama bank. So, the whole episode fell through, but it was still a miracle that I found the man.

Another time that we were in Columbus, we had been visiting the president of the Farmers and Merchants Bank. We found that there was a lawyer with an office on an upper floor of the same building who had my same surname. Deciding to try to meet him, we got on the elevator. On our way up, we met the man. After conversing for awhile, we showed him a picture of another First Charter note. He said that sometimes he had estates to settle and that he would keep watch for them. On the way to each Memphis Paper Money show we stop to see him. Y'all keep your fingers crossed for me!

I guess that I am just naive enough to think there is one out there, somewhere. I have now learned that the First National Bank of Columbus, Mississippi only issued fifties and hundreds. Now I am dreaming of a fifty that will improve the only fifty dollar note that we now have. Well, when you are dreaming, you might as well go all the way.

THE AMON CARTER STORY

I first met Amon at the 1957 ANA Convention in Philadelphia where he had some "Lazy Twos" on exhibit. An incident occurred where the hotel cashier did not want to accept his check. The story goes that Amon threatened to buy the hotel. At the 1961 ANA Convention in Atlanta I had my collection displayed on eight boards 21 inches high and six feet long. I showed one or more notes of each state along with the state bird, flower, tree, seal, motto, etc. Amon told me that he was investigating the possibility of locating a brewery in Atlanta.

Amon earnestly tried to help new and fellow collectors. He would attend most all of the ANA conventions and other major shows. Bringing several bundles of rare notes, the collectors (myself included) would sit at his table, look at these extremely rare and valuable notes, and drool over them. By watching these hungry collectors, Amon would "get his kicks."

There are lots of different stories about Amon, one of which I like particularly well. One new collector who did not know Amon looked at several of those high-powered notes and said to Amon, "Wow! Those must have cost a bundle. Mister, what do you do for a living?" Amon said, "I sell newspapers ... about 200,000 a day."

Sometimes when attending a large show, Amon would share a table with another collector/dealer. His identifiable trademark was a large black cigar which was always in his mouth. He rarely had anyone to assist him with records; he relied on his marvelous memory. I was amazed at the way he could remember every detail. He would often answer letters himself, even those I wrote to him. His short, typewritten letters would often start with "Off tomorrow to Mexico for a hunting trip ..." (or Wyoming, or Colorado, or wherever) "... but I do want to acknowledge your letter ..." Amon was a very avid collector, be it on Mexico, Canada, or some of the British Commonwealth possessions or Islands. He would collect each, but would pursue a particular series at different times. He was always knowledgeable about each of his notes and could discuss them with experts in the different fields.

Amon would trust a fellow collector implicitly. I was amazed how he trusted others, many who were almost strangers. In 1968 the ANA convention was in Houston, Texas. I visited his table, looked at some notes, and told him that I would like to copy the "specs" from several notes to assist in my research. He said that he had an appointment shortly and spontaneously added, "Take them along with you to your motel, copy the different specifications, and bring them back tomorrow morning." Incredulous, with the lot in my hands I said "Aren't you going to count them?" He made as not to bother, so, right there in front of him, I counted them. There were 24 different notes, all rare as the dickens. I still have the list of detailed information I copied from those notes that night, and I am still amazed by the trust that he could have in others. Perhaps (at least in this case), the busier and greater the man, the more generous he is.

SOME RECOLLECTIONS OF "MR. PHIL"

William A. Philpott, Jr., of Dallas, Texas, was quite a dapper gentleman. With a natty straw hat and spats, he cut a neat figure, despite his advanced age. Rather short of stature, he was nonetheless a "tall" character in numismatics. All through his seventies he was quite a golfer and very few, even younger men, could keep up with him.

Choice paper money was his field and shoe boxes full of old large-size currency in all types were his stock in trade. The quality of his notes became his trademark; he liked to be called "Mr. Phil," so his material soon became known as "Mr. Phil quality."

I first met "Mr. Phil" at the Cadillac Hotel in Detroit at the 1962 ANA Convention where I went to his room to see some of those fabulous notes. The saying about quality, not to mention quantity, is no exaggeration, for when he opened a closet door in his hotel room, there on the shelf were three shoe boxes (men's shoes) full of notes in individual plastic holders. On the closet floor sat three pairs of shoes with shoe stretchers to keep each shoe in perfect condition. He brought out one of the boxes and I picked out three National Bank Notes.

I remember visiting him at his office in Dallas. In the office building across the street from the Baker Hotel we found him "at home" in his office. He sat my wife and daughter down in front of his desk, went over to a drawer, and pulled out a 1935 Silver Certificate signed by Robert A. Anderson and autographed by Robert A. Anderson. He brought it over, handed it to my wife, and said, "This note was autographed by my friend Robert Anderson; I am giving to you. Now if Dewitt wants it, you charge him $25.00 for it." Needless to say, the note found its way into my collection. He was very proud of his library of numismatic books and pointed out several of these, as well as trophies and other memorabilia on the shelves behind his desk. At the time of our visit he was Secretary of the Texas Banker's Association. While at his office I picked out three more "Philpott quality" nationals (First Charter and brownbacks).

While my wife and daughter went to shop at Nieman-Marcus, he took me to his bank, the First National Bank of Dallas. From one of his safe deposit boxes he showed me some of his prize notes. I especially remember seeing quite a few choice brownbacks on Oklahoma and Indian Territory, such as Caddo, and a ten and twenty on Newkirk. He then took me up to the observation deck on the fiftieth floor of that new building and showed me all of Dallas. He pointed in one direction and said "That's where I live. It's five miles and often when the weather is nice, I walk to the office." He did not drive and had a sister who was a demanding housekeeper. His wife had died on Christmas Day, some years previously, which was quite a blow to "Mr. Phil."

We met the ladies back at the Baker Building. He called a cab, herded us in the back, climbed in front by the driver. We went out to the book depository where he had the cabbie wait while we visited the scene where President John F. Kennedy was killed. Back at the hotel and across the street from his office, he took us to his "Club" where he ate regularly. He called for his favorite waiter. He told us to order whatever we wanted, which we did, for I suspect the price had been included in the cost of the notes that I had selected. I remember the prime roast of beef that he wanted well done, selecting the outer cuts. For dessert, he

had the waiter roll over the three-tiered oval cart from which we made our selections. He recommended the black forest cake, which had thin slivers of chocolate on it. Thus ended our visit with "Mr. Phil."

"Mr. Phil" told me how, over the years, he had bought up so many of his notes. Many he bought at face value. He had many agents looking for notes of interest for him. In the early days he would sometimes have to borrow money to pay for them — especially after the sale of the famous A. A. Grinnell Collection, which was conducted as seven sales from 1944 to 1946 by Barney H. Bluestone of Syracuse, N.Y. Many of the famous rarities came to him from these sales, for example the fifty- and hundred-dollar brownbacks of Albuquerque, Territory of New Mexico, with the opposite backs. Looking again at the seven sales of the A. H. Grinnell Collection of United States Paper Currency, I find many "pedigreed notes" which I have seen change hands several times. Fortunately, several of these "gems" have found their way into our collection.

Years ago I wrote to "Mr. Phil," wanting to buy about fifteen very rare notes. He told me that he was interested in selling them all at once to "someone of means." I was smart enough to know that this let me out. So, sadly, I missed these and Amon Carter got them. It took some ten to fifteen years to gather in several of these rare notes. The last of these that we recently acquired was the twenty-dollar First Charter Series 1875 on Ogden, "State of Utah," with the territorial seal.

"Mr. Phil" wrote quite a few articles for *The Numismatist*, the journal of the American Numismatic Association, as well as for other publications. These articles were primarily about type notes. He was of the "old school." He thought that currency should be collected according to the U.S. treasury seals and treasury signatures, "star notes," matched serial numbers, low serial numbers, and runs of these in different series, especially the type notes. One would do well to read these articles from *The Numismatist*, the *Numismatic Scrapbook*, and others.

"Mr. Phil" died quite unexpectedly a few years ago at the age of 83 and has been sorely missed by our fraternity.

THE TUCSON STORY

The year was 1968. The ANA convention was held in the El Capitan Hotel in San Diego. My wife, daughter and I were on our second trip west, up and down the country visiting the state capitols and collecting the "official" seal of each state. We stopped and visited our son and his family. At that time he was in the Navy and attending the Naval Postgraduate School in Monterey, California, but they were living about fifteen miles away in Marina.

From nearby San Francisco I flew to San Diego to attend the convention. There was a dealer there from Catlettsburg, Kentucky who showed me a very rare note on Tucson, Arizona Territory (five-dollar First Charter Period). I asked how much he wanted for it and he answered "Fifteen hundred dollars." I knew I just had to have it. I offered him $800 which he rejected. The next morning I was ready to raise my offer, but the note had already been sold (a lesson I was to learn more than once). If you get a chance to hold a rare note in your hot little hands, do not let it go! The man who bought that note was William A. Anton, Sr. who gave the man 1500 silver dollars for it. It was ten or eleven years before I again had the opportunity to acquire it. Needless to say the sky was the limit. With inflation and the appreciation of collectibles as a whole, the price was several times what it had sold for in 1969. Suffice it to say, for the benefit of the collection, I couldn't afford to let it go this time at any price.

Only three First Charter Notes are known on Arizona Territory, all fives, and from one bank, the only bank in the territory to issue National Bank Notes. This example is missing the right top corner, but I still consider it the finest known.

THE TALLAHASSEE STORY

On March 11 through 13, 1965, there was a public auction held at the Waldorf Astoria Hotel, New York City, by Abner Kreisberg, Jerry Cohen, and Hans M. F. Schulman. Robert Friedberg, the publisher of our paper money "bible," had recently died. Many, if not all of the rare paper money type notes were in this auction, several of which were the same notes illustrated in his *Paper Money of the United States*. At that time I was "hot" into type notes, one dollar through one hundred dollars, so I bid on several notes, a few successfully. I had no real knowledge of the true value of the notes, but more or less went by the estimate of each lot or by pulling a figure out of the air.

With the auction catalog in front of me now, after the fact, I can admire my purchases. Lot #963 was a date-back Second Charter Period one-hundred dollar note signed by Napier and McClung on the First National Bank of Albuquerque, New Mexico Territory. This note I later traded to Amon Carter. Lot #967 contained the rare "FIFTY DOLLARS" (spelled out on the back) note on the Canal National Bank of New Orleans, one of four of this type. Lot #1013 was the rare 1891 one-hundred dollar Treasury or Coin Note, a very rare and desirable note indeed.

Lot #958 was a one-hundred dollar note dated 1882 on the First National Bank of Tallahassee, Florida. This crisp uncirculated brownback note was signed by Rosecrans and Huston, serial number B9702 and bank serial #317. Notes of this series in this condition from Florida are rare. At that time this note was estimated by the cataloguer to be worth $1750; I bid $950 and got it. Unfortunately, I had not narrowed my interest in collecting to the National Bank Notes, nor did I realize what a rarity this was. I already had a twenty dollar brownback on Pensacola, and still needed money to buy other notes. In a little over two years I was ready to sell it.

In August 1967 I was at the ANA convention in Miami Beach, Florida. On the bourse floor, I showed the one-hundred dollar Tallahassee note to three or four dealers. Walk-

ing on to the next table, a man tapped me on my shoulder, asking to see the note. Moving away from the tables, he examined it closely. Then he asked me how much I wanted for it. I said "One thousand dollars." He motioned me over to one side, out of the traffic near the stage curtains. Here he examined it minutely, taking it out of the holder, holding it up to the light, laying it flat on one finger, balanced, to see if there was even the slightest fold. Apparently satisfied, he started pulling cash out of every pocket he had, even his vest pockets, and finally counted out $1000. I went back to the motel that night feeling pretty good, picked up my wife, and swung her around the floor, despite knowing that I had made only $50 in a little over two years.

The new owner, who had moved to Florida some thirty years before, kept it about two or three years, and was wondering what to do with the Tallahassee note. A female collector from Tallahassee bought it for $2600 through an intermediary who made $100 for arranging the transaction. This collector kept it perhaps six years. Then my Florida syngraphic friend stopped by to see this lady and in less than a year, bought it back from her for $12,000. Now you will find this hard to believe — that same year, 10 years after my original purchase of it, I bought it back at $17,500. Now that's what I call INFLATION! I know a lot of you out there are saying "What a fool! Buys it for $950 and about ten years later, buys it back for that price!" But I had good reason. On today's market, I think it's worth it. Remember, everyone trying to collect a large-size note from each capitol city needs a Tallahassee note. There are only three known, the second one being nearly equal to this one. The third one is a later issue (according to the bank serial number) and is much circulated. The First National Bank of Tallahassee (charter #4132) operated from 1889 through 1916. It issued brownbacks, Series 1882 and date-back Series 1902, Third Charter Period only. It issued fifties and hundreds only. The Lewis Brothers did not want to get writer's cramp signing notes. Here is some information on their issues:

The First National Bank of Tallahassee (Charter #4132)
—Chartered in 1889 with a capital of $50,000
—Succeeded B.C. Lewis & Sons
—Placed in voluntary liquidation on July 12, 1916
—Circulation issued:
Second Charter Period brownbacks
   967 sheets, one fifty and one hundred to each sheet, Serials 1 to 967
Third Charter 1902-1908 date-backs
   50-100 plate = $75,000; Serials 1 to 500
   50-50-50-100 plate = $5,000; Serials 1 to 20
—Total circulation issued: $225,050
—Amount outstanding at close: $48,250
—Amount outstanding in October, 1916: $45,250

(Note: Some of the Lewis Brother heirs are still in the banking business operating as The Lewis State Bank. Also, see this note, NOTE #27C, pictured on following page.)

NOTE #27C:

DENOMINATION/ SERIES: One Hundred Dollars/1882 Brownback
BANK/CHARTER: The First National Bank of Tallahassee, #4132
FEDERAL DATA: Serial #B9702–, signed by Rosecrans and Huston
BANK DATA: Dated October 2, 1889, Plate letter "A," Bank serial #317. Organized in 1889, this bank only issued 967 sheets, one fifty-dollar and one-hundred-dollar note on each sheet, and also Third Charter date-

backs, also fifty- and one-hundred-dollar notes. Outstanding at close was $45,250.
BANK SIGNATURES: B.C. Lewis, Cashier, and J.W. Lewis, President, signed in pen.
BACK: Large charter number (4132)
SEAL: Florida seal as found on National Bank Notes
CONDITION: Bought as Uncirculated
SOURCE: Robert Friedberg Estate
RARITY: Rare. Best of only 3 notes known on Tallashassee.

THE WINNEMUCCA STORY

In August 1970 my wife and I went to the St. Louis ANA Convention. I went principally to buy the Winnemucca note. If you have ever driven across country on U.S. 40, now I-80, or the old route before that, chances are that you drove through or gassed up without even noticing the town name, Winnemucca, Nevada, named for an Indian chief. The First National Bank of Winnemucca was one of the "Nevada 16," described by M. Owen Warns in his book, *Nevada Sixteen National Banks and their Mining Camps* (see Bibliography). This bank holds the distinction of being the only bank in Nevada to issue brownback notes. It is rumored that a five-dollar note exists on Winnemucca, but I have no hard evidence that it is out there. Until it is known, shown, and/or photographed, it must be classed as only a rumor. The only known Nevada brownback is a ten dollar note owned by Robert Medlar and is shown in this book through his courtesy. The firm of Hickman & Waters found this particular note in Texas. It seems that some lady had it in her Bible. Hickman & Waters reportedly paid her $800. They admitted to me that they knew I wanted and needed the note, and that whatever they had asked for it would have been too much for me (which it possibly would have been). They thought that the only fair way to sell it was to place it in auction, which they did.

The sale was late one Friday night during the St. Louis ANA Convention sale. I registered and got an auction identification number. Remember, this was 1970. The air that night was tense and electric. Evidently a book bid of $1500 started the bidding; from there on it was hard to keep up with the bidding from the floor ... $1600, $1700, $1800, $1900. I turned around and looked behind me. There sat Amon Carter and John Rowe bidding on it. My heart sank as I also sank deeper into my seat. I did not get my hand up once and thereby made one of the greatest mistakes of my life. Needless to say, I am still regretting it and kicking myself. At the time, I was about $3000 in debt and was very timid about going further into debt. At any rate, the bidding continued. Hands shot up ... $2000, $2100, $2200, $2300 ... Amon bid $2400 or $2450 and got the note. Immediately after the sale he said that he would have stopped at $2700 or $2750. I honestly doubt if Amon would have gone over $3000. Even though Amon was a man of means, he would not let anyone make a fool of him. He would not overpay. I honestly believe I could have gotten it for $3500 or less. Needless to say, I have been regretting it ever since, and through later years, I tried to buy it or trade him out of it. Each time he would say, "Dewitt, if I have more than one of an item, I'll divide with you," ... (and he would) ... "but if I have only one, I want to keep it."

In Memphis, May of 1982, I exerted a little pressure on him for this and one other note we then lacked (the Ogden, Utah State twenty-dollar First Charter Period note with the territorial seal, which we later bought from his estate). I remember his expression, his earnestness, and feel that he did really want to help me. So this time he left his table, came out into the aisle, and we walked a few feet toward the stage to be out of the line of traffic. With the inevitable cigar in his mouth, he told me again that if he only had one of an item he wanted to keep it. He told me that I could borrow them (there were a total of four notes involved) photograph them, use their pictures in a book, exhibit them, anything at all, but that he was just not ready to part with them.

Now I often wonder that if I had borrowed them at that time I might have had an inside track, or, at least a better chance at them later. For as you may know, Amon died on July 19, 1982 on his way to Love Field. This was a great loss to the hobby. Apparently Amon had promised the Winnemucca ten-dollar note to a fellow Texan, and it sold at $33,000! If and when it sells again, what will be the price?

CHAPTER FIVE
EUREKA! THE COLLECTION NEARS COMPLETION

After nearly 35 exciting, fun-filled years, with each suc-ceeding year passing more swiftly than the year before, this collection is nearing completion. The almost ten years since retirement have flown at an especially rapid rate. Both my wife and I say now that we don't see how we had time to work.

I have never learned who originated the idea to use the seals on the National Bank Notes. Most likely it was one of the designers of the First Charter Original Series. But re-gardless of whose idea it first was, it was a grand one. Apparently, each state sent a drawing of its state's seal. The artists at the bank note companies or the Bureau of En-graving and Printing had to reshape these to fit them into the space allowed in the upright oval. In the early days transportation was a problem, especially for states in the mountainous West, such as Montana and Nevada. Mail often had to go all the way around the Horn to San Fran-cisco and then still had mountains to hurdle. Slow trans-portation may have been the reason that no territorial seals appeared on Montana, Washington or Wyoming Territorial notes. This also may have been a factor in Nebraska's never showing a state seal after statehood since the territo-rial seal was used throughout the period. Poor transporta-tion seems an improbable cause, however, in the case of Iowa, where no seal was employed until the 1890's on the second portion of the brownbacks.

Were it not for all these mysteries, seeming lack of logic, etc., this pursuit would not be challenging. We would soon tend to lose interest if everything were laid out for us. But it certainly would be interesting to learn the reasons for these discrepancies.

This collection lacks the Winnemucca brownback note to complete the state seals. We lack the First Charter and brownback notes on Dakota Territory for towns and banks that are now located in North Dakota. Both of our Dakota Territory notes are in what is now South Dakota; since both Dakotas comprised Dakota Territory however, as far as the seals on the territorial notes are concerned, all seals are the same. This collection also lacks the only Washington Ter-ritory note known at this time. However, it shows *no* seal. Of course the Mississippi First Charter and the Juneau, Alaska brownback are still not known in any collection.

In addition to the notes listed and pictured within the pages of this book, the collection also contains a previ-ously unreported one-dollar note on Omaha, Nebraska Territory. My partner recently acquired this note on the First National Bank of Omaha, Nebraska Territory charter #209. So, this makes two ones and, I think, three twos known on Nebraska Territory. Mr. Aubrey E. Bebee owns the first one-dollar note and has had it for several years.

The next known was Amon's lazy two on the same bank as ours. There are two ones, both on Omaha (#209), and three twos extant all on the Otoe County National Bank of Nebraska City, Nebraska Territory (#1417). This fact is strange, inasmuch as the two-dollar notes were all printed on 1-1-1-2 plates. Since the eventually-rather-large bank (#1633 — Omaha National Bank, Nebraska Territory) opened for business in 1866, possibly a few months before statehood (March 1, 1867), it is possible this bank also issued Nebraska territorial notes, although none are known.

Also in this collection are quite a few other notes, mostly collected by my partner, some of which I have not even seen. He is strong in the Western, especially the Northwest-ern states. The collection contains First Charter Period and/or 1882 Series brownback notes from approximately half the state capitol cities. A few are duplicates, in the sense that they have been upgraded. So proud am I of them that I am tempted to list each one, but will spare you.

When I began to collect nationals in the Fifties and the "official" state seals in the Fifties and Sixties, it was an easy and natural step to sell my type notes (1972) to be more able to buy the rare First Charter and brownbacks as the opportunities occurred. At one time or another I owned almost every type of note issued, including the one-, two-, five-, ten-, twenty-, fifty-, and hundred-dollar bills. A well known paper-money dealer (now deceased) from New York City flew to Charlotte and purchased my type note collection which consisted of 145 pieces in far better than average condition. Naturally I kept my National Bank Notes. So now I was well on my way to forming what is today the most complete collection of its type in existence.

The collection is not the largest in number of pieces, not the greatest in value, perhaps, but it is the most complete as to known First Charter and brownback notes, there being one, two, three, or more notes from every state and territory in the United States.

The remainder of the book consists of photographs of the notes of the Prather Collection, drawings of the state seals, and descriptive and explanatory comments on both. A series of pages are allotted to each state in the order in which it entered the Union, followed by the District of Co-lumbia. When the state's territorial status impacts upon the history of the notes, territorial seals, notes, and data are included.

A few additional words of explanation might be helpful. Each state has many "official attributes," such as state bird, state flower, and so forth. To list each attribute for every state would require more space than is available in this book. Additionally, the seals can most efficiently be de scribed in the language of heraldry, but this language is arcane to most. Since it is inevitable that some of this language must be used in many of the descriptions, some introduction to the terminology is required. Therefore, I have used the state of Delaware to illustrate the extent of "official attributes" as well as a rather full introduction to heraldic terminology. I have also listed Maryland with these heraldic terms explained, because this state's seal (particularly the reverse of the seal) has much to offer.

This might be a good place to note that in the territories of the west, upon reaching statehood, the very small number of banks operating started issuing First Charter *state* notes, but not all did; (see Bibliography for *Territorials*, by Peter Huntoon). These are mostly very rare, more so than even most collectors of nationals realize. The territorial notes are the "glamour" notes, therefore they are much sought after. But in most cases these state notes are much more rare. Since they are state notes and not territorials, they do not presently command as large a premium.

As an exception regarding rarity, however, consider Nebraska. Nebraska was the 37th state, admitted in 1867. Although Nebraska had become a state, the Bureau (and the banks) kept on using the territorial seal all the way through the state brownback notes. In fact, territorial notes were issued long after statehood. Except for the last five states, Nebraska was the only state not to show the now "official" *state* seal on its currency. Steinmetz, in his book, states that there are "no territorial issues" from the three banks that might have issued them. We now know this to be in error. There are two one-dollar notes on Omaha, Nebraska Territory, and three two-dollar notes, all on Nebraska City, Nebraska Territory (Otoe County National Bank of Nebraska City, Nebraska Territory, charter #1417). One is in the Carter Collection (for sale, as of this writing), and one is in the J. L. Irish Territorial Notes collection. Ours is the third one, bank serial #307. Our note is probably the only one that actually circulated during the territorial period. I understand that all are similar in condition, about Very Good. It was less than three years from the issue of the first territorial notes to statehood; then twenty banks issued First Charter state notes. So the rarity rating on Nebraska State does not apply as above.

Before August 1, 1975, I had never met my partner. At this point, I cannot remember who contacted whom first, but we had been corresponding for possibly two years. Since I had just about reached the limits of my ability to buy the super-rare notes, was approaching retirement, and my children were not particularly interested in my collection, I was, frankly, thinking of selling it.

For a vacation my wife and I flew to Hawaii in June 1974. This made a total of 49 states (and capitols) we had visited. Returning home, at church I was talking to a good friend who had gone to Hawaii in January 1974 and had also now visited 49 of the 50 states. I said to him, "...you have been to 49 states and now I have, too. We need to get together and visit number fifty." July 3, 1975 we two couples left home in his motor home for a trip to Alaska. He drove each morning and then, after lunch, I drove. Each morning I kept the log — mileage, places visited, etc. We had a wonderful experience and in exactly eight weeks, reached home with precisely 13,106 miles under our tires. I have memories of the Alcan highway, the fun trip with the motor home on a flat car and us in the last coach of the Whitepass and Yukon narrow gauge railway from Whitehorse to Skagway, Alaska, and the inside passage from Skagway to Juneau. I also got to attend the 1975 ANA convention on that trip.

From previous correspondence we made plans to stop in east central Washington state and find my future hobby partner. I felt strange, having never seen him before, and bringing others with me, albeit we had our "beds" with us. We shared a memorable outdoor supper, and in the wee hours of the morning, a handshake sealed our deal.

I have never met a more honest and trusting man. He bought my collection on the basis of having seen an auction-type listing. At his insistence, I sent him a third of the collection only upon his payment of a third of the selling price, with the second and third portions following similarly. We thereby entered a relationship whereby we could continue to buy the super-rare notes. Ten, twelve, fourteen, and seventeen and a half thousand dollars — amounts that neither of us could afford by ourselves — were now available to us. I took my costs and put that amount into certificates of deposit. The profits went into rare gold coins. On the CD's I could borrow up to 90% on each CD, so, when one of these high powered rare notes became available it would be purchased with borrowed money. The savings and loans charged me two percent over the interest rates they were paying. My partner sent me a check each month for the interest which I then passed on to the savings and loan. My only benefit from these transactions was the huge pleasure of seeing and helping to complete this marvelous collection.

Now some nine years later we need two more notes for completion, one with a state seal and one without a seal.

Now you understand why I am happy to say "we" when speaking of this collection.

CHAPTER SIX

THE PRATHER COLLECTION

DESCRIBED

#1 — DELAWARE

NAME: After Lord De La Warr

NICKNAME: "The First State" or "The Diamond State"

ENTERED THE UNION: December 7, 1787

CAPITAL: Dover

SEAL: Delaware's seal today (see PLATE III) is similar to one adopted in 1777. The Swiss-born artist, Pierre Eugene du Simitere said in his notebooks that he made a drawing of the seal in January, 1777. From 1793 until 1847, however, the supporters, a husbandman and a rifleman, were omitted; in 1847 the motto "Liberty and Independence" was first used on the seal. The shield has a wheat sheaf and an ear of maize at the top and a ruminating ox below. The husbandman holds a hilling hoe; the rifleman holds a musket. By law the crest is a ship under full sail on an azure and argent (blue and silver) wreath. State documents, however, indicate the wreath colors as white and red. The dates on the rim refer to years in which authorization was granted for new dies. The seal is two and one-half inches in diameter emblazoned as follows: "Party per fess, or and argent, the first charged with a garb (wheat sheaf) in bend dexter, and an ear of maize (Indian Corn) in bend sinister, both proper; the second charged with an ox statant, ruminating, proper; fess, wavy azure — supporters on the dexter a husbandman with a hilling hoe, on the sinister a rifleman armed and accoutred at ease. Crest, on a wreath azure and

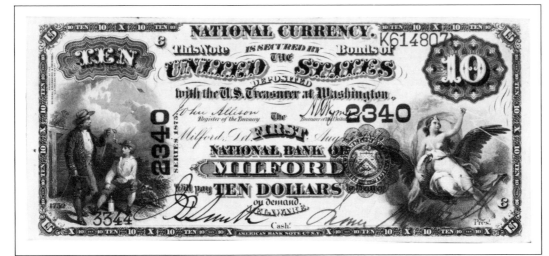

NOTE #1A:

DENOMINATION/SERIES: Ten Dollars/Series 1875

BANK/CHARTER: First National Bank of Milford (#2340)

FEDERAL DATA: Serial #K614807–2, signed by Allison and Wyman

BANK DATA: Dated August 15, 1876, Plate Letter "C," Serial #3344. The bank operated from 1876 to 1935 and issued Series 1875 and all three Second Charter

Period notes, but issued only the plain-back notes of the 1902 Series Third Charter Period. It also issued fives, tens, and twenties of both types of small size notes.

BANK SIGNATURES: J.L. Smith, Cashier, and James M. Hill, President

BACK: *Desoto Discovering the Mississippi.*

SEAL: Seal of the State of Delaware

CONDITION: Extra Fine, purchased as Uncirculated.

SOURCE: Purchased from R. Green, Chicago, IL, July 31, 1954

RARITY: All Delaware notes are scarce. Only eleven banks issued Original Series First Charter Period notes and fourteen issued Series 1875. The First National Bank of Milford had $4500 in large notes still outstanding in 1935.

argent, a ship under full sail, proper; with the words 'Great Seal of the State of Delaware,' and also the motto 'Liberty and Independence' engraved thereon."[1] The seal was adopted in 1777 and revised in 1793, 1847, 1871, and 1907.

TREE: By act of the Assembly on May 1, 1939, the American Holly *Ilex opaca aiton* became the official tree of Delaware.

BIRD: A tradition recorded by historians tells of the "Blue Hen's Chickens." During the early days of the Revolutionary War, the men of Captain Jonathan Caldwell's company, who had been recruited in Kent County, took with them game chickens noted for their fighting ability, said to be of the brood of a famous blue hen. When the soldiers were not fighting they amused themselves by pitting these "blue hen" chickens against all comers. The fame of these cock fights spread throughout the army and when in battle,

the Delaware men fought so valorously that they received the sobriquet "Blue Hen's Chickens."

FLOWER: The Peach Blossom was adopted as the state flower of Delaware because in the early years the state had so many peach orchards.

---

[1] From "The Great Seal of Delaware;" Delaware State Development Department pamphlet; Dover, Delaware.

[2] Symbols were sometimes used as suffixes to serial numbers. See note under "Serial Numbers," in Chapter 2.

NOTE #1B:

DENOMINATION/ SERIES: Ten Dollars/Brownback Series 1882

BANK/CHARTER: Citizen's National Bank of Middletown (#1181)

FEDERAL DATA: Serial #T73946–, signed by Bruce and Jordan

BANK DATA: Dated May 16, 1885, Plate letter "A," Serial #5560. Bank operated from 1865 to 1918.

BANK SIGNATURES: Jno. S. Crouch, Cashier, and Joseph Biggs, President

BACK: Large charter number (1181) in green lathe-work.

SEAL: Shows the Delaware seal

CONDITION: Extra Fine

SOURCE: Purchased from William P. Donlon, August 18, 1961

RARITY: There was $80,000 outstanding in large notes on this bank in 1918. Twenty-one Delaware banks issued brownback notes all of which are scarce.

#2 — PENNSYLVANIA

NAME: Named by Charles II for William Penn. The name means "Penn's Woods."

NICKNAME: The Keystone State (central to the colonies, hence "keystone")

ENTERED THE UNION: December 12, 1787

CAPITAL: Harrisburg

SEAL: Pennsylvania, classed as a Commonwealth, has a coat of arms (PLATE II), the central portion of which, the shield, is the seal. Living in Harrisburg as a young man, I remember the beautiful capitol building and how, even then, I was intrigued by the huge bronze doors and especially by the door knobs in bronze, each and all with the coat of arms thereon. The Pennsylvania seal has a blue background and also a reverse side in gold. United States National Bank Notes show the coat of arms, a black horse on the left side and a white horse on the right holding up the shield. The entire coat of arms shows up beautifully on the National Bank Notes. The seal of Pennsylvania (PLATE IX, the seal in use today) was adopted in 1776 with the obverse having a central shield, which has a ship at the top, a plow at the center, and three sheaves of wheat at the bottom. A stalk of maize and an olive branch and leaves surround the shield, and above it, as a crest, is an American eagle. The reverse of the seal shows Liberty, with a drawn sword in her right hand and a staff and a cap in her left, trampling a lion, representing Tyranny being crushed. An inscription, "Both Can't Survive," is in the border. Both First and Second Charter brownback National Bank Notes show the coat of arms, that is, horses supporting the shield and a motto: "Virtue, Liberty and Independence" underneath.

---

[3] Legibility of signatures affects interpretation in many cases. The author remains open for corrections.

NOTE #2A:

DENOMINATION/ SERIES: Five Dollar/ First Charter Original

BANK/CHARTER: The Gettysburg National Bank (#611)

FEDERAL DATA: Serial #N520210), signed by Colby and Spinner

BANK DATA: Dated December 14, 1864, Plate letter "A," Serial #4089

BANK SIGNATURES: Pen signed by J. Emry Bair,[3] Cashier, and G. Swope, President.

BACK: *Landing of Columbus, 1492.*

SEAL: Shows Pennsylvania seal

CONDITION: Very Fine

SOURCE: Purchased from Earl Minnick, January 20, 1950

RARITY: Not rare

NOTE #2B:

DENOMINATION/SERIES: Ten Dollars/1882 Brownback

BANK/CHARTER: The Gettysburg National Bank (#611), Regional letter "E"

FEDERAL DATA: Serial #A125744A, signed by Bruce and Wyman

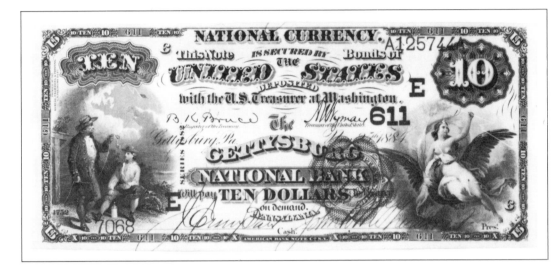

BANK DATA: Dated November 25, 1884, Plate letter "C," Bank serial #7068. Opening for business in 1864, this bank issued all except Second Charter Period date-backs and value-backs. Abraham Lincoln stayed across the street from this bank the night prior to his famous Gettysburg Address. In commuting back and forth from Harrisburg to Waynesboro in 1936/1937 I passed this bank many times.

BANK SIGNATURES:
Pen signatures of J. Emry Bair, Cashier and John (?), President
BACK: Large charter number (611)
SEAL: Pennsylvania coat of arms (seal)
CONDITION: Uncirculated
SOURCE: Purchased from Wm. A. Philpott, Jr., April 10, 1962
RARITY: Not rare
COMMENT: This collection also contained at one time the five- and twenty-dollar brownbacks on this bank.

#3 —
NEW JERSEY

NAME: Named after the island of Jersey, off the coast of England
NICKNAME: The Garden State
ENTERED THE UNION: December 18, 1787

CAPITAL: Trenton
SEAL: The seal of New Jersey (see PLATE II) was authorized in 1776 and shows three plowshares on a central shield, supported on the right by Ceres and on the left by Liberty. The crest is a helmet surmounted by a steed's head and the motto "Liberty and Prosperity" along with the date, 1776, located on a streamer at the bottom. National Bank Notes omit the helmet in the crest.

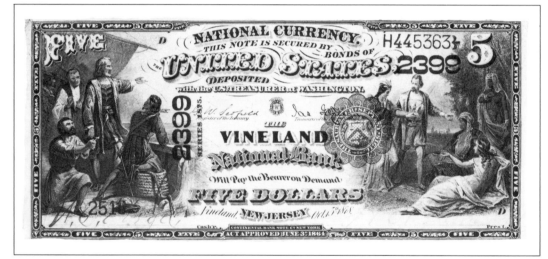

NOTE #3A:

DENOMINATION/ SERIES: Five Dollar/ Series 1875
BANK/CHARTER: The Vineland National Bank, Vineland, N.J. (#2399)
FEDERAL DATA: Serial #H445363–, signed by Scofield and Gilfillan
BANK DATA: Dated Oct. 15, 1878, Plate letter "D," Serial #2513. The Vineland bank operated only from 1878 to 1881 and issued only Series 1875 First Charter notes. Only $280 was outstanding in

1910. New Jersey notes are not rare, but this note is on a rare bank.
BANK SIGNATURES: Both illegible. Cashier's signature is a pen signature.
BACK: *The Landing of Columbus in 1492*
SEAL: The New Jersey seal
CONDITION: Extra Fine
SOURCE: Purchased from L.S. Werner, August 30, 1961
RARITY: Not rare.

NOTE #3B:

DENOMINATION/ SERIES: Ten Dollar/ 1882 Brownback

BANK/CHARTER: The Phillipsburg National Bank, Phillipsburg, N.J. (#1239)

FEDERAL DATA: Serial #K897562–, signed by Bruce and Jordan

BANK DATA: May 14, 1885, Plate letter "B," Serial #4539

BANK SIGNATURES: Pen signed by A. Bachman, Cashier and S. Rostipes, President

BACK: Shows large charter number (1239) in green with a brown border

SEAL: The New Jersey state seal

CONDITION: Extra Fine/About Uncirculated

SOURCE: Purchased from Paul Kagin at auction, December 19, 1959

RARITY: Not rare as either a state or a bank.

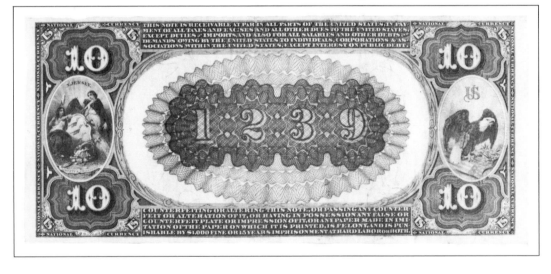

#4 — GEORGIA

NAME: Named for
King George II of England
NICKNAME:
The Peach State
ENTERED THE UNION:
January 2, 1788
CAPITAL: Atlanta

SEAL: The seal of Georgia (PLATE III) has an obverse and a reverse side. In the Governor's office in the Capitol in Atlanta, a secretary opened a drawer and handed me a wax pendant. A lavender ribbon on the inside looping at the top made two streamers at the bottom. The wax disk was about one quarter of an inch thick. I sliced through the center and melted the wax over low heat so that I could display the seal. Adopted in 1799, the obverse of the seal shows three columns supporting an arch emblazoned "Constitution." The left column is labeled "Wisdom," the center column reads "Justice," and the right column, "Moderation," with the date of statehood below. Between the center and right columns a man is standing with drawn sword. "State of Georgia" is written around the seal. The reverse shows a three-masted ship with the American flag at a wharf and at the left a man plowing with "Agriculture and Commerce" written above. Note: Limpert says the date on the obverse is the date of statehood, 1776. This is in error. The legislature in 1914 changed the date on the seal from 1799 (the year of the seal's adoption) to 1776 in honor of the Constitution and the Declaration of Independence. The left ovals of all Georgia National Bank Notes show the seal as I have described above.

NOTE #4A:

DENOMINATION/SERIES: Ten Dollar/First Charter Series 1875 (surcharged)
BANK/CHARTER: The First National Bank of Augusta (#1613)

FEDERAL DATA: Serial #K13001, signed by John Allison and Jno. C. New
BANK DATA: Dated Jan. 1, 1866, Plate letter "A," Bank serial #4487. This bank opened in 1865 and operated until 1912. It issued Original and Series 1875 First Charter notes; brownbacks (Series 1882);

and both red seals and value-backs in the Third Charter Period. The bank had $106,550 outstanding in 1912.
BANK SIGNATURES: A.C. Beam, Cashier, and Z.M. Cord, President
BACK: Large black picture *DeSoto Discovering the Mississippi*
SEAL: The Georgia state seal.
CONDITION: Extra Fine. We believe this to be the nicest First Charter Georgia note known. We traded a rarer note on Rome,

Georgia in order to improve the condition of the First Charter Georgia note in the collection.
SOURCE: Purchased from Lyn Knight, February, 1984. This note had probably been in the Amon Carter collection earlier.
RARITY: All Georgia First Charter Period notes are rare, with the total number known probably being less than fourteen.

NOTE #4B:

DENOMINATION/SERIES: Twenty Dollar/Series 1882 Brownback

BANK/CHARTER: The National Bank of Brunswick (#4944), Regional letter "S"

FEDERAL DATA: Serial #R601150R, signed by J. Fount Tillman and D.N. Morgan.

BANK DATA: Dated March 17, 1894, Plate letter "A," Serial #5164. Bank opened in 1894 issuing brownbacks and date-backs of Series 1882 and date-backs and plain-backs in the 1902 Series along with the small-size notes. There was $8,580 outstanding in large-size notes in 1935.

BANK SIGNATURES: Stamped signatures uncertain. One appears to be E.D. Walker.

BACK: The large charter number (4944).

SEAL: The Georgia seal

CONDITION: Extra Fine/About Uncirculated — in especially nice condition.

SOURCE: Purchased at auction, Kagin's, May 18, 1972

RARITY: Brownback notes on Georgia are not rare, but not common.

#5 —
CONNECTICUT

NAME: Mohican language for "long river place"
NICKNAME: The Constitution State, previously "The Nutmeg State"
ENTERED THE UNION: January 9, 1788

CAPITAL: Hartford
SEAL: Differing from all other states, Connecticut's seal (PLATE II) is an ellipse (upright oval) and is the result of many changes in the seal (1689, 1711, 1784, 1842, 1864, 1882, and 1931). The last several changes were modifications or corrections in the seal. The upright oval contains three grapevines, two on top and one underneath with the Latin motto, "Qui Transtulit Sustinet," meaning "He who transplanted, sustains." The seal as shown on National Bank Notes is embellished with a flag, cannon, and cannonballs at the left. Two nutmegs are underneath an ornate standard containing the three grapevines, described above, signifying the three original land grants given by the king of England, those of Hartford, Weatherford & Windsor, which together, comprised almost the whole of the present-day state of Connecticut. On a streamer below this fancy standard is the Latin motto, the "Qui" on the bottom left, and on the right and extending all the way up, as if in support, the rest of the Latin motto.

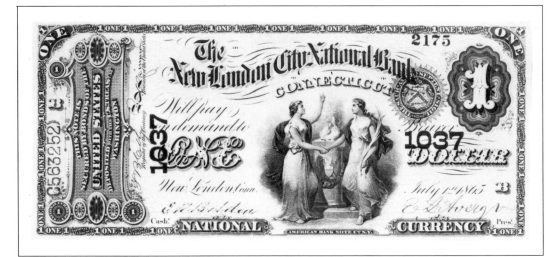

NOTE #5A:

DENOMINATION/ SERIES: One Dollar/Original Series (1863-1875)

BANK/CHARTER: The New London City National Bank (#1037)

FEDERAL DATA: Serial #C563252), signed by Colby and Spinner

BANK DATA: Dated July 1, 1865, Bank serial #2175, Plate letter "B." Opening in 1865, this bank released all issues except date-backs and value-backs of the

1882 series. In 1935 this bank had $8,390 outstanding.

BANK SIGNATURES: Beautiful pen signatures of E.N. Belden and E.D. Avery, "V" President.

BACK: *Landing of the Pilgrims*

SEAL: Left oval shows the Connecticut state seal.

CONDITION: Uncirculated

SOURCE: Purchased from Wm. A. Philpott, Jr., April 16, 1962

RARITY: Not rare.

DENOMINATION/ SERIES: Ten Dollar/1882 Brownback

BANK/CHARTER: The Central National Bank Of Middletown (#1340), Regional letter "N"

FEDERAL DATA: Serial #H807610H, signed by Rosecrans and Jordan

BANK DATA: Dated June 15, 1885, Serial #11298, Plate letter "C." This bank opened in 1865 and issued all series except date-backs and value-backs of Series 1882. The

amount of large-size notes outstanding in 1935 was $9,870.

BANK SIGNATURES: G.E.O. Barnes and A.S. Markham

BACK: Large charter number (1340) in green with a brown border

SEAL: The Connecticut seal. All seals on notes are similar.

CONDITION: Uncirculated

SOURCE: Purchased from Paul Kagin, December 19, 1959

RARITY: Connecticut notes are not rare.

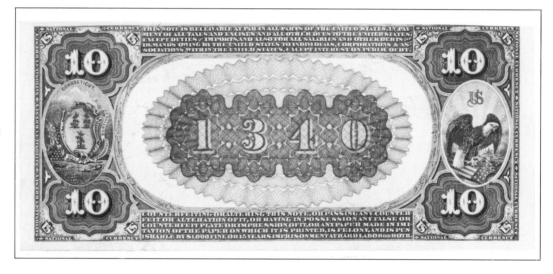

#6 —
MASSACHUSETTS

NAME: Indian
for "large hill place"
NICKNAME: The Bay State
ENTERED THE UNION:
February 6, 1788
CAPITAL: Boston

SEAL: The seal adopted in the first year of statehood (PLATE II) depicts an Indian with his bow in his right hand and an arrow in his left, with a star above the bow. As a crest there is a wreath supporting a right arm grasping a sword. The seal is a shield, the bottom point of which stands in the center of a streamer, which extends upward on each side, which has the Latin motto *Ense Petit Placidam sub Libertate Quietem,* meaning "Peace we seek by the sword, but only under Liberty." The legislative act describes the color of each section and device. It is taken from the Commonwealth's coat of arms. Other than my "official" gold seal, Massachusetts also uses a light green seal (the only state to use green).

COMMENTS ON NOTE #6A: This is the famous "Lazy Two," so called because of the extreme horizontal position of the figure "2." There is a vignette on the face left entitled "Maiden With Flag." The "lazy deuce" is very ornate in design, especially the back, and is much sought after by collectors.

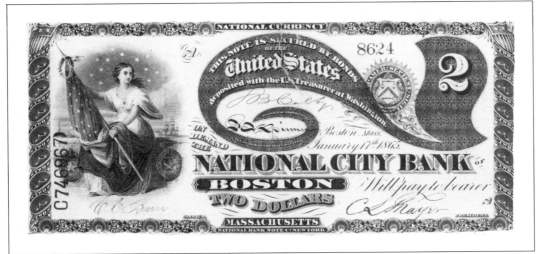

NOTE #6A:

DENOMINATION/ SERIES: Two Dollars/Original Series
BANK/CHARTER: The National City Bank Of Boston (#609 — not listed on note.)
FEDERAL DATA: Serial #C746967), signed by Colby and Spinner
BANK DATA: Dated January 17, 1865, Plate letter "A," Serial #8624. This bank began operating in 1864 and was liquidated on February 15, 1898. It issued only Original and

Series 1875 First Charter notes, and Series 1882 brownbacks. This bank had a total outstanding of $9,759 in 1910.
BANK SIGNATURES: C.C. Barry, Cashier and C.S. Thayer, President
BACK: The central picture in black shows a view of Sir Walter Raleigh in England in 1585 exhibiting products of the new American Colonies.
SEAL: State seal of Massachusetts
CONDITION: Extra Fine, but torn and mended at the top center.

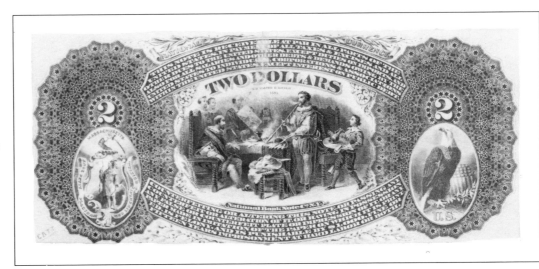

SOURCE: Purchased from French's, October 5, 1950, for less than $7.   **RARITY:** Not rare.

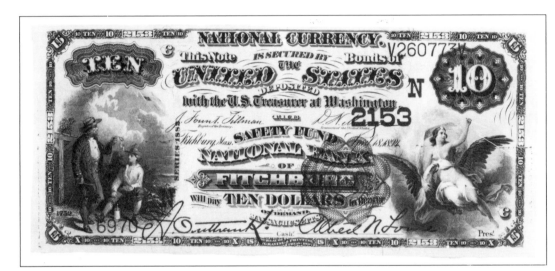

**DENOMINATION/
SERIES:** Ten Dollars/
1882 Brownback

BANK/CHARTER: The
Safety Fund National
Bank Of Fitchburg
(#2153), Regional letter
"N"

FEDERAL DATA: Serial
#V260773V, signed by
Tillman and Morgan

BANK DATA: Dated
April 18, 1894, Plate
letter "C," Bank serial
#6970. Opened in 1874
and released all issues
except value-backs
(1882) and red seals

(1902). Large-size notes
outstanding in 1935
totalled $10,800.

**BANK
SIGNATURES:** A.
Cuttrank, Cashier, and
Albert N. Lowe,
President

BACK: Large charter
number (2153).

SEAL: The seal is the
Massachusetts seal.

CONDITION:
Uncirculated

SOURCE: Purchased
from Wm. P. Donlon,
November 23, 1956

RARITY: Not rare, as
either a state or bank.

#7 — MARYLAND

NAME: Named after Queen Henrietta Marie of England
NICKNAME: The Old Line State
ENTERED THE UNION: April 28, 1788

CAPITAL: Annapolis

SEAL: The seal has both an obverse and a reverse (PLATE III). The original seal was a Calvert seal used by the Lords Baltimore during the years 1648-1692 and 1716-1776. A number of seals were used until 1876 at which date the Legislature re-established the 1648 seal. The obverse depicts Baron Baltimore in armor and plumed helmet with a sword, mounted on his prancing steed. The reverse shows a shield with the Calvert and Crossland arms quartered. The Calvert arms are in the first and fourth quarters, and consist of six pales (vertical stripes), alternately gold and black, with bend dexter counterchanged (diagonal stripe with colors reversed). The Crossland arms in the second and third quarters consist of a quartered field of red and silver, charged with a Greek cross or "botonee" with its arms in trefoils. Crossland arms are counterchanged (red is on silver ground and silver on the red ground). The Crossland arms appear because Alicia Crossland was the heiress mother of George, first Lord Baltimore. The shield is surrounded by an earl's coronet with full faced helmet, indicating Lord Baltimore's rank in America as Count Palatine (one with royal prerogative); his rank in England was only that of a baron. On the helmet is the Calvert crest: a ducal crown with two half bannerets, one gold, one black. The escutcheon (shield) is supported by a fisherman on the right and a farmer with his spade on

NOTE #7A:

DENOMINATION/ SERIES: Five Dollar/Series 1875

BANK/CHARTER: The National Union Bank At Baltimore (#1489)

FEDERAL DATA: Serial #X711039–, signed by Bruce and Gilfillan

BANK DATA: Dated September 1, 1865, Serial #26703, Plate letter "F." This bank operated from 1865 until 1929 and issued all large sizes except date-backs and value-backs, Series 1882. Outstanding in 1929 was $499,997.50. (See **COMMENTS** concerning large (high) serial numbers and plate letters.)

BANK SIGNATURES: R. Mickle, Cash., and Wm. A. Taylor (?), Pres.

BACK: *Landing of Columbus, 1492.*

SEAL: First seal on Maryland banknotes: Justice holding sword and scales; Baltimore harbor in background (PLATE IX).

CONDITION: Uncirculated

SOURCE: Purchased from Wm. A. Philpott, Jr., Dallas, January 20, 1958

RARITY: Since this is on a Baltimore bank, it is not very rare.

the left, symbolic of Baltimore estates in Avalon (Newfoundland) and Maryland. An ermine-lined mantle forms the background and the motto in Italian *Fatti Maschii Parole Femine* means "Deeds are manly, words are feminine." The first seal used on National Bank Notes (see PLATE IX) was an earlier seal showing Justice, blindfolded, holding a sword and scales, which was used on all Maryland First Charter Original and Series 1875 notes, as well as on the first part of the brownback issues up to 1890. This seal is described in more detail below.

COMMENTS: Maryland is the first state that shows a change in the seal on National Bank Notes. As mentioned earlier, there were eight states and the District of Columbia that changed their seals, along with the territories that changed their seals upon becoming states. These changes, some major, some minor, are really what fascinated me and fired my interest in the seals on National Bank Notes. But the changes appear only on the brownback notes (Series 1882), except for the territories which will be noted later.

All of these changes took place from 1890 to 1900: Maryland, #7, became completely different (see paragraph immediately below). In the cases of New York, #11, and North Carolina, #12, positions of both pairs of female figures in each of these two seals were transposed, and other minor additions and changes were made. Vermont, #14, was very different. Ohio, #17, changed the number of arrows from 5 to 17 (indicating its order of entry to the Union), and positions of wheat and arrows are transposed. The seal of Alabama, #22, became altogether different; the changes are explained elsewhere. For state #29, Iowa, an eagle used in place of a seal was changed to the true state

seal; for #30, Wisconsin, a number of changes, including showing the earlier young men grown up, indicating development. The District of Columbia's seal changed from showing Washington on a plaque to showing his figure standing on a pedestal.

First Charter Maryland greenbacks (and the earliest brownbacks) depict Justice holding up the scales in her right hand and an olive branch and sword in the left (PLATE IX). A merchant ship is at a wharf in the left background. If you look closely you will notice other things: a Fascist emblem (a bundle of rods tied with flat cords with an axe head extended) which shows strength in unity; a cornucopia with fruit and produce; and on the lower right side, a scene of Baltimore city. This seal appeared on all brownbacks beginning in 1882. Sometime after 1890 the seal was changed to the one in use today showing the arms of the Lords Baltimore described above. Note the pictures of the Maryland notes. You will see two brownback notes of the same bank, the First National Bank of Baltimore (charter #204), which opened in 1864. In 1883, after twenty years of operation, their charter was renewed. Even though the second note (a five-dollar brownback) bears the same date as the first, one may compare the bank and the federal serial numbers, and see that this note is a later issue. Also, the original five dollar plate was apparently worn out, as evidenced by the plate letter "G."

At the time of Dr. Frank A. Limpert's book *United States National Bank Notes* (the early Fifties), which this author's work humbly follows, updates and expands upon, Dr. Limpert apparently had not seen the first seal on a Maryland brownback note. The first seal on the brownback note is the scarcer of the two. John Hickman records ninety brownbacks with the second, or present day seal, against only twenty brownbacks with the first seal.

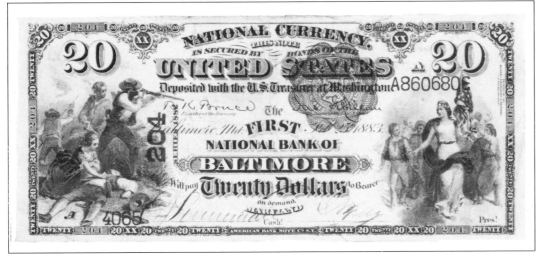

NOTE #7B:

DENOMINATION/ SERIES: Twenty Dollars/1882 Series Brownback

BANK/CHARTER: The First National Bank of Baltimore (#204)

FEDERAL DATA: Serial #A860680–, signed by Bruce and Gilfillan

BANK DATA: Dated February 25, 1883, Bank serial #4065, Plate letter "A." This bank operated from 1864 to 1916, issuing only Originals and Series 1875 First Charter

Period notes, brownbacks only of the Series 1882, then red seals and date-backs of the Third Charter Period Series 1902. Outstanding in 1916 was $235,600.

BANK SIGNATURES: Both signatures illegible

BACK: Large charter number (204)

SEAL: The first seal on Maryland banknotes, as on the note above. See comments on seal. This is not the first seal of Maryland, but rather the first seal used on National Bank Notes; it was used on all First Charter notes and the first part of the brownback notes (PLATE IX).

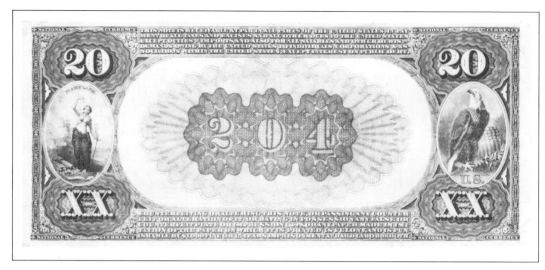

CONDITION: Extra Fine

SOURCE: Purchased from Kagin, February 26, 1962

RARITY: Not extremely rare, but brownbacks on Maryland are divided into the first and second (present-day) seals, this being the rarer of the two used on brownbacks.

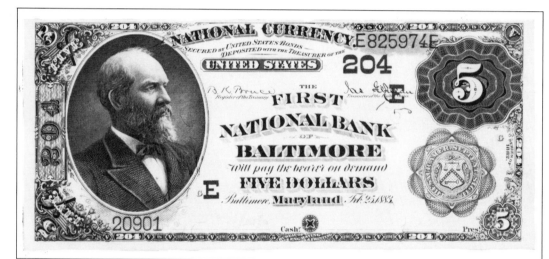

NOTE #7C:

DENOMINATION/ SERIES: Five Dollar/1882 Series Brownback

BANK/CHARTER: The First National Bank of Baltimore (#204), Regional letter E

FEDERAL DATA: Serial #E825974E, signed by Bruce and Gilfillan

BANK DATA: Dated February 25, 1883, the same date as above. This is a new issue; apparently when the first plate is worn out a new one is made, hence the

plate letter "G." The bank serial number is 20901. The remainder of data is the same as the note above.

BANK SIGNATURES: Stamped signatures have faded out.

BACK: Notice that the charter number is still the same (204).

SEAL: The seal is different. This is the second seal used on Maryland National Bank Notes, the one in use now. (PLATE III — see pictures and data on seals for comparison.)

CONDITION: Uncirculated, purchased as About Uncirculated

SOURCE: Purchased from Paul Whisonant, Lincolnton, N.C., April 2, 1969

RARITY: Not rare.

TO STATE 8:

SOUTH CAROLINA

☞

#8 —
SOUTH CAROLINA

NAME: After Charles II of England
NICKNAME: The Palmetto State
ENTERED THE UNION: May 23, 1788

CAPITAL: Columbia

SEAL: The seal of South Carolina has two upright ovals in the circle; these parts are referred to as obverse and reverse. Evidently these were originally back to back, for one source states that the seal is in the form of a circle, four inches in diameter (the largest I've noticed) and four tenths of an inch thick. The seal of South Carolina was first used in 1777, and the obverse shows a palmetto tree and logs,

the primary building material used in the construction of Fort Sumter, on Sullivan's Island in Charleston Harbor. A torn-up oak represents the British ships which were built of oak timbers. Two plaques are dated "March 26" (date of the state constitution) and "July 4" (Independence) and around, as a border, is the motto *Animis Opibusque Paratis* meaning "Prepared in Mind and Resources." The reverse shows a woman with an olive branch in her right hand walking on the seashore between daggers and swords. Above, in the border, is a motto, *Dum Spiro Spero* meaning "While I Breathe, I Hope." Beneath is the word *Spes,* meaning "Hope." All South Carolina First and Second Charter Period Brownbacks show only the obverse portion as described above.

Please see Plates III and IX

NOTE #8A:

DENOMINATION/SERIES: Ten Dollars/First Charter Original Series

BANK/CHARTER: The First National Bank of Charleston, S.C. (#1622)
FEDERAL DATA: Serial #D708623), signed by Colby and Spinner

BANK DATA: Dated January 1, 1866, Bank serial #10818, Plate letter "A." This moderately large bank operated from 1865 to 1926 and issued Original and Series 1875 First Charter notes, brownbacks only of Series 1882, and then all three issues of the 1902 Series. At its closing in 1926 it had outstanding $200,000.
BANK SIGNATURES: Unable to read signatures

BACK: Large picture in black, *De Soto Discovering the Mississippi*
SEAL: The South Carolina state seal as used on National Bank Notes
CONDITION: Extra Fine
SOURCE: Purchases from Hickman and Oakes auction sale
RARITY: Very rare. Nine First Charter notes are known on South Carolina. We think this one is the nicest available.

NOTE #8B:

DENOMINATION/ SERIES: Ten Dollars/ Brownback Series 1882

BANK/CHARTER: The First National Bank Of Charleston, S.C. (#1622), Regional letter "S"

FEDERAL DATA: Serial #B20445B, signed by Rosecrans and Jordan

BANK DATA: Dated December 12, 1885, Plate letter "C," Bank serial #6981. Balance of data same as for note above.

BANK SIGNATURES: Dwight Hughes, Cashier,

and John C. Limond, President, pen signed.

BACK: Large charter number (1622) in green in the center

SEAL: South Carolina seal (obverse) as used on all South Carolina notes

CONDITION: Uncirculated

SOURCE: Purchased from Stack's, May 6, 1956

RARITY: All large size early bank notes of South Carolina are scarce; all brownbacks are rare, especially in this condition.

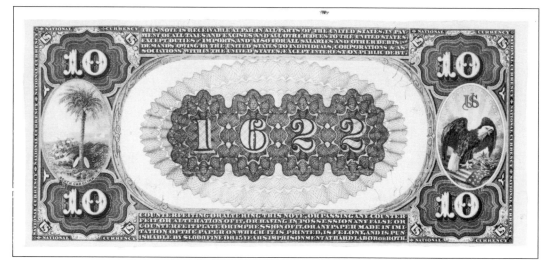

#9 —

NEW HAMPSHIRE

NAME: After
Hampshire County, England
NICKNAME:
The Granite State
ENTERED THE UNION:
June 21, 1788

CAPITAL: Concord

SEAL: The seal of New Hampshire was adopted in 1784 and shows a broadside view of the *Raleigh*, one of the first thirteen ships ordered by our Navy, built at Portsmouth in 1776. The Stars and Stripes flies at the stern and pennants

from the masts. A rising sun is shown on the horizon. Although New Hampshire has only nineteen miles of coastline, Portsmouth had facilities for shipbuilding, so this became very important in the state history. The seal on National Bank Notes shows the *Raleigh* in the shipbuilding process, including a number of workmen, lumber, a team of horses, etc., but no flag, pennant or sun. In fact, the banknote seal looks quite different from the official seal, which shows no workmen or construction; the ship already launched, and anchored in a bay.

Please see Plates II and IX

NOTE #9A:

DENOMINATION/SERIES: Two Dollars (Lazy Two)/Series 1875 First Charter

BANK/CHARTER: The Manchester National Bank, Manchester, New Hampshire (#1059)

FEDERAL DATA: Serial #A765706–, signed by John Allison and A.U. Wyman

BANK DATA: Dated June 15, 1877, Plate letter "A" (as were all twos), Bank serial #1102. This bank opened in 1865 and released all issues except date-backs and value-backs of the 1882 Series and in 1910 had $9,160 outstanding in large size notes.

BANK SIGNATURES: Chas. E. Patch, Cashier, and Nathan Parker, President

BACK: *Sir Walter Raleigh, 1585* exhibiting corn and smoking tobacco

SEAL: New Hampshire state seal (similar to present seal)

CONDITION: Extra Fine.

SOURCE: Traded from Dr. C.A. Bolt, Marshville, N.C.

RARITY: Not rare and not common

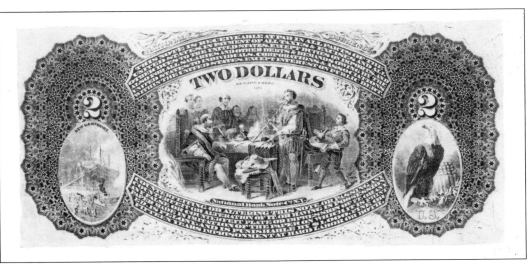

NOTE #9B:

DENOMINATION/SERIES: Ten Dollars/Brownback Series 1882

BANK/CHARTER: The First National Bank of Newport (#888)

FEDERAL DATA: Serial #K564195–, signed by B.K. Bruce and A.U. Wyman

BANK DATA: Dated February 18, 1885, Plate letter "C," Bank serial #2644. This bank opened in 1865 and issued all series except date-back and value-backs, Series 1882. Large size outstanding in 1935 was $14,200.

BANK SIGNATURES: Sam D. Lewis, Cashier and Dexter Richards, President

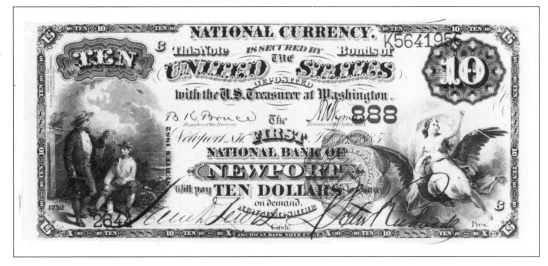

BACK: Large Charter number (888) in center

SEAL: New Hampshire state seal as adopted in 1784. Seals on banknotes show the actual building of the *USS Raleigh* including construction accoutrements, horses, and several workers in the foreground.

CONDITION: About Uncirculated

SOURCE: Purchased from Stack's on July 15, 1955

RARITY: Not rare, either as a state or bank

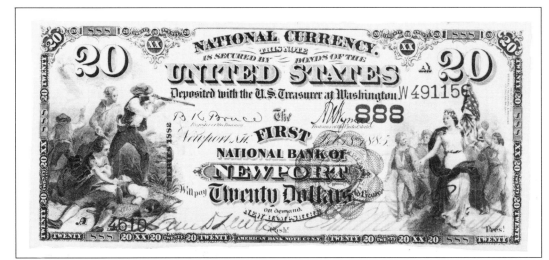

NOTE #9C:

DENOMINATION/ SERIES: Twenty Dollars/Brownback Series of 1882

BANK/CHARTER: First National Bank of Newport (#888)

FEDERAL DATA: Serial #W49115–, signed by B.K. Bruce and A.U. Wyman

BANK DATA: February 18, 1885, Plate letter "A," Bank serial #4610. (Same bank as above.)

BANK SIGNATURES: Sam D. Lewis, Cashier and Seth M. Richards, President

BACK: Large charter number (888) in center.

SEAL: Same seal as on note above. (Also see note below).

CONDITION: Uncirculated

SOURCE: Purchased from Wm. P. Donlon, May 29, 1966

RARITY: Not rare.

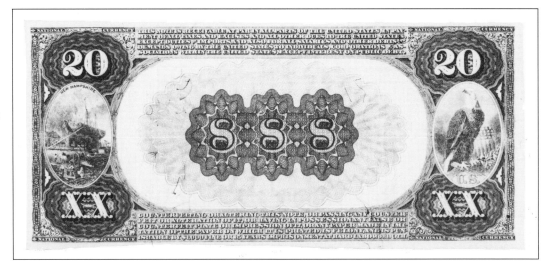

NOTE #9D:

DENOMINATION/SERIES: Five Dollars/1882 Series Brownback
BANK/CHARTER: The First National Bank of Newport (#888)
FEDERAL DATA: Serial #M770945–, signed by Bruce and Wyman

BANK DATA: Dated February 18, 1885, Plate letter "C," Bank serial #10095, (Same bank as NOTE #9B, above.)

BANK SIGNATURES: Sam D. Lewis, Cashier and Seth M. Richards, President

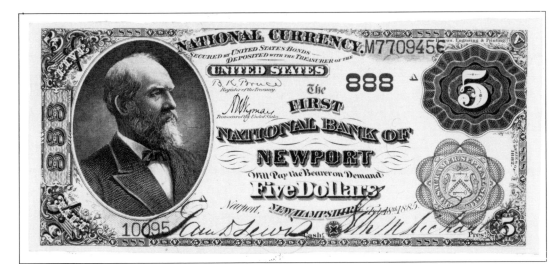

BACK: Same charter number (888) as above.

SEAL: Same seal as above also. Here one can see the different "stances" of eagles shown in the right ovals. All five- and ten-dollar notes, both First Charter and brownback notes, have the stooped or hunched eagle in a landing or take-off position, wings partially spread. The eagle is standing on a U.S. shield, with arrows under its right foot and a laurel branch. Seventeen stars are in a semi-circle around the top under which is "US" intertwined. All one-, two-, twenty-, fifty-, one hundred-, five hundred and one thousand-dollar denominations show an upright eagle in the right oval, with a U.S. flag to the right and "U.S." at the bottom.

CONDITION: Uncirculated

SOURCE: Wm. P. Donlon, purchase date unknown.

RARITY: Not rare.

#10 — VIRGINIA

NAME: After Elizabeth I, the Virgin Queen of England
NICKNAME: The Old Dominion
ENTERED THE UNION: June 25, 1788
CAPITAL: Richmond
SEAL: The seal of Virginia was authorized in 1776 and the obverse shows Virtus with a spear in her right hand and a sheathed sword in her left.

She has her left foot on the prostrate body of Tyranny whose crown is falling off and who has a club in his right hand and a broken chain in his left. "Liberty and Union" is written above the figures and beneath is *Sic Semper Tyrannis,* meaning "Thus ever to tyrants." The reverse depicts Liberty with wand and cap in the center and Ceres with a cornucopia at the right. At the left is Aeternita with a globe and bird. Above them is "Liberty and Union" and at the top is *Perseverando,* meaning "By Perseverance." Greenbacks and brownbacks show Virtus astride Tyranny with a spear in her left hand and a drawn sword in her right.
Please see Plate III

NOTE #10A:

DENOMINATION/SERIES: Twenty Dollars/First Charter Series 1875
BANK/CHARTER: The Peoples National Bank Of Lynchburg, Lynchburg, Virginia (#2760)

FEDERAL DATA: Serial #K869251–, signed by B.K. Bruce and Chas. Gilfillan
BANK DATA: Dated July 26, 1882, Plate letter "B," (apparently

printed in sheets of $10, $10, $20, $20,) Serial #10457. Opening in 1882, this bank lasted throughout the National Bank Note era issuing all series except Series 1882 (all three issues). This was one of the last banks to issue First Charter notes. Amount of large size outstanding in 1935 was $32,142.50.
BANK SIGNATURES: J.M. Ivey, Cashier, and Chas. M. Blackford, President
BACK: Large center picture in black, *Baptism Of Pocohontas*

SEAL: Virginia seal in use today (obverse of seal, Liberty over Tyranny)

CONDITION: About Uncirculated. Bought as Extra Fine. There could not be many in this excellent condition.

SOURCE: Bought at auction, Hickman and Oakes sale, April 10, 1976

RARITY: Rare. There are probably about a dozen First Charter notes known, certainly none better than this one.

NOTE #10B:

DENOMINATION/ SERIES: Twenty Dollars/Brownback Series 1882

BANK/CHARTER: The Norfolk National Bank, Norfolk, Virginia (#3368)

FEDERAL DATA: Serial #E623140–, signed by W.S. Rosecrans and C.N. Jordan

BANK DATA: Dated July 24, 1885, Plate letter "A," Serial #2349. A large bank which operated from 1885 to 1927 and issued brownbacks, no date-backs or value-backs, but all three Series 1902 Third Charter Period notes. Large size outstanding in 1926 was $983,400.

BANK SIGNATURES: O. Hardy, Cashier and C.N. Ramsey, President

BACK: Charter number (3368)

SEAL: State seal of Virginia

CONDITION: About Very Fine

SOURCE: Purchased from Morey Perlmutter on December 2, 1970

RARITY: Not particularly rare

#11 —
NEW YORK

NAME: After the Duke of York, later King James II
NICKNAME: The Empire State
ENTERED THE UNION: July 26, 1788

CAPITAL: Albany
SEAL: The seal, originally devised in 1777 and approved in 1778, was modified five times. The original description of the seal in writing was lost and reestablished on May 20, 1882, when the seal was changed to its present form, now described. The second and present-day seal has a central shield showing two ships on the water with three mountains and the rising sun in the background. The shield is supported on the right by Justice, blindfolded and holding scales, and on the left by Liberty. The crest is a globe surmounted by the American Eagle. "On Top of the World" is indicated. The motto *Excelsior* meaning "Ever

NOTE #11A:

DENOMINATION/SERIES: Fifty Dollars/First Charter Series 1875
BANK/CHARTER: The Second National Bank of Elmira (#149)
FEDERAL DATA: Serial #A88055–, signed by Bruce and Gilfillan
BANK DATA: Dated January 5, 1864, Bank serial #45, Plate letter "A." This bank survived from 1863 through 1935 and issued all but date-backs and value-backs Series 1882 and five-dollar small size of both Type I and Type II. Large size outstanding in 1935 was $17,700.

BANK SIGNATURES: Chas. R. Pratt, Cashier, and president's signature is illegible.
FACE: Upper left corner has an ornate "FIFTY" and *Washington Crossing the Delaware.* The right side shows three females representing Victory and below, *Washington Kneeling in Prayer at Valley Forge, PA.*

BACK: Large picture in black, center, shows *Embarkation of the Pilgrims*

SEAL: This is the first New York seal to be used on National Bank Notes.

CONDITION: Fine

SOURCE: Purchased from The Numismatic Gallery, California, October 20, 1951

RARITY: This is the only fifty-dollar First Charter Period note presently in this collection. This note

shows soil and wear and needs to be improved. Fifty-dollar First Charter notes are rarer than the hundreds. In fact, there are very few fifties known that are in top condition and in the great series of A.A. Grinnell sales in the Forties, only ten fifties were listed. Only one of these was noted as "Crisp Uncirculated" and one "Practically Uncirculated." There were twelve one-hundred dollar notes, four of which he lists as Practically Uncirculated.

Upward" (also Loftiest, Highest) is on a streamer below the shield. This was probably the last of the five modifications. First Charter bank notes show Liberty on the right and Justice on the left with a half-submerged globe on top of which stands an eagle with wings outstretched. This design is also shown on the first part of the brownbacks. Sometime after the change in the seal (probably around 1890), the seal as described above was placed on the brown-

backs. All National Bank Notes of New York are rather plentiful so it's hard to say which are the scarcer brownback seals. Although at first glance the seals appear similar, upon closer examination one will discover other differences. I always thought the first seal showed a partially submerged globe or half-globe. At least, it shows a half-dome.

Please see Plates II and X

NOTE #11B:

DENOMINATION/SERIES: Five Dollars/Brownback Series 1882

BANK DATA: Dated January 2, 1891, Plate letter "A," Bank serial #1. (First note on the first sheet.) This bank issued, beginning with the brownbacks, all series except value-backs Series 1882 and red seals of the 1902 Series (the first part of the Third Charter Period). The bank opened in 1891 and had large size outstanding in 1935 or $6,330.

BANK SIGNATURES: John Olmstead, Cashier and Geo. O. Mead, President

BANK CHARTER: The First National Bank of Walton (#4495)

FEDERAL DATA: Serial #K356412–, signed by W.S. Rosecrans and J.N. Huston

BACK: Large charter number (4495)

SEAL: This is also the first New York seal.

CONDITION: Nice clean Uncirculated crisp note. Bought as About Uncirculated.

SOURCE: Purchased from A. Kosoff in 1956.

RARITY: New York notes are not rare, but must be scarce in this condition on a small bank.

COMMENT: This could possibly be the note listed in Grinnell.

NOTE #11C:

DENOMINATION/ SERIES: Ten Dollars/Brownback Series 1882

BANK/CHARTER: The National Bank of Commerce in New York (#733)

FEDERAL DATA: Serial #U871893–, signed by Bruce and Wyman

BANK DATA: Dated January 14, 1885, Plate letter "F," Bank serial #72708. This very large bank opened in 1865 and closed in the crash of '29. It issued only

large size notes, i.e., Original and Series 1875 First Charters, brownbacks Series 1882, then red seals and date-backs of the 1902 Series. Outstanding in 1929 was $338,085. At one time this collection contained a five- and twenty-dollar notes like this ten.

BANK SIGNATURES: Vanity signatures of C. Randall, Cashier and J. Pierpont Morgan (famous signature but not very legible)

BACK: Large charter number (733)

SEAL: This shows the second or present day seal of New York. Look closely and you will see many differences compared with the first seal.

CONDITION: Uncirculated.

SOURCE: Purchased from Clyde Plyler (N.C.) in 1961

RARITY: New York notes are not rare, and notes on this bank are certainly not rare. John Hickman says that the second seal is more common than the first seal on brownbacks.

TO STATE 12:

NORTH CAROLINA

☞

#12 —

NORTH CAROLINA

NAME: After
Charles II of England
NICKNAME:
The Tarheel State
ENTERED THE UNION:
November 21, 1789

CAPITAL: Raleigh
SEAL: The seal of North Carolina, used since 1893, is the fourth one adopted since 1779. The original seal had Minerva, goddess of War, Wisdom, and the Liberal Arts, on the obverse. Ceres, goddess of Plenty, appears on the reverse. A later seal shows Liberty seated at the right with a scroll and liberty pole, and Ceres at the left with wheat and maize. The present seal was proposed in 1891 but not

actually adopted by the State Legislature until 1893. It depicts Ceres at the right and Liberty at the left with the date May 20, 1775 (Mecklenburg County Declaration of Independence) at the top. The motto *Esse Quam Videri*, meaning, "To be, rather than to seem," appears on a streamer at the bottom. First Charter and brownback bank notes (until the change in 1893) depict Liberty at the right and Ceres at left, while later brownback notes show the figures reversed. I feel that the transposition of the figures is a minor change. This transposition also appears in the two New York seals, as well as Wisconsin seals, which, in addition to the transposition, change the figures from youths to adults, indicating development and growth.

Please see Plates III and X

NOTE #12A:

DENOMINATION/SERIES: Ten Dollars/First Charter Original Series
BANK/CHARTER: The National Bank of New Berne (#1632 — number not on note.) Notice early spelling of Newbern, now all one word.

FEDERAL DATA: Serial #798175, signed by S.B. Colby and F.E. Spinner. (Note the federal serial number. This is an early number without a prefix or a suffix.)
BANK DATA: Dated February 14, 1866, Plate letter "C," Bank serial #1 (third note on first sheet.) Opened in 1866, one year after the close of the Civil War, this bank failed when the great depression began. It

issued all large-size notes except value-backs Series 1882 and red seals Series 1902. Outstanding in 1929 was $18,400.
BANK SIGNATURES: H.A. Thompson, Cashier, and D. Heaton, President, both pen signed.
BACK: Large black picture in center shows *Desoto Discovering the Mississippi*
SEAL: This is the first North Carolina seal shown on banknotes.
CONDITION: About Uncirculated, except for a clever repair job at the

bottom left corner. Because I am not an expert, it was a long time before I noticed it.
SOURCE: Purchased from Paul Whisonant, Lincolnton, N.C. back in the late Sixties.
RARITY: Very rare. All southern, western and territorial notes in this condition must be considered rare. There is a twenty-dollar note extant from the same sheet (#1). There are perhaps twelve to fifteen First Charter North Carolina notes known to collectors.

COMMENTS ON NOTE #12C: The First National Bank of Charlotte (#1547) was the first bank chartered in North Carolina (1865) and was re-chartered in 1885 (date on note). This note was issued in 1893 or some time thereafter. The plate had to be changed to accommodate the "S" regional letter and the new version of the state seal. This probably accounts for the plate letter "F" as it is not likely that the first plate was worn out. While I was still a boy, I remember, this bank built a new twenty-story building, the highest in the city (and probably in the state) at that time. But the great crash of 1929 and the general economic crisis caused this bank to close its doors early in 1930, when so many other banks were folding. My wife's father, having recently moved to Charlotte and having always put his money in "The First National Bank of ..." in other towns, naturally followed suit, and with the bank's failure, lost the larger part of his meager savings.

NOTE #12B:

DENOMINATION/SERIES: Five Dollars/Brownback Series 1882
BANK/CHARTER: The First National Bank of Salisbury, N.C. (#2981)

FEDERAL DATA: Serial #N761489–, signed by Bruce and Wyman
BANK DATA: Dated June 20, 1883, Plate letter "A," Bank serial #3676. Bank opened in 1883 and continued in business through 1935, issuing brownbacks, no date-back or value-backs Series 1882,

but all the rest, including small fives, tens, and twenties of both Type I and Type II notes. Large size outstanding in 1935 was $4,330.

BANK SIGNATURES: I.H. Faust, Cashier and R.J. Helms, President (pen signed).

BACK: The charter number appears in large letters (2981)

SEAL: Again, the first seal of North Carolina

CONDITION: Uncirculated

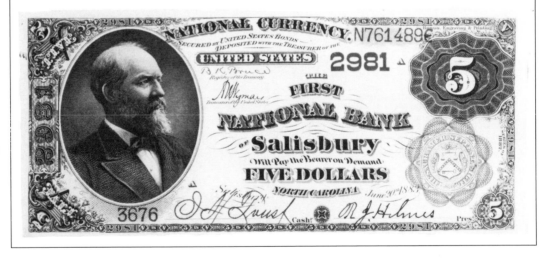

51

SOURCE: Purchased from Wm. P. Donlon, November 23, 1956.

RARITY: Brownback notes of North Carolina are not common. A total of 43 banks issued brownback notes. Probably about four or five dozen are known, but in 1893 the present seal was adopted so this reduces the number available with each seal. We think that the second seal is more common than the first.

NOTE #12C:

DENOMINATION/ SERIES: Ten Dollars/ Brownback Series 1882

BANK/CHARTER: The First National Bank of Charlotte, N.C. (#1547), Regional letter "S"

FEDERAL DATA: Serial #K125469K, signed by Rosecrans and Jordan

BANK DATA: Dated August 21, 1885, Plate letter "F," Bank serial #6850. Bank opened in 1865 and went "broke" in 1930. It issued all types of notes (but not all denominations, of course) through the fives, tens, and twenties of Type I small size except date-backs and value-backs of the Series 1882. Large size outstanding (1930) was $42,920.

BANK SIGNATURES: H.M. Victor, Cashier and J. Frank Gilreath, President.

BACK: Charter number (1547)

SEAL: This is the second and present seal of North Carolina. Notice that the figures have been transposed. Also notice that the ladies are not as buxom as those on the first seal. This reflected the earlier period's belief that buxomness indicated good health.

CONDITION: Extra Fine/About Uncirculated, bought as Extra Fine.

SOURCE: Purchased from Wm. P. Donlon 1958 or 1959.

RARITY: Not as rare as notes with the first seal.

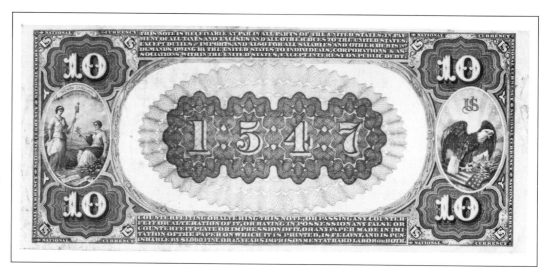

TO STATE 13:

RHODE ISLAND

☞

#13 —
RHODE ISLAND

NAME: "Red" island, after its red clay
NICKNAME: Little Rhody
ENTERED THE UNION: May 29, 1790
CAPITAL: Providence

SEAL: The seal of Rhode Island existed as early as 1647 when it was still a province. The central element of this early seal was an anchor. The present seal, based on the earlier design, was officially adopted in 1875. The state name is unusual since "Rhode Island" is actually an incomplete title; its name since the original land grant in 1636 is actually "Rhode Island and Providence Plantations." The seal shows a central shield upon a solid rock offshore, with an anchor and the motto "Hope" above it. The seal on National Bank Notes, like most, was embellished by artists at the bank note companies. I must say that they (the artists) enhanced the seals' appearance greatly by giving them a more artistic look. The bank note seals also show two ships, one on each side.

Please see Plate II

NOTE #13A:

DENOMINATION/SERIES: One Dollar/Series 1875 First Charter
BANK/CHARTER: The National Bank of North America of Providence, Rhode Island (#1036)

FEDERAL DATA: Serial #B607848–, signed by John Allison and A.U. Wyman
BANK DATA: Dated June 30, 1877, Plate letter "B," Bank serial #9294. This bank opened in 1865 and closed in 1904. It issued only

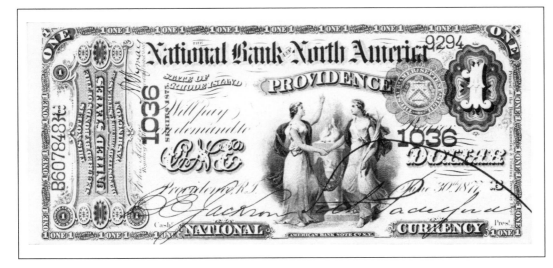

Original and Series 1875 First Charter and brownback Series 1882. Amount outstanding in 1910 was $24,060.

BANK SIGNATURES: C.E. Jackson, Cashier and ? (illegible)

BACK: At center, a painting, *The Landing of the Pilgrims*, in black, surrounded on each side with the government obligation and penalty regulations. In the right-hand oval is the upright eagle. Other than the painting and lettering, the rest of the printing is in green.

SEAL: The state seal of Rhode Island

CONDITION: Uncirculated

SOURCE: Purchased from The Numismatic Gallery, California (Kosoff and Kreisberg) Supplemental Sale, in which they lowered the grade of each lot in order to sell everything remaining from the first sale.

RARITY: Rhode Island notes are not rare.

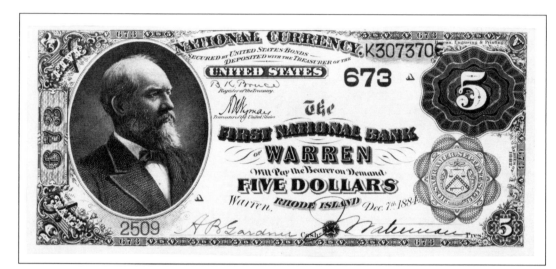

NOTE #13B:

DENOMINATION/ SERIES: Five Dollars/ Brownback Series 1882

BANK/CHARTER: The First National Bank of Warren, Rhode Island (#673)

FEDERAL DATA: Serial #K307370–, signed by Bruce and Wyman

BANK DATA: Dated December 7, 1884, Plate letter "A," Bank serial #2509. This bank operated from 1864 to 1904 and issued only Original and Series 1875 First Charters and

brownback Series 1882 notes. Balance outstanding in 1910 was $5,596.

BANK SIGNATURES: Pen signatures of A.B. Gardner, Cashier, and J. Waterman, President.

BACK: Charter number (673) in center

SEAL: Rhode Island state seal. All seals are similar.

CONDITION: Uncirculated

SOURCE: Purchased from Wm. A. Philpott, Jr., January 20, 1958.

RARITY: Not rare.

#14 —
VERMONT

NAME: French for "green mountain"
NICKNAME: The Green Mountain State
ENTERED THE UNION: March 4, 1791

CAPITAL: Montpelier

SEAL: The principle figure in the seal is a pine tree, rising from the center of a thick growth of evergreens with conical tops. Above these tops start the limbs of the pine, and the bases of the evergreens extend in a horizontal line across the seal. A sheaf of grain stands on each side at the top of the pine tree. Under the right sheaf a cow stands facing right; under the left sheaf is a fancy sword handle or

horizontal *fleur de lis*. Just under the line of evergreens, centered, is "Vermont" with "Freedom" below and an upright sheaf of wheat at each side. On the bottom is "& Unity." (NOTE: The seal described refers to the "official" seal, the gold seal wafer now in use. This bears little resemblance to the two seals found on the National Bank Notes — See PLATE X, bottom right.) Vermont notes also show two different seals on their banknotes; like the other 7 states and the District which changed their seals, the two different seals both appear on notes of the brownback period. The first seal on banknotes appears on a shield shaped like an artist's palette (PLATE X, lower left). The greater upper portion of a pine tree on the left and a mountain in the right background, a large dairy cow facing

NOTE #14A:

DENOMINATION/SERIES: Five Dollars/Original Series

BANK/CHARTER: The National Bank of Poultney, Vermont (#1200 — charter number not on the note)

FEDERAL DATA: Serial #C148894, signed by Colby and Spinner

BANK DATA: Dated July 1, 1865, Plate letter "D," Bank serial #7. Bank operated only from 1865 to 1879 and

issued only Original and Series 1875 First Charter notes. Amount outstanding in 1916 was $1,442.50.

BANK SIGNATURES: Pen signatures of M. Clarke, Cashier and O.P. Hooker, President.

BACK: Similar to all First Charter fives: *Landing of Columbus, 1492*

SEAL: This shows the first seal of Vermont which was shaped like an artist's palette.

CONDITION: Bought as Extra Fine; I call it Uncirculated.

SOURCE: Out of the James M. Wade collection, purchased from Aubrey E. Bebee in 1969 or 1970.

RARITY: Vermont notes are not rare, but with this pedigree and in this condition this note has to be rare.

"FREEDOM," the right segment continues, also just above, with "AND UNITY," while the central segment reads "VERMONT." The central device in the shield is the pine tree, darker and showing the upper four-fifths of the tree and in front a cow (looks like a Hereford beef cow) facing left, and in front of the cow, standing, are three large sheaves of wheat. As a background is the row of conifers and a mountain on each side behind the trees. All in all, this is a beautiful pair of seals. As mentioned earlier, Dr.

Limpert pioneered this work on the seals and here again he mentions only one seal. I quote: "National Bank Notes show similar seals but without stag-head or motto." This is difficult to understand for the second shows the stag head and both show the motto, albeit on the first seal the motto at the top is much slimmer. It is possible that the last seal is scarcer because the last bank to issue brownbacks was Swanton (#4943), which bowed out in 1904.

Please see Plate IV

NOTE #14B:

DENOMINATION/SERIES: Ten Dollars/Brownback Series 1882
BANK/CHARTER: The Waterbury National Bank, Vt. (#1462)

FEDERAL DATA: Serial #K206732–, signed by Rosecrans and Jordan

BANK DATA: Dated June 24, 1885, plate letter "A," Bank serial #1706. Operated from 1865 to 1911 and issued Original and 1875 First Charters, brownbacks of Series 1882, then red seals and date-backs of the 1902 Series (Third Charter Period). Outstanding in 1912 was $4,350.
BANK SIGNATURES: A.W. Wells, Cashier, and W.T. Dillingham, President.
BACK: Charter number (1462)

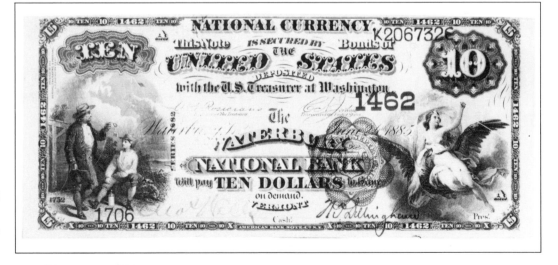

57

SEAL: First seal of Vermont, as was on the previous note. It shows an artist's palette, Holstein (milk) cow facing right and no crest. (Please refer to section on Vermont seals, above.)
CONDITION: Extra Fine
SOURCE: From the Dr. Limpert collection sold by Stack's, September 24, 1955
RARITY: Vermont brownback notes are not very rare, but they are divided between the two seals.

NOTE #14C:

DENOMINATION/SERIES: Ten Dollars/Brownback Series 1882
BANK/CHARTER: The Allen National Bank of Fair Haven, Vermont (#2422), Regional letter "N"
FEDERAL DATA: Serial #T576379J signed by Lyons and Roberts

BANK DATA: Dated April 6, 1899, Plate letter "A," Bank serial #1985. Opening in 1879 this bank operated during the entire period of National Bank Note issue. Beginning with the Series of 1875 (First Charter Period) it issued all series except red seals and date-backs of the Third Charter Period, Series 1902. Total large size outstanding in 1935 was $2,430.

BANK SIGNATURES: Thos. H. Allen, Cashier and Frank E. Allen, President. An unusual example of a family owned and operated bank.
BACK: Large charter number (2422)
SEAL: This is the second seal used on Vermont notes (similar to PLATE IV.) Although it has some of the same main features, at first glance it appears very different. A smaller cow faces left; it shows a larger, bolder tree and

wheat shocks. The wreath-type circle contains the main features: the bold three-sectioned motto at the bottom and, not the least, an elk's head as a crest. Vermont's "official" seal, gold in color (PLATE X), which features most of the items here on the note, but drawn in styl-

ized form, appears very different. The coat of arms (PLATE IV) is very colorful and very pleasing to the eye.
CONDITION: About Uncirculated
SOURCE: Purchased from the A.N.A. sale, August 10, 1971 (St.Louis)

RARITY: Not rare. We believe the second seal on the brownbacks to be more common. It appears there were 28 banks which issued notes with the first seal against 26 banks issuing brownbacks with the second seal. Probably most of these were rechartering banks. By counting the banks, the two seals would be about equal. But that assumes that the Bureau started placing the second seal on the brownbacks beginning early in 1890.

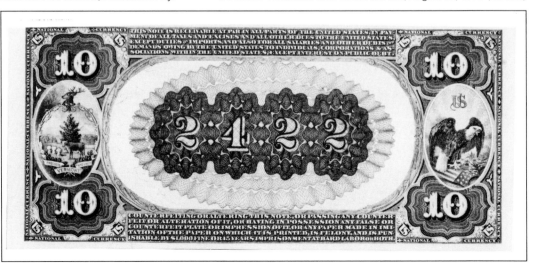

TO STATE 15:

KENTUCKY

☞

#15 —
KENTUCKY

NAME: Wyandotte language for "meadowland"
NICKNAME: The Blue Grass State
ENTERED THE UNION: June 1, 1792

CAPITAL: Frankfort

SEAL: The Commonwealth of Kentucky adopted its seal on December 20, 1792. It depicted two friendly hunters with clasped hands standing on the edge of a precipice and the motto "United We Stand. Divided We Fall." A later seal shows the friends in dress clothes with a table and document in the background and the motto below (similar to arms, PLATE IV). Some sources say two friends are embracing. One drawing appears to show the pair in black dress clothes (not evening clothes), hands clasped, standing about a foot apart. The "official" seal is like this, with the motto at the bottom extending upward in a semi-circle on each side. Another drawing shows the men closer together (semi-embracing) with the motto in small letters "united we stand" at top and at bottom "divided we fall." All Kentucky banknotes show the seal this way, with KENTUCKY at the top. The figures look like two statesmen, hands clasped. The one on the left wears a white front shirt, black tie, and a coat with tails. The man on the right wears a swallow-tailed coat and white trousers.

NOTE #15A:

DENOMINATION/SERIES: One Dollar/First Charter Series 1875

BANK/CHARTER: The German National Bank of Covington, Ky. (#1847)
FEDERAL DATA: Serial #A602040–, signed by Allison and Wyman

BANK DATA: Dated July 15, 1871, Plate letter "C," Bank serial #356. This bank operated from 1871 to 1928 and issued only large size, except no value-backs (Series 1882) and no red seals (1902 Series). Outstanding in 1928 was $326,900. This was a rather large bank just across the Ohio River from Cincinnati, Ohio, and was one of several banks around the country with an ethnic name.

BANK SIGNATURES: James Spelman, Cashier, and H. Feltman (?), President

BACK: Center circle painting in black, *Landing of the Pilgrims.*

SEAL: Seal of Kentucky: "United We Stand, Divided We Fall"

CONDITION: Crisp Uncirculated Gem

SOURCE: Purchased from Wm. A. Philpott, Jr.

RARITY: Not rare, but in this condition?

NOTE #15B:

**DENOMINATION/
SERIES:** Twenty
Dollars/Brownback
Series 1882

BANK/CHARTER: The
First National Bank of
Maysville, Kentucky
(#2467), Regional letter
"S"

FEDERAL DATA:
Serial #R167735R,
signed by J.W. Lyons
and
Ellis H. Roberts

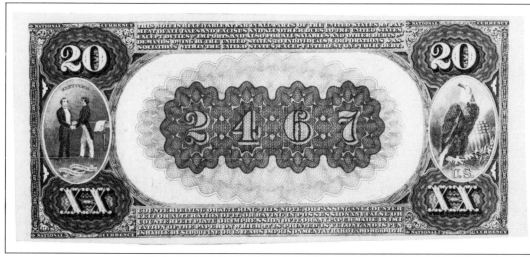

BANK DATA: Dated
March 5, 1900, Plate
letter "A," Bank serial
#1648. This bank
opened in 1880
(therefore the above
date, 1900, is the
re-charter date), and
closed in 1916. This
bank issued First
Charters (Series 1875)
and all three Series
1882 Second Charter
notes only. There
remained $75,000
outstanding in 1916.
BANK SIGNATURES:
Have faded out.

BACK: Large charter number (2467)
SEAL: Kentucky state seal
CONDITION: Extra Fine +

SOURCE: Wm. A. Philpott, Jr., Dallas, Texas, April 10, 1962
RARITY: Kentucky brownbacks are not rare, but scarce in nice
condition.

#16 — TENNESSEE

NAME: Name of Cherokee Village

NICKNAME: The Volunteer State

ENTERED THE UNION: June 1, 1796

CAPITAL: Nashville

SEALS: The Tennessee seal was adopted on November 14, 1801 and was first used in 1802. The circular seal shows a ship at sea, sailing East, with the word "Commerce" at the bottom. At the top is XVI, indicating Tennessee as the sixteenth state. Below is a plow at the left, wheat at the center, and a cotton plant at the right with the word "Agriculture" beneath. Drawings agree, more than most. All banknotes show the same seal, similar to the one described above, except for the artist's adjustment to the oval shape. A fancy floral design decorates the upright shield, with the number XVI and "Agriculture" above the plow with what looks like a cotton plant to the left in front of the plow. Below is a ship (I always assumed it was a river boat) with open deck showing cargo, a helmsman on the right end, and a single mast near the stern with furled (rolled up) canvas, with "Commerce" below and near the very bottom the word "Tennessee" on a scroll or slab (or monument marker).

Please see Plate IV

NOTE #16A:

DENOMINATION/SERIES: Five Dollars/First Charter Series 1875.

BANK/CHARTER: The Mechanics National Bank Of Knoxville, Tennessee (#2658)

FEDERAL DATA: Serial #Y551652–, signed by Bruce and Gilfillan

BANK DATA: Dated April 12, 1882, just two or three months before the Second Charter Period began. Plate letter "D," Bank serial #5234. Operated from 1882 to 1907 and issued only First Charter Series 1875 notes and red seal notes of 1902 Series. Amount outstanding in 1910 was $23,600.

BANK SIGNATURES: O.G. Bates, Cashier and F.R. Cuttrell, President (pen signatures)

BACK: *Landing of Columbus, 1492*

SEAL: Tennessee state seal (Agriculture and Commerce)

CONDITION: Fine

SOURCE: From the Limpert collection, auctioned by Stack's, N.Y.C., September 24, 1955

RARITY: Tennessee First Charter notes are rare, especially in nice condition.

NOTE #16B:

**DENOMINATION/
SERIES:** Ten Dollars/
Brownback Series 1882

BANK/CHARTER: The
East Tennessee National
Bank of Knoxville,
Tennessee (#2049),
Regional letter "S"

FEDERAL DATA:
Serial #V280451V,
signed by
W.S. Rosecrans and
E.H. Nebeker

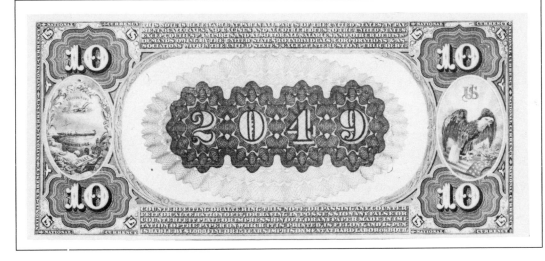

BANK DATA: Dated
August 24, 1892, Plate
letter "D," Bank serial
#15748. This rather
large bank that opened
in 1872 issued all series
except value-backs
Series 1882 and red
seals, Series 1902, and
Type I, small-sized
five-dollar notes. Amount
of large size outstanding
in 1935 was $54,822.50.

BANK SIGNATURES:
Pen signed by
D.V. Carten, Cashier and
F.D. Lesher, President

BACK: Large Charter number (2049)
SEAL: Tennessee seal. All seals are similar.
CONDITION: About Uncirculated

SOURCE: Purchased from Wm. P. Donlon, March 1, 1969.
RARITY: Not particularly rare.

#17 — OHIO

NAME: Indian word for "great river"
NICKNAME: The Buckeye State
ENTERED THE UNION: March 1, 1803
CAPITAL: Columbus
SEAL: The first seal of Ohio was adopted in 1803. Legend has it that a group of officials worked all night on affairs at the Capitol. When they were standing on the lawn at daybreak before separating, the sunrise became the inspiration for the new state seal, which shows the rising sun between mountains with a bundle of arrows and a sheaf of wheat in the foreground. Ohio changed its seal on April 16, 1867, but it had to be some time later that the second seal appeared on the brownbacks, between 1890 and 1900, as with the other seal changes shown during that time. (PLATE XI, upper left, is this seal, the first, with *five* arrows, shown on First Charter notes and the first part of the brownbacks). There are numerous drawings of the seal which differ in the number and arrangement of the mountains and the sun and its rays. But the "official" seal (more similar to arms, PLATE IV, with fewer arrows) shows five mountains with long rays and sun showing about four-fifths full above the second mountain from the left. On the right stands a large sheaf of wheat. Below on the left are seventeen arrows indicating Ohio's entry into the Union. This view appears on the last part of the brownbacks.

NOTE #17A:

DENOMINATION/SERIES: Ten Dollars/First Charter, Series 1875

BANK/CHARTER: The Fourth National Bank of Columbus, Ohio (#2423)

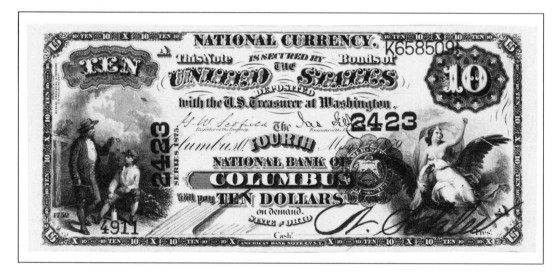

FEDERAL DATA: Serial #K658509–, signed by Scofield and Gilfillan

BANK DATA: Dated May 15, 1879, Plate letter "A," Bank serial #4911. Bank operated from 1879 to 1897, about eighteen years, and issued only Series 1875 First Charter Period notes. Amount outstanding in 1910 was a paltry $2,670.

BANK SIGNATURES: Vanity signatures of (illegible) and Nicholas Schlee, President. Please see if you can read the vanity signature.

BACK: Beautiful painting, *De Soto Discovering the Mississippi*

SEAL: First seal of Ohio (five arrows on the right and sheaf of wheat on the left)

CONDITION: Uncirculated Gem

SOURCE: Wm. A. Philpott, Jr., date unknown.

RARITY: Not rare as a state. Someone must have laid some aside for it is not difficult to find.

NOTE #17B:

DENOMINATION/SERIES: Five Dollars/Brownback Series 1882

BANK/CHARTER: The Dayton National Bank, Dayton, Ohio (#898)

FEDERAL DATA: Serial #Y370825–, signed by Bruce and Wyman

BANK DATA: Dated January 29, 1885, Plate letter "A," Bank serial #3537. Bank operated from 1865 to 1925 and issued all large sizes except date-backs and value-backs Series 1882. Outstanding in 1925 was $233,200.

BANK SIGNATURES: Pen signed by Jas. Martin, Cashier, and Wm. H. Simmons, President.

BACK: Charter number (898).

SEAL: First seal, same as above.

CONDITION: Uncirculated

SOURCE: Purchased from Paul M. Whisonant, Lincolnton, N.C., April 2, 1969.

RARITY: Not rare but uncommon quality.

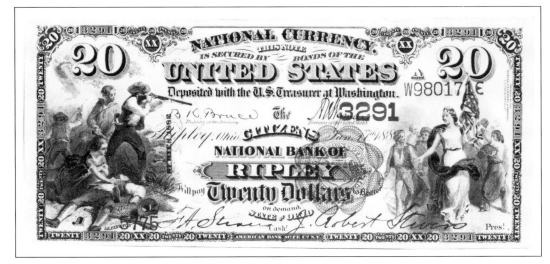

NOTE #17C:

DENOMINATION/ SERIES: Twenty Dollars/Brownback Series 1882

BANK/CHARTER: The Citizens National Bank of Ripley, Ohio (#3291)

FEDERAL DATA: #W980171–, signed by Bruce and Wyman

BANK SIGNATURES: F.A. Strong, Cashier, and J. Robert Stevens, President, signed in pen.

BANK DATA: Dated January 17, 1885, Plate letter "A," Bank serial #5775. The bank opened in 1885 and lasted through the end of the National Bank Note issuing period. It issued brownbacks Series 1882, and all three Third Charter Period notes of Series 1902. It also issued tens and twenties of both Type I and Type II small-size notes. Large size outstanding in 1935 was $7,610.

BACK: Large charter number (3291)

SEAL: This is the second and present day seal of the State of Ohio.

CONDITION: Uncirculated

SOURCE: Purchased from Wm. A. Philpott, Jr., Dallas, Texas, April 10, 1962.

RARITY: Ohio is not rare.

TO STATE 18:

LOUISIANA

☞

#18 —
LOUISIANA

NAME: After Louis XIV
of France
NICKNAME:
The Pelican State
ENTERED THE UNION:
April 30, 1812

CAPITAL: Baton Rouge
SEAL: The seal of Louisiana was probably designed shortly after statehood by the first governor. A large brown pelican, a bird quite numerous in the state, is depicted as stripping its breast to feed its young. During the Civil War,

the Confederate portion of the state adopted a similar seal with the pelican's head turned left and including several (the number is disputed) young birds (most like arms, PLATE IV, bottom center); the federal version of the state seal had the bird's head turned right with but four young. The present (and official) seal, adopted in 1902, is a compromise with the head turned left and three young. The bank notes show the head turned right with four young. The mottos, "Union" and "Justice" around and over the top of the bird with "Confidence" below the nest, do not show on National Bank Notes.

NOTE #18A:

**DENOMINATION/
SERIES:** Twenty
Dollars/First Charter
Series 1875
BANK/CHARTER: The
First National Bank of
Baton Rouge, Louisiana
(#2633)
FEDERAL DATA: Serial
#K871498–, signed by
Bruce and Gilfillan
BANK DATA: Dated
February 21, 1882,
Plate letter "A," Bank
serial #3590. This bank
operated from 1882 to
1910 and issued only
First Charter Series
1875 and brownbacks

and date-backs of the Series of 1882. Opening just before the Second Charter Period began in the middle of 1882, it had the privilege of issuing First Charter Series 1875 notes for twenty years, if it so desired, or, more likely, if plans and needs made it desirable. We know that a bank could re-order notes from the Bureau. However, since this bank issued brownbacks and date-backs yet bowed out in 1910, one of these issues had to be short-lived. Amount outstanding in 1910 was $85,000.

BANK SIGNATURES: A. Komert, Cashier and D.M. Reymond, President, both signed by hand.
BACK: Large picture in black in center, *Baptism of Pocahontas*.
SEAL: State seal of Louisiana
CONDITION: Very Good, but borders are ragged.

SOURCE: Purchased from Wm. A. Philpott, Jr., February 13, 1958
RARITY: A very rare note on a scarce state and on a rare bank. Most Louisiana First Charter notes encountered are on New Orleans. This is a rare Southern state and capital city note. I know of only one other First Charter note on this bank, a ten, one or two grades better than this note.

NOTE #18B:

DENOMINATION/ SERIES: Ten Dollars/ Brownback Series 1882

BANK/CHARTER: The New Orleans National Bank, New Orleans, Louisiana (#1778)

FEDERAL DATA: Serial #A217494–, signed by Rosecrans and Huston, Regional letter "S"

BANK DATA: Dated August 2, 1890, Plate letter "A," Bank serial #15544. This bank operated from 1871 to 1919. It issued both First Charters, brownbacks and date-backs Series 1882, and date-backs of the Third Charter Series 1902 only. Amount outstanding in 1919 was $385,900.

BANK SIGNATURES: Wm. Palfry and A. Baldwin, Jr.

BACK: Large charter number (1778)

SEAL: Louisiana state seal

CONDITION: Extra Fine

SOURCE: Bought at auction from A. Kosoff, October 10, 1957

RARITY: Scarce, but not rare

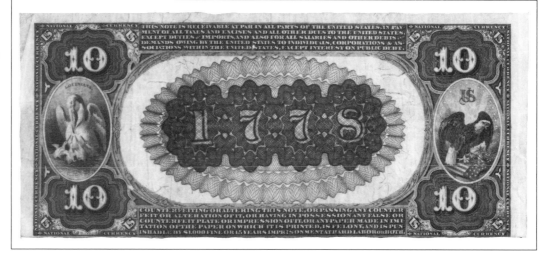

#19 — INDIANA

NAME: "Land of the Indian"
NICKNAME:
The Hoosier State
**ESTABLISHED AS
TERRITORY:** 1800
ENTERED THE UNION:
December 11, 1816
CAPITAL: Indianapolis

SEAL: The seal of Indiana is based on a design observed on territorial papers as early as 1801. After becoming a state in 1816 the basic design was retained; this depicts a pioneer felling a tree and a buffalo running, with mountain ranges in the background. There are minor differences in drawings of the seal. The "official" seal shows the buffalo running to the left, facing toward the front over a fallen tree (most like arms, PLATE IV, lower right). National Bank Notes show the buffalo running to the right front.

NOTE #19A:

**DENOMINATION/
SERIES:** One
Dollar/First Charter
Original Series
BANK/CHARTER: The
National State Bank of
Lafayette, Indiana (#930
— charter number not
on note)
FEDERAL DATA: Serial
#B571235), signed by
Colby and Spinner
BANK DATA: Dated
July 1, 1865, Plate letter
"A," Bank serial #7107.
Operated for twenty
years only (1865 to

1885). Issued only
Original and Series
1875 First Charters. In
1910 there was
$7,972 out.
BANK SIGNATURES:
J.C. Packenburgh and
M.F. Niles, hand signed
BACK: *Landing of the
Pilgrims*
SEAL: Indiana state
seal. All are alike.
CONDITION: Very
Good
SOURCE: New
Netherlands Coin Co.,
New York, April 24,
1954
RARITY: Not rare; one
of the more common
states.

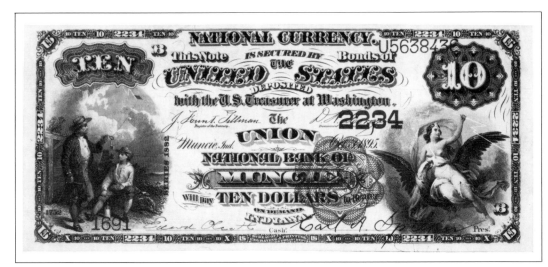

NOTE #19B:

DENOMINATION/ SERIES: Ten Dollars/Brownback Series 1882

BANK/CHARTER: The Union National Bank of Muncie, Indiana (#2234)

FEDERAL DATA: Serial #U563843–, signed by J. Fount Tillman and D.N. Morgan

BANK DATA: Dated October 3, 1895, Plate letter "B," Bank serial #1691. Bank opened in 1875 and ran the full course of years and issued all but

value-backs (1882) and red seals (1902). Large-size outstanding was $18,687.50.

BANK SIGNATURES: Edward Olcott, Cashier and Carl A. Spelker, President.

BACK: Large charter number (2234)

SEAL: Seal of Indiana

CONDITION: About Uncirculated, Crisp

SOURCE: Hollinbeck's sale of March 31, 1954

RARITY: Not rare

#20 — MISSISSIPPI

NAME: Choctaw for "Father of Waters"
NICKNAME: The Magnolia State
ESTABLISHED AS TERRITORY: 1798
ENTERED THE UNION: December 10, 1817
CAPITAL: Jackson
SEAL: The seal of Mississippi is based on the territorial seal and was adopted the first year of statehood, 1817. It shows an American eagle with an olive branch in his right talon and arrows in the left with a stars and stripes shield on its breast. I find three drawings that are different in small ways (compare Arms on PLATE V). One reference says there should be only one arrow in the left talon. The "official" seal has three arrows in the eagle's left talon. This is a very plain but beautiful seal, especially in color. The seal on the brownbacks shows an American bald eagle with upraised wings, facing left, standing on a rock in the water, right talon raised and holding a stars and stripes shield upright. The eagle stands on his left leg with arrows in his left talons (PLATE IX). You will notice I said brownbacks showed this seal. I state it this way because the First Charter period notes are still unknown. Although three banks issued First Charter notes, none are known at the present and some paper money experts doubt that any are still extant. Vicksburg, #803, only in business for three years, issued only Original Series notes. In 1916 there was only $57.50 which had not been redeemed. (Actually there was $55 outstanding; evidently the Treasury redeemed one-half or more of a damaged five dollar note.) The second bank, Jackson (#1610), operated from 1865 to 1867, less than the first bank. Jackson issued only Original Series of the First Charter Period and had $125 outstanding in 1910. The third bank was #2638, just before the end of the First Charter period, in business from 1882 to 1894, which issued only Series 1875 (First Charter). This bank's records from 1910 show just $2200 outstanding, but it

NOTE #20A:

First Charter notes of Mississippi are unknown.
Please help.

72

issued only $50 and $100 notes! Although sixteen banks then issued brownback notes, only ten or twelve brownback notes are known today. (NOTE: In November 1985 this writer saw a reverse proof of the back of a Mississippi sheet [$50 and $100, Columbus, Mississippi] and can now definitely state that if First Charter Period note[s] ever come to light, they will show the same seal as the brownbacks.)

COMMENTS: On the subject of those that got away from me, there is a Mississippi story. A collector friend from Mississippi decided to quit collecting notes. He wrote and offered me his two Mississippi brownbacks at a reasonable price. One was a five-dollar note on the First National Bank of Meridian, also About Uncirculated. The other was well circulated with three heavy folds (Very Good or better), a five dollar note on Starkville, Mississippi. Both are rare, and

I should have bought them.

This writer knows of nine brownback notes. There were three national banks in Mississippi that issued First Charter notes. The first was Vicksburg (charter #803) which operated for only three years, issued only Original Series, and as of 1916 had only $57.50 outstanding, as stated above. (I asked why the $2.50. My friend John Hickman, a "walking encyclopedia," said someone apparently redeemed a

NOTE #20B:

DENOMINATION/SERIES: Five Dollars/Brownback Series 1882
BANK/CHARTER: The Meridian National Bank, Meridian Mississippi (#3176)

FEDERAL DATA: Serial #M311846–, signed by Bruce and Wyman
BANK DATA: Dated May 6, 1884, Plate letter "A," Bank serial #6361. This bank operated from 1884 to 1903 and issued brownback Series

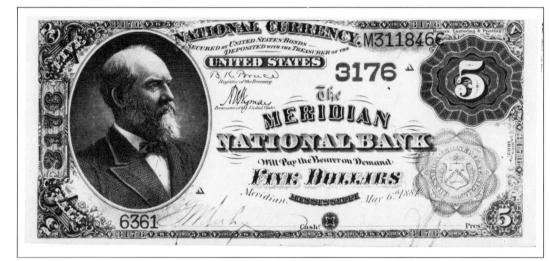

of 1882 only. In 1910 it had an outstanding circulation of only $5,970.

BANK SIGNATURES: The cashier is G.M. Lahy, and the other stamped signature is illegible.

BACK: Large charter number (3176)

SEAL: The Mississippi state seal. The seal shows a large rampant eagle on a rock holding a United States shield upright, with one of its talons.

CONDITION: About Uncirculated.

SOURCE: From the Limpert Collection sale by Stack's, Lot #209, September 24, 1955

RARITY: Very rare. First Charters are unknown and only sixteen banks issued brownbacks Series 1882, only three issued any date-backs and only two issued any value-back Series 1882. There are less than a dozen brownback notes known on the entire state.

mutilated half [or larger] note. To my mind, this leaves $55 outstanding.) The second bank in the state was Jackson (charter #1610) in business from 1865 to 1867, a little less time than Vicksburg. It also only issued Original Series and the 1910 records say $125 was outstanding. The third and last bank in Mississippi to issue First Charter notes (Series 1875) was Columbus (charter #2638), in business from 1882 to 1894 (among the last banks to issue First Charter [1875]). As of 1910, it had an outstanding circulation of just $2200. Here is another case of the bank officers' not wanting to sign a lot of notes. They only issued fifty- and hundred-dollar notes. Some in our hobby believe that no Mississippi First Charter Period notes exist, but I am foolish enough to believe that there is at least one note out there somewhere. Perhaps wishful thinking?

The following is a breakdown of the first four banks in the state of Mississippi which includes data on the banks and their orders to the Bureau for notes for circulation:

The National Bank of Vicksburg, (Charter #803)
— Chartered on February 14, 1865 with a capital of $50,000
— Placed in receivership on April 24, 1868; capital = $50,000
— Reason for failure: incompetent management
— Circulation issued:
  First Charter Original Series
    5-5-5-5 plate = $20,000; serials 1 to 1000
    10-10-10-20 plate = $5,500; serials 1 to 110
— Total amount of circulation issued = $25,500
— Amount outstanding at close = $25,500
— Amount outstanding in 1916 = $57.50

The First National Bank of Jackson, charter #1610
— Chartered on November 15, 1865
— Placed in voluntary liquidation on December 26, 1867; capital = $100,000
— Circulation issued:
  First Charter Original Series
    5-5-5-5 plate = $13,000; serials 1 to 650
    10-10-10-20 plate = $27,500; serials 1 to 550

— Total amount of circulation issued = $40,500
— Amount outstanding at close = $40,500
— Amount outstanding in 1910 = $125

The First National Bank of Columbus, charter #2638
— Chartered on February 28, 1882 with capital of $75,000
— Succeeded Williams, Johnston & Co.
— Placed in voluntary liquidation on May 30, 1894; capital $75,000
— Succeeded by the First State Bank
— Circulation issued:
  First Charter Series of 1875
    50-100 plate = $201,150; serials 1 to 1341
— Total amount issued = $201,150
— Amount outstanding at close = $66,600
— Amount outstanding in 1910 = $2,200

The First National Bank of West Point, charter #2891
— Chartered in 1883 with capital of $52,500
— Succeeded Stockard, Bonner & Co.
— Assumed the First Savings Bank of West Point by consolidation on December 29, 1931
— Circulation issued:
  Second Charter brownbacks
    50-100 plate = $147,300; serials 1 to 982
  Third Charter red seals
    10-10-10-20 plate = $165,000; serials 1 to 3300
  Third Charter 1902-1908 backs
    10-10-10-20 plate = $290,000; serials 1 to 5800
  Third Charter plain-back blue seals
    10-10-10-20 plate = $624,100; serials 5801 to 18282
Small Size
  Ten dollar Type I = $122,760; serials 1 to 2046
  Twenty dollar Type I = $65,280; serials 1 to 544
  Ten dollar Type II = $43,450; serials 1 to 4345
  Twenty dollars Type II = $24,300; serials 1 to 1215
— Total circulation issued = $1,482,190
— Amount outstanding in July 1935 = $95,900
— Amount outstanding of "large" in July 1935 = $5,240

TO STATE 21:

ILLINOIS

#21 — ILLINOIS

NAME: Algonquin for "man"
NICKNAME:
The Prairie State
**ESTABLISHED AS
TERRITORY:** Illinois
Territory in 1809, but a part of
Northwest Territory in 1787
ENTERED THE UNION:
December 3, 1818

CAPITAL: Springfield
SEAL: The seal of Illinois underwent about eight changes

in its evolution. The original seal was adopted soon after statehood and depicts an American eagle with a streamer reading "State Sovereignty," "National Union," a stars and stripes shield, and also an olive branch and arrows. The "official" seal shows the eagle with upraised wings with both feet resting on a standing stars and stripes shield, with the sun in the right background, with two dates under the sun and eagle's tail feathers (See inset for present-day seal. For comparison, see PLATE V, probably an earlier seal). The date on top is 1868, being the renewal date of a former seal, and just under that date is 1818, the year of

NOTE #21A:

DENOMINATION/SERIES: Ten Dollars/First Charter Series 1875
BANK/CHARTER: The First National Bank Of Paris, Illinois (#1555)

FEDERAL DATA: Serial #H963333–, signed by John Allison and Jno. C. New

BANK DATA: Dated October 2, 1865, Plate letter "B," Bank serial #3209. This bank operated for twenty years (1865-1885) and issued only First Charters, Original and Series 1875, and in 1910 the amount outstanding was only $2,821.

BANK SIGNATURES: Wm. Seibert, Cashier and A.J. Parker, President, pen-signed

BACK: *DeSoto Discovering the Mississippi*

SEAL: Illinois state seal
CONDITION:
Uncirculated
SOURCE: Purchased from A. Kosoff, November 23, 1956
RARITY: The low outstanding amount indicates this bank's notes to be scarce. However, there are several known on this bank. Like several other banks, someone put a few away in uncirculated condition to give syngraphists today a grand opportunity to have type notes of quality.

statehood. Also in the concentric circles and below that described above is the date August 26, 1818. This date is just before statehood and must refer to the state Constitution. The seal as shown on all state National Bank Notes shows no dates whatsoever (PLATE XI). A large eagle facing upright, head left, has a long streamer in its beak in two segments which reads "State Sovereignty" in the top line and "National Union" underneath. The eagle has an olive branch in his right talons and three arrows in his left with a large shield covering all its body and the lower part of the upraised wings. The shield shows only three stars across the top over the stripes (seven red and six white).

NOTE #21B:

DENOMINATION/SERIES: Five Dollars/Brownback Series 1882.

BANK/CHARTER: The Oakland National Bank, Hyde Park, Illinois (now Chicago) (#3916)

FEDERAL DATA: Serial M840496–, signed by W.S. Rosecrans and James W. Hyatt

BANK DATA: Dated August 1, 1888, Plate letter "C," Bank serial #2596. This bank operated from 1888 to 1931 and issued brownbacks Series 1882 and all three Charter Period notes of the 1902 Series. Also issued small-sized Type I five-, ten- and twenty-dollar notes. Large size circulation outstanding in 1931 amounted to $47,832.50.

BANK SIGNATURES: Henry Sheffield, Cashier and A.C. Hoskins (?), President, signed in pen.

BACK: Charter number (3916)

SEAL: Illinois seal (all are similar)

CONDITION: Extra Fine

SOURCE: Bought from Paul Whisonant, Lincolnton, N.C., April 2, 1969

RARITY: Illinois notes are not rare.

#22 —
ALABAMA

NAME: Name of an Indian tribe
NICKNAME: The Heart of Dixie
ESTABLISHED AS TERRITORY: 1817
ENTERED THE UNION: December 14, 1819
CAPITAL: Montgomery
SEAL: Alabama has two seals on its bank notes, altogether different from each other. The original seal shown in the inset and on PLATE XI (also now the official seal), was suggested in 1817 by the Territorial governor, whose likeness also appears on the Alabama Commemorative half-dollar. It was re-adopted in 1819 soon after becoming a state. Evidently the first seal was considered a territorial

seal. It shows a map of the state, a tract of land bounded on the north by Tennessee, on the east by Georgia, on the south by Florida and a small portion of the Gulf of Mexico, and on the west by Mississippi. The courses of the Alabama, Tombigbee, Black Warrior, and Tennessee rivers are shown. This seal, as described, is the "official" seal. A second newer seal was introduced in 1868, apparently under duress (author's opinion) to calm things down after the Civil War. This newer seal (most like arms, PLATE V) shows an eagle with raised wings, standing on a shield, and bearing a ribbon in its beak with the words "Here we rest." In 1939, through the efforts of the United Daughters of the Confederacy, the original seal was restored. All First Charter notes and, I think, most of the brownback notes show the first seal shown on bank notes, pictured in this volume

NOTE #22A:

DENOMINATION/SERIES: Five Dollars/Original First Charter Series
BANK/CHARTER: The City National Bank Of Selma, Ala. (#1736 — not shown on the note)

FEDERAL DATA: Serial #E792542–, signed by Allison and Spinner
BANK DATA: Dated January 16, 1871, Plate letter "D," Bank serial #1026. This bank opened in 1870 and "went all the way," releasing all issues except value-backs Series 1882, red seals Series of 1902

and small-size fives and twenties of both Types I and II. The amount of large-size notes outstanding in 1935 was $25,640.

BANK SIGNATURES: Both illegible

BACK: *Landing of Columbus, 1492*

SEAL: This shows the first seal of Alabama, showing a large map and rivers of the state, especially significant in that day when rivers were the highways.

CONDITION: Uncirculated

SOURCE: Bought from A. Kosoff sometime before 1955 (1951?)

RARITY: First Charter notes on Alabama are rare, especially on Huntsville, Eufaula and banks other than Selma, there being only four or five known, all in rather poor condition. But here again, someone put away a handful in top condition, giving collectors today a wonderful opportunity.

only on the notes themselves. On these notes it is quite different: a large map is draped over a large rock with Alabama in bold letters across the center of the map with cotton on the right side, other plants on the left, and a large tree as a background. It must have been 1890 or 1893 when the second seal (as on PLATE V), began to appear on the brownbacks. If you will check the pictures of the notes you will see a ten dollar brownback on the Isbell National Bank of Talladega (#4838). This bank opened in 1893, and the note is dated January 11, 1893. This note has the first seal. However the twenty-dollar brownback of the First National Bank of Montgomery (#1814), the fifth bank to open (1871) in the state, (rechartered in 1891) shows a date of April 19, 1891. Montgomery (#1814) apparently went through its recharter day in 1891 with the same first seal (a large map of the state). Because Talladega (#4838) opened in 1893 and also showed the first seal, the seal must have been changed sometime after 1893, perhaps 1895 or later. But the later the date, the more ineffective the message "Here we rest" seems. It has already been determined that the nine changes in state

seals all occurred between 1890 and 1900. The unrest which the carpetbaggers stirred up should have been settled long before 1900.

The twenty-dollar note shows the second seal (with the eagle on a shield and "Here we rest."). I believe the latter seal to be scarcer. A comment is in order on the First Charter notes. Someone long ago did all us syngraphists a huge favor and put aside some five dollar notes (Original Series, no charter number thereon) of the City National Bank of Selma. A total of ten more banks issued original and Series 1875 notes, but other than Selma (in nice condition), the other notes could probably be counted on one hand. I know of only three or four such as Eufaula and Huntsville, all well worn. To appreciate and study the seals in detail requires notes to be new, or in better condition. So we have upgraded most of the badly worn notes in the collection, sacrificing some rarer notes. Probably the remaining note in worst condition is the five-dollar brownback of Helena, Montana Territory and it shows no seal, only another eagle in the left oval.

NOTE #22B:

DENOMINATION/SERIES: Ten Dollars/Brownback Series 1882

BANK/CHARTER: The Isbell National Bank Of Talladega, Ala. (#4838)

FEDERAL DATA: Serial #H440521–, signed by Rosecrans and Nebeker

BANK DATA: Dated January 11, 1893, Plate letter "C," Bank serial #1. This bank opened in 1893 and released some of all issues except value-backs Series 1882, red seals Series 1902 and five-dollar small-size of Type I. Amount of large outstanding in 1935 was $3,255.
BANK SIGNATURES: R.C. Ivey, Cashier (in red ink), and president's signature is illegible, but both were signed by hand.

BACK: Large charter number (4838)

SEAL: First seal of Alabama, as above.

CONDITION: Extra Fine

SOURCE: From Limpert Collection, sold by Stack's, New York, NY, September 24, 1955

RARITY: There are not very many nice Alabama brownbacks around, especially when you consider that some have the first seal and some have the second seal.

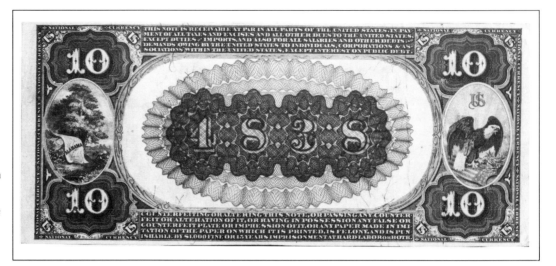

NOTE #22C:

DENOMINATION/ SERIES: Twenty Dollars/Brownback Series 1882

BANK/CHARTER: The First National Bank Of Montgomery, Ala. (#1814)

FEDERAL DATA: Serial #T325030T, signed by Rosecrans and Huston, Regional letter "S"

BANK DATA: Dated April 19, 1891, Plate Letter "B," Bank serial #4213. This bank

opened in 1871 and went all the way. It was the largest bank of the first twelve in the state. This bank did not issue any value-backs Series 1882 or red seals Series 1902 and no Type I small-size notes. Amount of large outstanding in 1935 was $30,227.50.

BANK SIGNATURES: A.B. Woolfolk, Cashier and A.N. Baldwin, President, pen-signed.

BACK: Large charter number (1814)

SEAL: This is the second seal of Alabama, which says "Here we rest."

CONDITION: Very Fine

SOURCE: Purchased from Kagin's, May 18, 1972

RARITY: Brownbacks are scarce, especially divided between two seals.

TO STATE 23:

MAINE

☞

#23 — MAINE

NAME: After the ancient French province
NICKNAME: The Pine Tree State
ENTERED THE UNION: March 15, 1820
CAPITAL: Augusta
SEAL: The seal of Maine was adopted June 9, 1820 and shows a central shield with an moose reclining under a pine tree. At the right is a sailor and at the left a husbandman. Above the shield as a crest is the North Star and "Dirigo," meaning "I direct" (PLATE V). The example of Maine's "official" seal given me is impressed on a royal blue wafer (differing from the usual gold), but in full color it is handsome. The old political adage "As goes Maine, so goes the nation" is the principal reason for the Latin motto, "I direct." The seals on Maine bank notes are all alike, though there are some differences which resulted (mostly artist's license) in the transition from the round official seal to the upright oval. The star appears more like the sun because of the light it radiates. The husbandman has a scythe which stands on the ground, and he is supporting it in the crook of his left arm, the blade extending to the left back of his head. This is different from the "official" seal and drawings which show the scythe blade a little less than chest height. Also, instead of the sailor standing on an anchor, on the bank notes he is holding a sextant in his left hand.

COMMENT ON NOTE #23A: The hundreds were issued from 1864 to 1901 in sheets of 50-50-50-100, and rarely 50-100 and 100-100, plus a few other rare combinations.

NOTE #23A:

DENOMINATION/SERIES: One Hundred Dollars/First Charter Series 1875
BANK/CHARTER: The Union National Bank Of Brunswick, Maine (#1118)

FEDERAL DATA: Serial #A18236–, signed by Allison and New.
BANK DATA: Dated July 1, 1865, Plate letter "A," Bank serial #100 (Note the serial of #100 on a 100 dollar note.) This bank operated from 1865 to 1929 and apparently bowed out in the crash of 1929. It issued Original and Series 1875 First Charter notes, brownbacks only in the Series of 1882 and all three issues of the Third Charter 1902. It issued only tens and twenties of the small size. Amount of large size outstanding in 1929 was $22,817.50.

BANK SIGNATURES: J.A. Randall, Cashier and Stephen J. Strong, President, signed in pen.

BACK: Another of the famous paintings reproduced from those in the rotunda of the Capitol, entitled *Declaration Of Independence*, in black.

SEAL: This shows the seal of Maine.

CONDITION: Very Fine/Extra Fine but trimmed close at the bottom (face)

SOURCE: Bought at auction from Numismatic Gallery, Beverly Hills, California, October 20, 1951

RARITY: Rare — probably less than fifteen to twenty First Charter one-hundred-dollar notes extant today on all states and in all conditions.

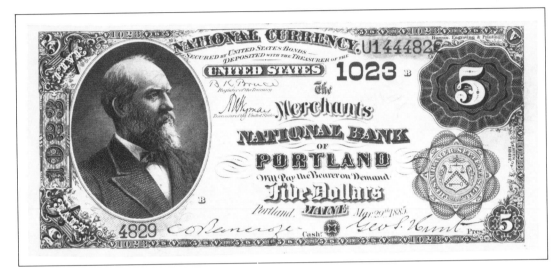

NOTE #23B:

DENOMINATION/ SERIES: Five Dollars/Brownback Series 1882

BANK/CHARTER: The Merchants National Bank Of Portland, Maine (#1023)

FEDERAL DATA: Serial #U144482–, signed by Bruce and Wyman

BANK DATA: Dated March 29, 1885, Plate letter "B," Bank serial #4829. This bank operated from 1865 to 1905, issuing only

Original and Series 1875 First Charter and 1882 brownback Series and red seals Series 1902 notes. In 1910 the amount outstanding was $14,936.

BANK SIGNATURES: C.O. Bancroft, Cashier and Geo. S. Hunt, President, pen signed.

BACK: Charter number (1023)

SEAL: Maine state seal; all are similar.

CONDITION: Uncirculated

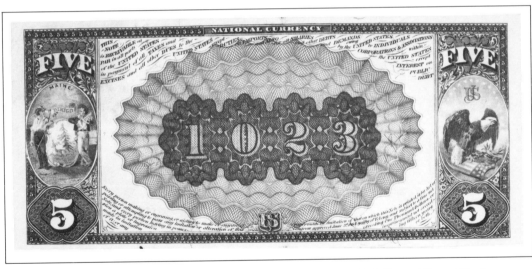

SOURCE: Purchased from Paul Whisonant, Lincolnton, N.C., April 2, 1969

RARITY: Nice notes of Maine, both First and Second Charter brownbacks, are hard to find.

#24 — MISSOURI

NAME: Algonquin for "canoe haver"
NICKNAME: The Show Me State
ESTABLISHED AS TERRITORY: 1812
ENTERED THE UNION: August 10, 1821
CAPITAL: Jefferson City
SEAL: The seal was adopted on January 11, 1822 and has a central elliptical shield, the right half of which is said

to indicate the United States and the left half the State. The crescent, upper left, indicates that Missouri was the second state formed out of territory not in the original limits of the nation, Louisiana being the first. The bear, lower left, indicates resources of the state. As a crest, the helmet signifies sovereignty with the star above and the motto "Salus Populi Suprema Lex Esta" below the shield means "Let the good of the people be supreme law." Supporting the shield are two black bears standing on each end of the ribbon bearing the motto (PLATE V). All National Bank Notes of

NOTE #24A:

DENOMINATION/SERIES: One Dollar/Original First Charter Series
BANK/CHARTER: The Moniteau National Bank Of California, Missouri (#1712 — charter number not on the note).

FEDERAL DATA: Serial #C74439–, signed by Allison and Spinner.
BANK DATA: Dated October 1, 1870, Plate letter "A," Bank serial #1487. The Moniteau Bank operated from 1870 and went to the end

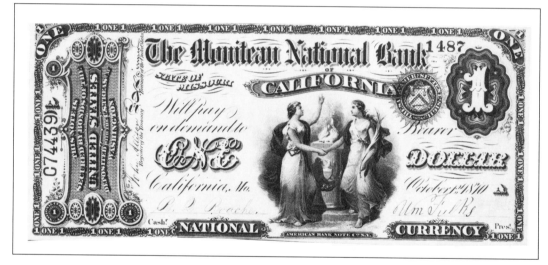

of the National Bank Note issuing period in 1935. The bank issued all but value-backs Series 1882 and red seals Series 1902 and five dollars of Type I and Type II small-size notes. Outstanding in 1935 was $3,620 in large-size notes.

BANK SIGNATURES: R.Q. Roache, Cashier and Wm. Fulks, President, pen signed.
BACK: *Landing of the Pilgrims, 1620*
SEAL: Missouri state seals are all alike on the National Bank Notes.

CONDITION: Uncirculated

SOURCE: Stack's sale of the Limpert Collection, Lot #149, September 24, 1955

RARITY: Even though it is a small bank someone laid some notes back so that this bank is well represented today with choice specimens. Missouri is not rare as a state nor as a bank.

Missouri show the seal as described above except that I find no star or stars. On two drawings all three bears are white and as also shown on the official seal (see inset) there are twenty-four stars, the largest one (standing for Missouri) just above the helmet crest and around the inside circle of the shield "United We Stand. Divided We Fall" which is barely visible on the banknote seal. Also not shown on the banknote seal is the large Roman numeral at the bottom, MDCCCXX (1820) which is probably the territorial date.

COMMENTS: You will notice that this bank (and state) is represented in this collection by four notes: a one-, a two- (Original Series), a five-, and a ten-dollar brownback. On one of our trips west we visited the town of California, Missouri and the bank. Yes, it is still there. Without looking up the population, I'd say the town had about 10 or 12 thousand people, about the same size as Waynesboro, Pennsylvania, where we lived for twenty years.

NOTE #24B:

DENOMINATION/ SERIES: Two Dollars/ First Charter Original Series

BANK/CHARTER: The Moniteau National Bank of California, Missouri (#1712)

FEDERAL DATA: Serial #C74414–, signed by Allison and Spinner

BANK DATA: Dated October 1, 1870, Plate letter "A," Bank serial #1462.

BANK SIGNATURES: R.Q. Roache, Cashier and Wm. Fulks, President

BACK: *Sir Walter Raleigh, 1585*

SEAL: All Missouri seals are similar.

CONDITION: Choice Uncirculated

SOURCE: Purchased from Louis S. Werner, New York, N.Y., August 21, 1964

RARITY: Not rare.

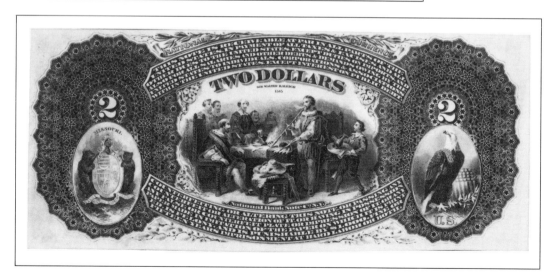

NOTE #24C:

DENOMINATION/ SERIES: Five Dollars/ Brownback Series 1882

BANK/CHARTER: The Moniteau National Bank of California, Missouri (#1712)

FEDERAL DATA: Serial #Z353959–, signed by Rosecrans and Huston

BANK DATA: Dated September 1, 1890, Plate letter "B," Bank serial #2241. (See Note #24A.)

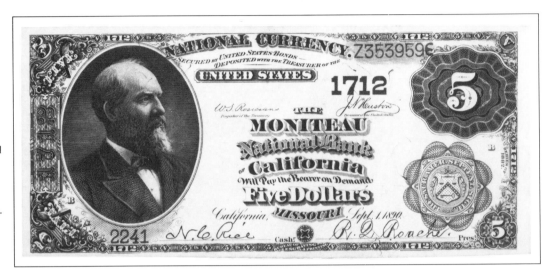

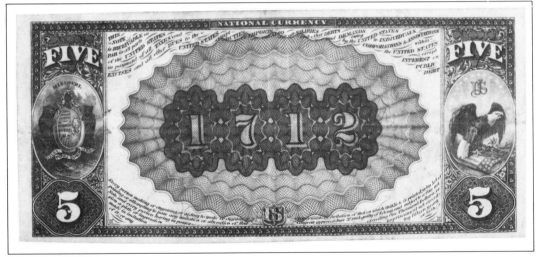

BANK SIGNATURES: Pen signed — N.C. Rice, Cashier and R.Q. Roache, President

BACK: Charter number (1712)

SEAL: Missouri state seal.

CONDITION: Extra Fine/About Uncirculated, cut close at bottom

SOURCE: Purchased from Wm. A. Philpott, Jr., Hotel Sheraton Cadillac, Detroit, Michigan, August 17, 1962

RARITY: Not rare.

NOTE #24D:

DENOMINATION/ SERIES: Ten Dollars/ Brownback Series 1882

BANK/CHARTER: The Moniteau National Bank Of California, Missouri (#1712)

FEDERAL DATA: Serial #W444270–, signed by Rosecrans and Huston

BANK DATA: Dated September 1, 1890, Plate letter "A," Bank serial #1.

BANK SIGNATURES: Pen signed — N.C. Rice, Cashier and R.Q. Roache, President

BACK: Charter number (1712)

SEAL: Seals on all Missouri notes are similar.

CONDITION: Extra Fine/About Uncirculated, cut close at bottom.

SOURCE: Stack's auction of the George O. Walton Collection, October 2, 1963

RARITY: Not rare.

#25 — ARKANSAS

NAME: Sioux for south wind people
NICKNAME: The Land of Opportunity
ESTABLISHED AS TERRITORY: 1819
ENTERED THE UNION: June 15, 1836
CAPITAL: Little Rock
SEAL: Part of the Louisiana Purchase, Arkansas became a Territory in 1819. The seal of Arkansas was adopted in 1864 from the territorial seal designed in 1820. The Goddess of Liberty, encircled by thirteen stars, is shown at the top, holding a wreath in the right hand and a liberty pole

and cap in the left hand. Beneath is an erect American eagle with a streamer reading "Regnant Populi" meaning "The People Rule." An olive branch is in the right foot and four arrows in the other; the eagle's breast is covered by a shield with a steamboat at the top, a plow and beehive below and a sheaf of wheat below that. An Angel of Mercy is posed at the left of the shield with the Sword of Justice at the right on the official seal (see inset, also compare PLATE V). National Bank Notes of Arkansas (both First and Second Charter Periods) are quite different from the seal described above. They show the shield with the steamboat across the top third, a plow in the left portion of the second third, and a beehive in the right portion. In the

NOTE #25A:

DENOMINATION/SERIES: Ten Dollars/First Charter Series 1875
BANK/CHARTER: The Merchants National Bank Of Little Rock, "Little Rock City" Arkansas (#1648)
FEDERAL DATA: Serial #H838842–, signed by Allison and Wyman
BANK DATA: Dated April 16, 1866, Plate letter "C," Bank serial #4468. This bank operated from 1866 to 1893 and issued only

Original and Series 1875 First Charter and brownbacks Series 1882. The amount outstanding in 1916 was $4,184.
BANK SIGNATURES: Lucian M. Coy, "a" (for assistant) Cashier and Logan Hunt (??), President, pen signed.
BACK: *De Soto Discovering the Mississippi*
SEAL: This shows the Arkansas seal as used on all National Bank Notes.
CONDITION: Fine +. This one is the best of the three by a whole grade.

SOURCE: Out of the Hickman and Oakes State Seal and State Capital Sale April 10, 1976, Lot 13. We believe this note is out of the former Pickett Collection.
RARITY: So far as this collector knows there are only three First Charter notes known on the entire state of Arkansas. All three are on

this bank, and all three are now in this collection. There is one five, my first, obtained years ago through Kagin's auction. This ten, along with one twenty, was acquired recently out of the Amon G. Carter, Jr. Collection. Arkansas First Charter notes are very rare.

bottom third of the shield is a star. The entire shield is supported by two large eagles. Supporting the shield are 2 cornucopias; underneath all is the motto. Standing on top of the shield is Liberty with a wreath in her left hand and liberty pole and cap in her right hand. There is no "Angel of Mercy" or "Sword of Justice" (please see PLATE XII).

This is a beautiful and very scarce seal for there are perhaps a dozen and a half known brownback notes and only three First Charter notes (Series 1875: a five-dollar, a ten-dollar and a twenty-dollar note) all on the Merchants National Bank of Little Rock City (#1648). All three of these First Charter notes repose in this collection.

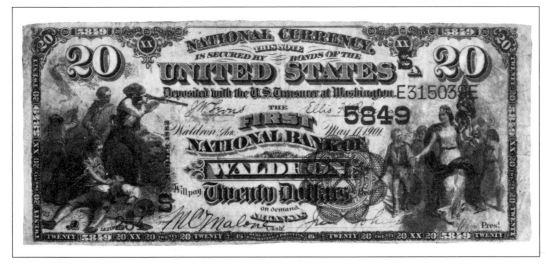

NOTE #25B:

DENOMINATION/ SERIES: Twenty Dollars/Brownback Series 1882

BANK/CHARTER: The First National Bank Of Waldron, Arkansas (#5849), Regional letter "S"

FEDERAL DATA: Serial #E315039E, signed by Lyons and Roberts

BANK DATA: Dated May 17, 1901, Plate letter "A," Bank serial #254. This bank opened

in 1901 and closed in 1931, and issued all three Series 1882, only plain-backs Series 1902 and tens and twenties (small size) of Type I. The amount of large size out in 1931 was $2,800.

BANK SIGNATURES: Pen signed — M.C. Malone, Cashier and J.M. Johnston, V Pres.

BACK: Charter number (5849)

SEAL: Arkansas seal used on bank notes.

CONDITION: Fine (four pin holes)

SOURCE: Limpert Collection, sold by Stack's, Lot #183, September 24, 1955

RARITY: Rare. There are perhaps a dozen or 18 brownback notes known on Arkansas.

#26 —
MICHIGAN

NAME: Chippewa for "great lake"
NICKNAME:
The Wolverine State
ESTABLISHED AS TERRITORY: Became

Michigan Territory, 1805
ENTERED THE UNION: January 26, 1837
CAPITAL: Lansing
SEAL: Cut from the Northwest Territory, Michigan

became a separate territory in 1805. The seal of Michigan was designed by Lewis Cass, second territorial governor (1813-1831) and adopted in 1835 two years before statehood. The central shield depicts a soldier in front of the American flag and his tent, looking across a body of water at the sun. Above the scene is *Tuebor* meaning "I will defend." As a crest is an American eagle and a streamer reading *E Pluribus Unum* meaning "One of many." Supporting the shield is a moose at the right and an elk at the left. Another streamer below is inscribed *Si Quaeris*

NOTE #26A:

DENOMINATION/ SERIES: Five Dollars/ First Charter Series 1875
BANK/CHARTER: The First National Bank of St. Clair, Michigan (#1789)
FEDERAL DATA: Serial #X625737–, signed by Allison and Gilfillan
BANK DATA: Dated February 15, 1871, Plate letter "C," Bank serial #4311. This bank

operated only from 1871 to 1886 and issued only Original and Series 1875 First Charter notes leaving an outstanding balance of $1,079 in 1910.

BANK SIGNATURES: J.H. Watkins, Cashier and Wm. J. Hopkins (?) President

BACK: *Landing of Columbus, 1492*

SEAL: Michigan state seal, all are alike

CONDITION: Extra Fine (bought as Uncirculated with one crease)

SOURCE: Purchased from Stack's sale of the Henry A. Pirtle Collection, April 18, 1953

RARITY: Michigan notes are not rare, but this small bank must be rare.

Peninsulim Amoenam Circumspice meaning "If you seek a pleasing peninsula, look about you." Two drawings I have found and the "official" seal are alike except that I find no tent for the soldier on the shore as on the seal first described (PLATE V). All Michigan bank notes (of these two series) show the seal as described. The only small difference I can find is that the supporters of the shield are standing less upright. Also, in the shield the National Bank Notes show the shore of land on the right side (instead of left, facing) with soldier, gun, flag, and tent. This is a beautiful seal.

NOTE #26B:

DENOMINATION/ SERIES: Five Dollars/Brownback Series 1882

BANK/CHARTER: The First National Exchange Bank Of Plymouth, Michigan (#4649)

FEDERAL DATA: Serial #M720184–, signed by Rosecrans and Nebeker

BANK DATA: Dated November 14, 1891, Plate letter "B," Bank serial #1909. This bank operated from 1891 to 1903 and issued only brownback notes. Amount outstanding in 1910 was $1,335.

BANK SIGNATURES: R. Disher (?) Cash. and D.D. Allen, President, signed in pen.

BACK: Charter number (4649)

SEAL: Michigan seals are all similar.

CONDITION: Uncirculated

SOURCE: Purchased from Paul Whisonant, Lincolnton, N.C., April 2, 1969

RARITY: Small bank, but several of its notes are known to collectors.

#27 — FLORIDA

NAME: Spanish for "flowery"
NICKNAME:
The Sunshine State
ESTABLISHED AS
TERRITORY: West Florida
declared independent of
Spain in 1810; 1812 West
Florida became a U.S. Territory. East Florida purchased from Spain by U.S. in 1819.
ENTERED THE UNION: March 3, 1845
CAPITAL: Tallahassee
SEAL: Florida became a territory in 1819. The seal of Florida was authorized in 1845 and showed a map of the state. This seal was replaced by one adopted on August 6,

1868. The new design depicts an Indian maiden strewing blossoms, a ship, a palm, and high hills in the distance with the motto "In God We Trust." Bank notes of the First Charter Period and brownback notes show the seal as described last. The two drawings I have and the "official" seal show minor differences. The script describing one of these drawings says "hills"in the background, except one drawing and the "official" seal show no hills at all. In the first drawing the "hills" look more like mountains and everyone knows there are no mountains in Florida. I'm told the hills represent the highest elevation in Florida, 700 odd feet, near Lake Wales and the Bok Singing Tower. One drawing shows a distinct flower or plant in the lower right; the other drawing has no plant distinguishable. There is

Please see Plates VI and XII

NOTE #27A:

DENOMINATION/SERIES: Five Dollars/First Charter Series 1875

BANK/CHARTER: The First National Bank of Pensacola, Florida (#2490)

FEDERAL DATA: Serial #K789640–, signed by Scofield and Gilfillan

BANK DATA: Dated August 30, 1880, Plate letter "A," Bank serial #1056. This bank operated from 1880 to 1914 and issued only Series 1875 First Charters and brownbacks and date-backs of the Series of 1882.
BANK SIGNATURES: Signed in pen by W.W. Wheeler, Cashier, and Louis P. Knowles, Vice President.
BACK: *Landing of Columbus, 1492*

SEAL: Florida state seal. All are alike.
CONDITION: Fine +
SOURCE: From Hickman and Oakes sale, April 1976, Lot #45
RARITY: Very rare. There are only three First Charter notes known on the state of Florida. All three are drawn on this bank and this is the nicest. Jacksonville (#2175) also issued them but they are unknown.

also some disagreement about the Indian, whether it is a maiden, woman, or man. Logically, my first thought was that she was dropping orange blossoms, but again, the script says flower blossoms. The seal on bank notes show some differences. The ship is a sailing vessel under sail. The other seals show a side-wheeler. One source says that the tree is a cocoa tree, but in Florida I was told that it is a Sabal Palm, the state tree. Also on the notes, the Indian is very definitely a "maiden" wearing a small feather head-

dress, a skirt, and little else. Dr. Limpert says, "No Florida First Charter notes are known to exist," but by this time three have come to light, all on Pensacola (#2490, 1880-1914). Only one other bank issued all three (Original, Series 1875, and brownbacks), but no First Charter notes are known on this bank. These notes are very rare and the brownbacks are not common. A friend of mine who has seen most of them can account for a total of thirty-three.

NOTE #27B:

DENOMINATION/ SERIES: Twenty Dollars/Brownback Series 1882

BANK/CHARTER: The First National Bank of Pensacola, Florida (#2490), Regional letter "S"

FEDERAL DATA: Serial #K994296K, signed by Lyons and Roberts

BANK DATA: Dated July 11, 1900, Plate letter "A," Bank serial #7546.

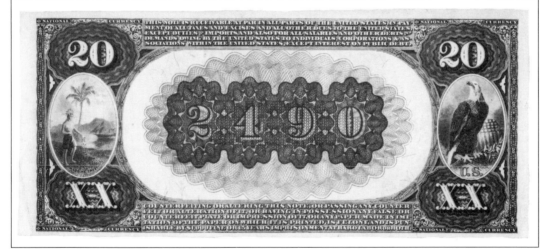

BANK SIGNATURES: P.K. Fifer, Cashier and R.H. Knowles, President, pen-signed

BACK: Charter number (2490)

SEAL: Florida seal

CONDITION: Extra Fine/About Uncirculated

SOURCE: From Stack's sale of the Limpert Collection, Lot #193, September 24, 1955

RARITY: Florida brownback notes are scarce.

#28 — TEXAS

NAME: Indian for "friend"
NICKNAME:
The Lone Star State
**ESTABLISHED AS
TERRITORY:** Became part
of Mexico 1821; Republic
of Texas formed 1836
ENTERED THE UNION: December 29, 1845
CAPITAL: Austin

SEAL: The seal of Texas is a five-pointed star encircled by a wreath of live oak and olive branches and was authorized in the first year of statehood in 1845. Legend has it that during the era of the Republic of Texas, an official, needing a seal, used a brass button from his greatcoat to make the impression, the button having a star-like appearance. National Bank Notes of Texas have a similar seal.

Please see Plates VI and XII

NOTE #28A:

**DENOMINATION/
SERIES:** Ten
Dollars/First Charter
Series 1875
BANK/CHARTER: The
City National Bank Of
Dallas, Texas (#2455)
FEDERAL DATA: Serial
#K837626–, signed by
Scofield and Gilfillan
BANK DATA: Dated
March 15, 1880, Plate
letter "B," Bank serial
#67187. This bank
operated from 1880 to
1929 and issued Series
1875, all three Second

Charter Series 1882 and
plain-backs Series 1902
(the last and most
common, usually, of all
the large-size notes). It
also issued small five-,
ten- and twenty-dollar
notes of the Type I only.
The amount of large-size
notes outstanding in
1929 was $444,220.
BANK SIGNATURES:
Both pen-signed
signatures are illegible.
BACK: *De Soto
Discovering the
Mississippi.*
SEAL: Texas state seal
CONDITION: Fine. A
well circulated note, soiled.
SOURCE: Purchased personally from Wm. A. Philpott, Jr.
Dallas, Texas

RARITY: A large bank but Texas First Charter notes are
definitely rare.

NOTE #28B:

DENOMINATION/ SERIES: Twenty Dollars/Brownback Series 1882

BANK/CHARTER: The City National Bank Of Wichita Falls, Texas (#4248), Regional letter "S"

FEDERAL DATA: Serial #A987596A, signed by Rosecrans and Huston

BANK DATA: Dated March 5, 1890, Plate letter "A," Bank serial #2876. This bank operated from 1890 to

1933 and issued brownbacks and value-backs Series 1882, date-backs and plain-backs of the Third Charter Series 1902 and fives, tens, and twenties of Type I only, small-size notes (1929) Series. Amount of large-size notes outstanding in 1935 was $41,400.

BANK SIGNATURES: P.P. Langford, Cashier and Jas. A. Kemp, President, pen signed

BACK: Charter number (4248)

SEAL: Texas seal. All are similar.

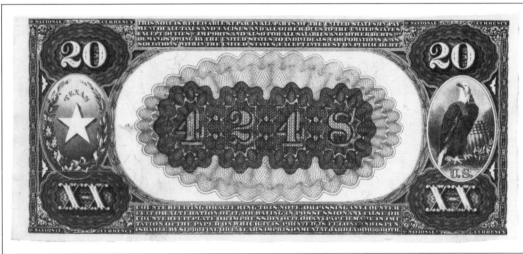

CONDITION: Uncirculated

SOURCE: Purchased from M. Perlmutter, May 11, 1970

RARITY: Brownback notes on Texas are not rare.

#29 — IOWA

NAME: Sioux for "beautiful land"

NICKNAME: The Hawkeye State

ESTABLISHED AS TERRITORY: Part of Louisiana Purchase. Became Iowa Territory in 1838

ENTERED THE UNION: December 28, 1846

CAPITAL: Des Moines

SEAL: Iowa became a territory in 1838. The Legislature of Iowa adopted the state seal on February 25, 1847, soon after statehood. The seal depicts a soldier with the national flag in his right hand and a rifle beside him on his left. In the right background is a smelting mill and some pig lead along with a plow; at the left is a sheaf of wheat and in the distance is a steamer on the Mississippi River. At the top is an eagle with a streamer worded "Our Liberties We Prize and Our Rights We Will Maintain." Iowa is another of the states to change seals. Actually, the first "seal" of Iowa was not a seal, and we don't know why the Treasury or Bureau of Printing and Engraving placed a large eagle there. It is a different eagle than any of the others. But we do know that all First Charter period notes and some of the

---

NOTE #29A:

DENOMINATION/SERIES: Twenty Dollars/First Charter Series 1875

BANK/CHARTER: The Sioux National Bank Of Sioux City, Iowa (#2535)

FEDERAL DATA: Series #K438636–, signed by Bruce and Gilfillan

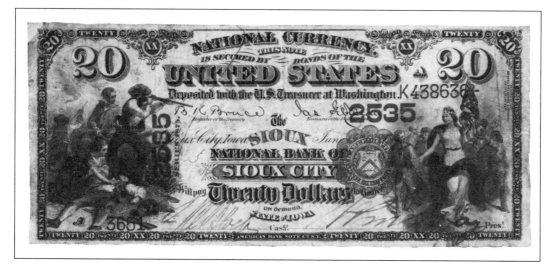

BANK DATA: Dated June 15, 1881, Plate letter "A," Bank serial #3651. This bank operated from 1881 to 1896 and issued only First Charter Period notes of 1875. Amount outstanding in 1915 was $1,120.

BANK SIGNATURES: Pen signed, A.W. Black (or Bloch?), Cashier, and (?) Pres.

BACK: *Baptism Of Pocahontas*

SEAL: First seal, probably used only on National Bank Notes. We do not know why the eagle was used instead of a seal.

CONDITION: Very Fine

SOURCE: Purchased from Numismatic Gallery, October 20, 1951

RARITY: While Iowa First Charter notes are not particularly rare, this small bank's notes must be.

brownbacks showed this particular eagle. The latter portion of brownback notes show the "official" seal as described above except that the soldier in the foreground is larger, the pig lead and smelting mill are much larger, and the Mississippi River and the side-wheeler are shown in the left background instead of on the right side. There are differences in the farm tools also: the later brownback notes show a rake standing on its handle in the center of a large shock of wheat instead of lying on the ground. (Please see seal on note picture #29C).

Please see Plates VI and XII

NOTE #29B:

DENOMINATION/SERIES: Five Dollars/Brownback 1882 Series
BANK/CHARTER: The First National Bank of Charles City, Iowa (#1810)

FEDERAL DATA: Serial #K434988–, signed by Rosecrans and Huston

BANK DATA: Dated January 31, 1891, Plate letter "C," Bank serial #512. This bank operated from 1891 to 1932 and issued brownbacks and date-backs Series 1882 and date-backs and plain-backs of 1902. Also, it issued tens and twenties of Type II small size. The amount of large-size notes out in 1929 was $43,547.50.

BANK SIGNATURES: Pen signed — S.B. Hall, Cashier and ?? (can not make it out)

BACK: Charter number (1810)

SEAL: First seal, a large eagle (substitute for seal)

CONDITION: About Uncirculated

SOURCE: Received in trade with Dr. Limpert, April 18, 1953

RARITY: Not very rare but scarce in this condition, more so with the number of brownbacks divided between two seals. We believe the first seal to be the scarcer of the two.

NOTE #29C:

DENOMINATION/SERIES: Twenty Dollars/Brownback Series 1882

BANK/CHARTER: The Citizens National Bank of Knoxville, Iowa (#4633), Regional letter "M"

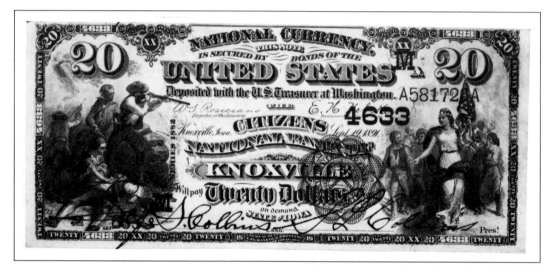

FEDERAL DATA: Serial #A581726A, signed by Rosecrans and Nebeker

BANK DATA: Dated September 19, 1891, Plate letter "A," Bank serial #633. This bank operated from 1891 to 1932 and issued brownbacks and date-backs Series 1882 as well as date-backs and plain-backs Series 1902. Also it issued tens and twenties of Type II small-size notes. The amount of large-size outstanding in 1932 was $12,137.50.

BANK SIGNATURES: Signed in pen by Lafe S. Collins, Cashier and S.L. Collins, P. (brothers)

BACK: Charter number (4633)

SEAL: Second seal on brownback notes. This is the state seal in use now.

CONDITION: About Uncirculated

SOURCE: Received in a trade from Dr. Limpert, November 29, 1952

RARITY: Not real rare but scarce in this condition, especially when divided between the two seals. Hickman says that the last seal on brownbacks (the present day seal) is about four times more common than the brownbacks with the large eagle used as the first seal.

98

TO STATE 30:

WISCONSIN

☞

#30 —
WISCONSIN:

NAME: Chippewa for "gathering of the waters"
NICKNAME: The Badger State
ESTABLISHED AS TERRITORY: Part of Northwest Territory, 1787. Became Wisconsin Territory, 1836
ENTERED THE UNION: May 29, 1848
CAPITAL: Madison
SEAL: The seal of Wisconsin is said to have been designed in 1857, three years after statehood, while the Governor and Chief Justice of the state were sitting on the steps of a bank on Wall Street, New York City. Note that Wisconsin became a territory in 1836, a state in 1848, and began using a state seal in 1851. By 1881 the old seal die

was worn out and a new seal was adopted on April 1. The old seal was to be used until July 4, 1881 after which the new seal was to be used. We will describe the worn out seal later. Two drawings and the present "official" seal appear as follows (compare PLATE XIII): A quartered central shield with a small United States shield, encircled with *E Pluribus Unum* at the center, with a crossed pick and shovel in the upper right quarter and a plow in the upper left. There is an anchor in the lower right and an arm and hammer in the lower left quarter. The shield rests on a small stack of lead bars and a cornucopia, and is supported on the right by a man with a pick and on the left by a sailor with a coil of rope. Above the shield as a crest is a badger and the word "Forward." At the bottom are thirteen stars. As hinted above, Wisconsin also shows two

NOTE #30A:

DENOMINATION/SERIES: Two Dollars/First Charter Series 1875

BANK/CHARTER: The La Crosse National Bank, La Crosse, Wisconsin (#2344)
FEDERAL DATA: Serial #A503433–, signed by Allison and Wyman

BANK DATA: Dated December 15, 1876, Plate letter "A," Serial #94. This bank operated for 20 years, 1876 to 1896 and issued Series 1875, First Charter notes only. The amount outstanding in 1910 was only $2,112.
BANK SIGNATURES: S.S. Burton, Cashier, and G.C. Nixon, President, pen signed.
BACK: *Sir Walter Raleigh, 1585*
SEAL: This is the first seal of the state of Wisconsin on bank notes.

CONDITION: Uncirculated
SOURCE: From the Friedberg Collection sold by Abner Kreisberg, New York, N.Y., March 12, 1965
RARITY: State is not rare. From the above figures, notes on this bank have to be scarce. As has happened in other states, someone put several away.

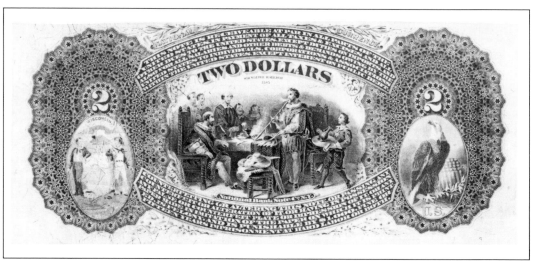

100

different seals on its bank notes (see PLATE VI). Although most of the objects shown on the last (current) seal appear on the first seal, glancing at them side-by-side they appear quite different. In the first seal the two men appear as young men, and the sailor is on the right side rather than the left and is holding a sextant in his right hand. The youth on the left is bareheaded and holding a short scythe or weeding froe. The objects at the bottom are indistinct and the shield is resting on the ground (compare the seals on the notes). But what makes the biggest difference in appearance is the fact that the first seal has no quartered shield. The first has a shield but is very light colored and the objects are not as distinct. In essence, the second seal shows attainment, fulfillment, and full development; Wisconsin has more items named and acclaimed as attributes than any other state. For example, beside the usual items of state flower, bird, and tree, it has named the state large game animal, small game animal, game fish, etc. All Wis-

consin First Charter and part of the brownback notes have the first or earlier seal. The latter part of the brownback notes show the present seal as described above. In this collection we show a "Lazy Two" of La Crosse (#2344) dated December 15, 1876. This bank was in business from 1876 to 1896 and issued only first Charter Series 1875 notes. Also showing the first seal is the Northern National Bank of Ashland (#3607) dated December 21, 1886. There is also a twenty dollar brownback note on the Wisconsin National Bank of Milwaukee (#4817), a large bank that changed its title several times along with its charter number (#64, #2715, #4817, and #6853). This note shows the second seal. This note is dated November 12, 1892 and was probably issued about the time that the second seal began to be used (perhaps as the early banks were rechartered?). After all is said and done, both seals are handsome.

NOTE #30B:

DENOMINATION/SERIES: Five Dollars/Brownback Series 1882
BANK/CHARTER: The Northern National Bank Of Ashland, Wisconsin (#3607)

FEDERAL DATA: Serial #W715048–, signed by Rosecrans and Jordan

BANK DATA: Dated December 21, 1886, Plate letter "B," Bank serial #8360. This bank operated from 1886 to 1933 and issued brownback Series 1882 as well as all three issues of the 1902 Series and then small-size Type I of five-, ten-, twenty-, fifty-, and one-hundred-dollar denominations. The amount of large size outstanding in 1933 was $18,190.

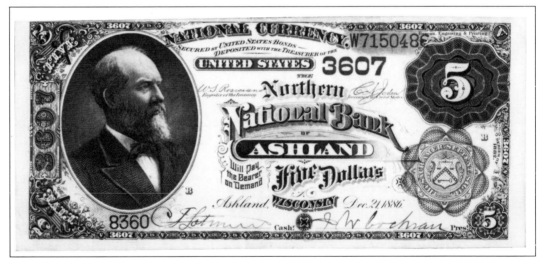

BANK SIGNATURES:
Pen signed —
C.S. Latimer, Cashier
and J.W. Cockran,
President

BACK: Charter number
(3607)

SEAL: This is also the
first seal used on
National Bank Notes.
(See seals, PLATES VI,
XIII.)

CONDITION: Very
Fine/Extra Fine. This
note has one of the
most beautiful layouts to
be found. Very
distinctive "tombstone"
and ornate "Five
dollars."

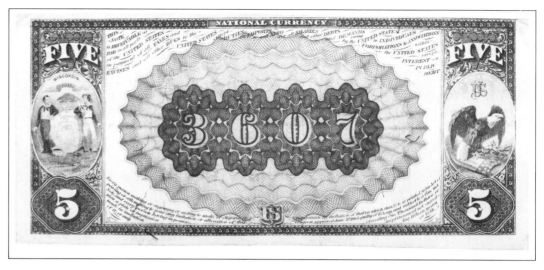

SOURCE: Purchased from Paul Whisonant, Lincolnton, N.C.,
February 15, 1972

RARITY: Not rare, but in this condition it must be very scarce.

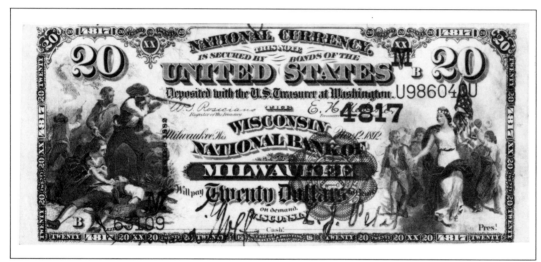

NOTE #30C:

**DENOMINATION/
SERIES:** Twenty
Dollars/Series 1882
Brownback

BANK/CHARTER: The
Wisconsin National
Bank of Milwaukee, WI
(#4817),
Regional letter "M"

FEDERAL DATA: Serial
#U986040U, signed by
Rosecrans and Nebeker

BANK DATA: Dated
November 12, 1892,
Plate letter "B," Bank
serial #63109. This
large bank operated

from 1892 to 1919 and issued only large-size notes, namely
brownbacks and date-backs Series 1882, date-backs and plain-back
Series 1902. The amount outstanding in 1919 was $665,995.

BANK SIGNATURES: (stamped ?) ? Wolf, Cashier and L.J. Petit,
President

BACK: Large Charter number (4817)

SEAL: Second seal
found on the later
portion of the
brownback notes and is
the state seal used
today.

CONDITION:
Uncirculated

SOURCE: Purchased
from Paul Kagin,
October 17, 1972

RARITY: Not rare. We
believe that the last seal
is about twice as
common as the first on
brownback notes.

TO STATE 31:

CALIFORNIA

☞

#31 — CALIFORNIA

NAME: Named for a treasure island in the Spanish tale, "Las Sergas de Esplandian"
NICKNAME: The Golden State
ESTABLISHED AS TERRITORY: Part of Mexico, 1822. Mexico ceded California to U.S., 1848
ENTERED THE UNION: September 9, 1850
CAPITAL: Sacramento
SEAL: The seal of California was adopted on October 2, 1849 and depicts the Goddess Minerva seated, with a spear and a circular shield; a bear and miners with mountain ranges in the background appear with "Eureka," meaning "Have found it," and 31 stars around the top. "Eureka" could signify that California became a state without going through the process of being a territory, but the most common explanation is that "Eureka" refers to the discovery of gold. National Bank Notes all show this seal with some minor changes made by the artist to get all elements of the seal into the upright oval space. "Eureka" is placed at the bottom. The first eight banks of California operated as National Gold Banks under the National Banking Act. These showed a large picture of various gold coins

NOTE #31A:

DENOMINATION/SERIES: Five Dollars/First Charter Original National Gold Bank Series
BANK/CHARTER: The First National Gold Bank Of San Francisco, Ca. (#1741)

FEDERAL DATA: Serial #K276407), signed by Allison and Spinner
BANK DATA: Dated November 30, 1870, Plate letter "B," Bank serial #7270. This large bank opened in 1870 and "went all the way." This bank issued both Original and 1875 Series in gold-back bank notes

(picturing gold coins). The bank then converted to regular national bank status; then starting with First Charter Series 1875 it released some of all issues except value-backs Series 1882 and red seals of the 1902 Series. The amount of large size outstanding in 1935 was $277,795.

BANK SIGNATURES: D. Morgan, Cashier and R.C. Woolworth, President, pen-signed.

BACK: This note shows in the center a large picture depicting a group of gold coins.
SEAL: State seal of California
CONDITION: Very Good or better. California gold-back notes saw lots of circulation and those in choice condition are few.
SOURCE: Purchased from Earl Minnick, Waynesboro, Pa., January 12, 1957
RARITY: Not rare, except in top condition.

on the backs of the notes and also, at the left, the same California seal. Seven of these eight National Gold Banks converted to regular bank status. These seven and the next four banks all issued First Charter State National Bank Notes, but like most western states, the First Charter State national notes are rare. Ours is on Los Angeles, a large bank. There are perhaps six to ten First Charter notes known of these eleven banks. The time of issue of these notes falls between the National Gold Bank issues and the brownback Series 1882. I personally know of two other notes and have a picture of a five-dollar note on Alameda.

Please see Plate VI

COMMENTS: The discovery of gold in California soon created a problem for the banks and business in general. It took too long for the gold dust and nuggets to reach Washington and for the gold coins to return, hence the establishment of private coinage firms in California. Twenty years of private coinage relieved pressure for a medium of exchange until the nine National Gold Banks in California were ushered in. There was also one in Boston, the Kidder National Gold Bank, but it never actually released any notes to the public. The National Gold Banks in California speedily advanced the state's rapid growth.

NOTE #31B:

DENOMINATION/SERIES: Ten Dollars/First Charter Series 1875
BANK/CHARTER: The First National Bank Of Los Angeles (#2491)

FEDERAL DATA: Serial #K721008–, signed by Scofield and Gilfillan
BANK DATA: Dated September 10, 1880, Plate letter "B," Bank serial #4810. This bank opened in 1880 and lasted through 1931.

Beginning with Series 1875 First Charters this bank released some of all issues except red seals and date-backs of the 1902 Series. Also issued fifty- and one-hundred-dollar small-size Type I. The amount of large-size notes outstanding in 1935: $91,110.

BANK SIGNATURES:
Pen-signed —
Frank W. Gibson, Cashier, and J.M. Elliott, President

BACK: Reproduction of the famous painting *De Soto Discovering the Mississippi.*
SEAL: California seal
CONDITION: Extra Fine
SOURCE: Purchased from Paul Kagin, September 30, 1967
RARITY: Rare. First Charter notes on California after the National Gold Bank issues only lasted about two years. There are only a very few notes known at the present time.

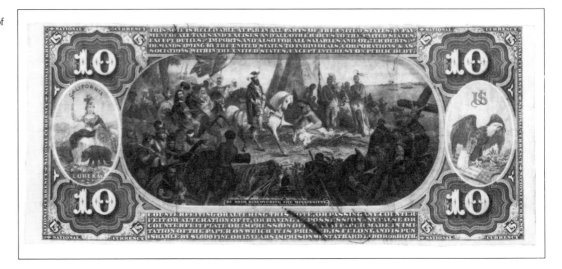

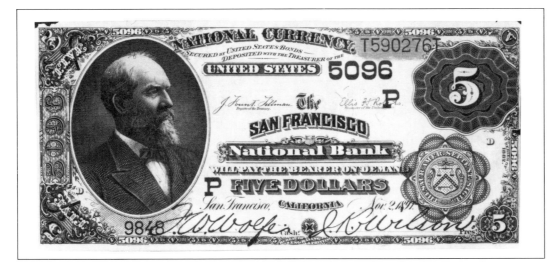

bank, it operated from 1897 to 1910 and issued only brownbacks and date-backs Series 1882. There remained outstanding in 1910 $806,497.50.

NOTE #31C:

DENOMINATION/ SERIES: Five Dollars/Series 1882 Brownback

BANK/CHARTER: The San Francisco National Bank, San Francisco, California (#5096), Regional letter "P"

FEDERAL DATA: Serial #T590276T, signed by Tillman and Roberts

BANK DATA: Dated November 2, 1897, Plate letter "D," Bank serial #9848. A large

BANK SIGNATURES: Pen-signed — F.W. Wolfe, Cashier, and J.K. Wilson, President
BACK: Charter number (5096)

SEAL: California state seal

CONDITION: Was Uncirculated, but the author (long ago, and carelessly) placing it in an album, was punching holes in the plastic holders and nicked the top two corners as well as the right center.

SOURCE: Purchased from New Netherlands Coin Co., New York, N.Y., April 29, 1953

RARITY: Not rare

TO STATE 32:

MINNESOTA

☞

#32 —
MINNESOTA

NAME: Sioux for "sky colored water"
NICKNAME: The North Star State
ESTABLISHED AS TERRITORY: 1849
ENTERED THE UNION: May 11, 1858
CAPITAL: St. Paul
SEAL: Minnesota became a territory in 1849. The seal of Minnesota was adopted July 16, 1858, during the first year of statehood. It depicts a pioneer plowing and warily watching an Indian on a horse galloping west toward the sun and St. Anthony's Falls. The settler's rifle and powder horn are resting on a nearby tree stump. Minnesota is the only state with a French motto, *L'Etoile du Nord*, meaning "Star of the North." This indicated the state's geographic position in the union (before Alaska was acquired). All Minnesota National Bank Notes show similar seals.

Please see Plate VI

NOTE #32A:

DENOMINATION/ SERIES: Five Dollars/ Series 1875 First Charter

BANK/CHARTER: The Farmers National Bank Of Owatonna, Minn. (#2122)

FEDERAL DATA: Serial #Z560348–, signed by Allison and New

BANK DATA: Dated August 15, 1873, Plate letter "C," Bank serial #6518. This bank operated from 1873 to 1892 and issued only Original and Series

1875 First Charter notes. In 1910 the amount remaining outstanding was $1,186.

BANK SIGNATURES: C.J. Backus, Cashier, and S.C. Nesmith, President, pen-signed.

BACK: *Landing of Columbus, 1492*

SEAL: Minnesota state seal.

CONDITION: Crisp Uncirculated

SOURCE: From the B. Max Mehl estate through A. Kosoff (1957)

RARITY: Scarce state and scarce bank.

108

NOTE #32B:

DENOMINATION/ SERIES: Ten Dollars/ Brownback Series 1882

BANK/CHARTER: The Rochester National Bank, Rochester, Minnesota (#2316), Regional letter "M"

FEDERAL DATA: Serial #K725376K, signed by Tillman and Morgan

BANK DATA: Dated December 21, 1895, Plate letter "C," Bank serial #658. This operated from 1876 to

1924 and issued Series 1875 First Charter, brownbacks and date-backs of Series 1882 and plain-backs Series 1902. In 1922 this bank had $11,800 outstanding.

BANK SIGNATURES: C.C. Storing, Cashier, and H.M. Nowell, President, signed in pen.

BACK: Charter number (2316)

SEAL: Minnesota seal; all seals are alike.

CONDITION: Uncirculated

SOURCE: Wm. P. Donlon, 1961

RARITY: Not very rare, either as bank or state.

#33 — OREGON

NAME: Algonquin for "beautiful water"
NICKNAME: The Beaver State
ESTABLISHED AS TERRITORY: 1848
ENTERED THE UNION: February 14, 1859

CAPITAL: Salem

SEAL: The seal of Oregon was approved in the first year of statehood and has a central shield (another source calls this an escutcheon) supported by a three-quarter circle of 33 stars, indicating the number of states when Oregon was admitted to the Union. The upper part of the shield shows the Pacific Ocean coast; in the distance is a British man-o'-war departing and an American ship arriving, representing an end of the joint occupancy of Oregon by Great Britain and the United States. A covered wagon and an elk from a forest is shown just above a streamer (called an "ordinary" in another source) with "The Union" upon it. A plow, pick, and rake are shown in the lower part of the shield while above it, as a crest, is the American Eagle with an olive branch in the right talon and four arrows in the left (the arms, PLATE VII, shows three). Two drawings I have of the seal and the "official" seal are very much alike. The seal as shown on Oregon bank notes of both periods looks quite different (PLATE XIII). The eagle is shown on top standing on a branch with a small U.S. shield on its breast

NOTE #33A:

DENOMINATION/SERIES: Ten Dollars/First Charter Series 1875
BANK/CHARTER: The First National Bank of Pendleton, Oregon (#2630)

FEDERAL DATA: Serial #K983061–, signed by Bruce and Gilfillan
BANK DATA: Dated February 10, 1882, "C" is the plate letter, Bank serial #3383. This bank operated from 1882 to 1932 and issued First Charter Period notes of 1875, all three Second Charter Series 1882, then plain-backs of Series 1902 plus 10- and 20-dollars of Type I

small-size notes. The amount of outstanding large size in 1935 was $12,255.

BANK SIGNATURES: E.B. Meek (?) Cashier, and Wm. Matthews, President, pen-signed.

BACK: *De Soto Discovering the Mississippi.*

SEAL: State seal of Oregon. This is the National Bank Note version of the seal.

CONDITION: Very Fine/Extra Fine

SOURCE: Purchased from Morey Perlmutter, May 18, 1970

RARITY: First Charter Oregon notes are rare. Only two banks issued First Charters. Portland, the largest city, and a larger bank (#1553), issued both Original and Series of 1875. Pendleton issued only Series 1875 notes. But there are probably more Pendleton First Charter notes in real nice condition than there are Portland notes; I would say four, or perhaps six Pendleton Series 1875 notes exist.

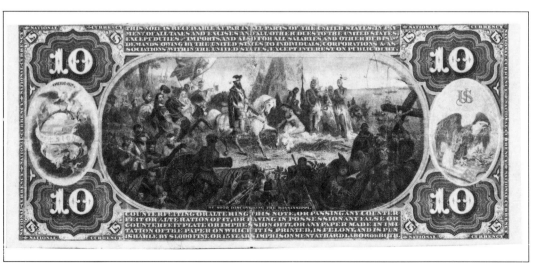

and has a streamer in its beak which loops down on the left side and opens out across the center of what at a glance appears to be a globe but is supposed to represent a shield. The streamer says "The Union." The covered wagon is above the streamer with a plow and sheaf below. Again, the changes are the result of the artist's rendition. The Oregon "official" seal is beautiful.

COMMENTS: Among the data I have gathered on seals is a pamphlet titled "Oregon, Without a Seal of State" (See Appendices). It shows the evolution of the Oregon seal in nine stages along with drawings of each. In 1846 the seal used by the provisional government shows only two ob-

jects, wheat and salmon with "Oregon" at the top. This was called the "Salmon Seal" and was used before Oregon became a territory. On August 14, 1848, an act created Oregon Territory.

The second seal was the first seal of Oregon Territory and shows five stars below within concentric circles. In the center is a shield occupying about one-third of the space. The shield is supported on the left by an Indian with a bow in the right hand and a mantle of skins over his shoulder. The dexter supporter (the one facing the right side) is an eagle and over the shield between these two is a banner or ribbon with *Alis volat propriis* ("I fly with my own wings".) Two compartments are in the shield's upper half containing a ship under full sail, and in the center are mountains,

NOTE #33B:

DENOMINATION/SERIES: Twenty Dollars/Brownback Series 1882.
BANK/CHARTER: The Capital National Bank of Salem, Oregon (#3405), Regional letter "P"

FEDERAL DATA: Serial #D423370D, signed by Rosecrans and Jordan

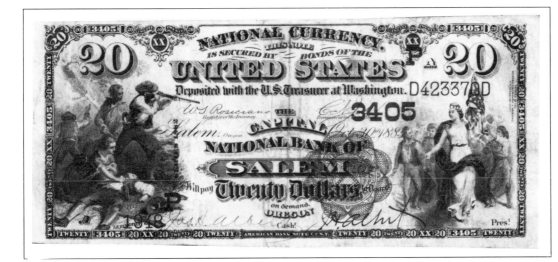

BANK DATA: Dated October 30, 1885, Plate letter "A," Bank serial #1948. This bank operated from 1885 to 1933. It issued brownbacks first and then all three Third Charters of 1902 plus ten- and twenty-dollar Type I small-size notes. The amount of large size outstanding in 1935 was $6,020.
BANK SIGNATURES: Pen-signed — Jas. H. Albert, Cashier, and J. H. Albert, President (brothers?)

BACK: Charter number (3405)
SEAL: Oregon seal as rendered by the Bureau artists. A handsome seal.
CONDITION: Fine
SOURCE: From the Dr. Limpert Collection sold by Stack's, Lot #226, September 24, 1955.
RARITY: Only two Salem banks issued brownback notes. 45 Oregon banks issued brownbacks; Oregon brownbacks as a whole are scarce.

and below that a plow. As a crest appears a beaver.

The third version of the seal deletes the plow. The fourth seal uses a Norman shield with "State of Oregon" written around the edge; "State" begins in the lower left corner, "of" is at the top, and "Oregon" ends at the bottom right. The escutcheon (the smaller shield inside the larger shield) has an eagle as a crest and a circle of stars supporting the inner shield. In the shield the ships and wagon in the upper two-thirds are separated by a banner which reads "The Union" from the plow and farm implements in the bottom third.

The fifth seal shows the same details more clearly. The whole now is a circle, "State" on the left, "of" at the top, and "Oregon" at the right with the date "1857" at the bottom. There are seventeen stars on the left and eighteen on the right with the sum (35) being too many to indicate the order of statehood. The sixth seal is essentially the same but shows nineteen stars on each side (a total of 38).

The seventh seal is again identical to the last with the exception of a return to 35 stars and the change of the date at the bottom to 1859. The eighth variation is the first version to say "Seal of the State of Oregon," but has reduced the number of stars to 32. The ninth seal has the correct number of stars (33), but leaves off the date. The author of this pamphlet ends with some memorable words: "We have no seal and never had one. What are you going to do about it? We would respectfully suggest that a state seal be secured which will meet all requirements of the law in relation thereto. It would not be amiss if a new act was passed providing that the state seal should have objects thereon indicative of the days of the 'prairie schooner,' coupled with the pioneers' vision of what Oregon is and can become; and that all past efforts, together with facsimiles shown, be turned over to keepers of historical relics and placed in the curio department."[4] In other words, they never had a correct seal; all contained errors, but all were used. In fact, most are still used by different departments. My "official" seal, the most correct to date, does not say "The Great Seal...," but only "State of Oregon."

4 From "Oregon Without a Seal of State" by F.H. Saylor, from *Oregon Native Son,* V,1, May 1899–April 1900, reprinted in its entirety in the appendix courtesy of the Oregon State Library.

TO STATE 34:

KANSAS

☞

#34 — KANSAS

NAME: Sioux for "south-wind people"
NICKNAME: The Sunflower State
ESTABLISHED AS TERRITORY: Part of Louisiana Purchase 1803; Kansas-Nebraska Act established Kansas Territory 1854
ENTERED THE UNION: January 29, 1861
CAPITAL: Topeka
SEAL: The seal of Kansas was adopted on May 25, 1861, shortly after statehood. In the foreground of the seal is a plowman and team of horses, with his log cabin and covered wagon in the distance. Also shown is a hunter pursuing buffalo and a mountain range. At the top, above 34 stars, is the motto, *Ad Astra per Aspera*, meaning "To the stars through difficulties." The two drawings I have and the "official" seal are all similar. The artist's conception on the bank notes (both First Charter Period and the brown-backs) show no river or steamboat; one of the drawings shows the covered wagon with one pair of oxen,

COMMENTS ON NOTE #34A: This handsome note has much going for it. The marriage of the bank serial number and the charter number is very unusual.

NOTE #34A:

DENOMINATION/SERIES: Two Dollars/First Charter Series 1875
BANK/CHARTER: The First National Bank of Emporia, Kansas (#1915)

FEDERAL DATA: Serial #A67171–, signed by John Allison and Jno. C. New
BANK DATA: Dated January 15, 1872, Plate letter "A," Bank serial #1915 (note that this is the same as the charter number). This bank

opened in 1872 and closed in 1898, issuing only Original Series 1875 First Charter notes and the first issue of the Series 1882 brownback notes. There remained on the records a balance of $3,578 (in 1915!!).
BANK SIGNATURES: R.H. Holderman, Cashier, and H.C. Cross, President, pen-signed.
BACK: *Sir Walter Raleigh, 1585.*
SEAL: Kansas state seal.

CONDITION: Uncirculated. New, borders irregular.
SOURCE: Bought from L.S. Werner, May 21, 1964. I traded some 1886 Silver Certificates (five silver dollars on the back) for two "Lazy Deuces."
RARITY: While not rare, early bank notes on Kansas are quite scarce. This bank is scarce to rare as indicated by the outstanding balance. There are, however, several ones on this bank around.

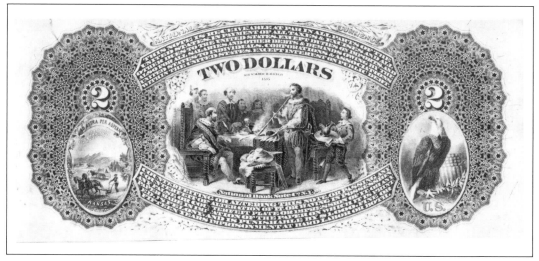

others show two covered wagons with two pairs of oxen in one example and in the other drawing, two pairs of horses or mules instead of the oxen (PLATE VII). The "official" seal shows one hunter and two or three buffalo whereas the drawings show two hunters (or Indians) and four to six buffalo. Kansas' motto has always impressed me. It seems to me that Kansas has had more than its share of "difficulties" — extremes of heat and cold, crop failures, drought, Indian massacres, and its own internal civil war over slavery prior to becoming a free state.

Please see Plate XIII

NOTE #34B:

DENOMINATION/ SERIES: Ten Dollars/ Brownback Series 1882

BANK/CHARTER: The First National Bank of Emporia, Kansas (#1915)

FEDERAL DATA: Serial #N2613–, signed by Rosecrans and Nebeker

BANK DATA: Dated December 15, 1891, Plate letter "B," Bank serial #521. (Same bank as last note.)

BANK SIGNATURES: Pen signed — D.M. Davis, Cashier, and C.S. Cross, President

BACK: Charter number (1915)

SEAL: State seal of Kansas

CONDITION: Fine

SOURCE: Purchased at auction from Paul Kagin, December 19, 1959.

RARITY: Scarce but not rare.

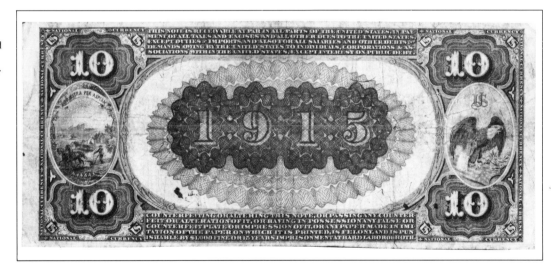

#35 —
WEST VIRGINIA

NAME: Derived from Virginia's name
NICKNAME: The Mountain State
ENTERED THE UNION: June 20, 1863

CAPITAL: Charleston

SEAL: West Virginia was created by separation from Virginia during the throes of the Civil War. The seal of West Virginia was adopted during the first year of statehood. This seal is also one with an obverse and reverse. The obverse shows a large ivy-clustered rock at the center which is engraved with the date of statehood. At the right of the rock is a miner with a pick and a sledge with an anvil nearby; at the left is a frontiersman with an ax and plow. Two crossed rifles and a Liberty-cap are in the foreground along with the motto *Montani Semper Liberi,* meaning "Mountaineers are always free." National Bank Notes show

Please see Plate VII

NOTE #35A:

DENOMINATION/ SERIES: Twenty Dollars/First Charter Series 1875

BANK/CHARTER: The National Exchange Bank Of Weston, West Virginia (#1607)

FEDERAL DATA: Serial #E741297–, signed by Allison and Wyman

BANK DATA: Dated January 1, 1866, Plate letter "A," Bank serial #1530. This bank operated from 1865 to 1932. It issued no date-backs and value-backs of the Series 1882 and no Type II small-size notes. It released some of all the other issues. There remained outstanding in 1935 in large-size notes the amount of $7,540.

BANK SIGNATURES: Pen signatures of S.M. Bailey, Cashier, and A.H. Kunst, President

BACK: *Baptism of Pocahontas*

SEAL: West Virginia state seal. All are similar.

CONDITION: Extra Fine

SOURCE: Purchased from Wm. A. Philpott, Jr. Dallas, TX, April 10, 1962.

RARITY: West Virginia First Charter notes must be considered rare but not extremely so. There were 18 banks to issue them.

the seal as described. The reverse of the seal shows a landscape with mountains on the left, a cultivated slope on which is a log-frame house that is peculiar to this region. On the side of a mountain is the viaduct of the Baltimore and Ohio Railroad which is located in Preston County; this was included because it was a great engineering triumph of its age. On the viaduct is a train. Near the center of the reverse is a factory, a river, boats, and on the river bank to the right is a derrick and shed representing the production of salt and petroleum. In the foreground are cattle and sheep and above the mountains appear the sun and the motto *Libertus e Fidelitate,* or "Liberty from Loyalty."

NOTE #35B:

DENOMINATION/SERIES: Five Dollars/Brownback Series 1882

BANK/CHARTER: The National Exchange Bank Of Wheeling, West Virginia (#5164), Regional letter "S"

FEDERAL DATA: Serial #N974572N, signed by Lyons and Roberts

BANK DATA: Dated December 16, 1898, Plate letter "D" (bottom note of sheet), Bank serial #11999. This bank opened in 1898 and went the full term. From the brownbacks it issued all series except red seals and date-backs of the Third Charter Period Series 1902 and in 1935 had a balance of $29,115 in large-size notes.

BANK SIGNATURES: Pen signed — Laurence E. Sands, Cashier and J.N. Nance, President

BACK: Charter number (5164)

SEAL: West Virginia seal

CONDITION: Extra Fine. Face cut close on top, but the back is perfect. This is an example where the face and back of the sheet printing were not perfectly matched in place. Also note the bottom guidelines and the number on the bottom border.

SOURCE: Purchased from New Netherlands Coin Co., New York, N.Y., (Charles M. Wormser), June 24, 1952

RARITY: Not rare, this bank even common.

#36 — NEVADA

NAME: Spanish for "snow-clad"

NICKNAME: The Silver State

ENTERED THE UNION: October 31, 1864

CAPITAL: Carson City

SEAL: The seal of Nevada was approved on February 24, 1866 and is a scene depicting a quartz mill at the right and a tunnel at the left opening to silver in a mountain. A wagon load of ore, drawn by two horses, is approaching the mill. In the background are mountain ranges, pine trees, and a train on a trestle. The 36 stars in the border of the seal indicate the number of states in the Union when Nevada became a state by President Lincoln's proclamation. The motto "All for our Country" is at the bottom of the seal. This same seal appears on Nevada bank notes. There are 37 stars on the bank note seal, apparently an error since the "official" seal has the 36 stars which match Nevada's entry to the Union.

Please see Plates VII and XIII

Some additional discussion of this "error" is warranted. The die-proof of the oval seal for Nevada was prepared by the Continental Bank Note Company of New York City for use on the backs of the First and Second Charter notes. In redesigning the round "official" seal into the upright oval, Continental apparently made the error; whether intentional or unintentional, an extra star has been added.

BANKS: Nevada had the fewest banks issuing First Charter and brownback notes (before Alaska and Hawaii). Only three banks operated from 1865 to 1903. The first bank in the early capitol city of Austin (#1331) issued only

NOTE #36A:

DENOMINATION/ SERIES: Twenty Dollars/First Charter Series 1875

BANK/CHARTER: The First National Bank Of Reno, Nevada (#2478)

FEDERAL DATA: Serial #A67928–, signed by Scofield and Gilfillan

BANK DATA: Dated June 25, 1880, Plate letter "B," Bank serial #1081. This bank operated from 1880 until 1896 and issued

only First Charter Series 1875. In 1910 the bank had only $1,400 outstanding. All the notes ordered and issued by this bank were twenty-dollar notes. That means that there were just 70 notes outstanding.

BANK SIGNATURES: C.T. Bender, Cashier and D.A. Bender, President (brothers?), pen signed.

BACK: *Baptism of Pocahontas*

SEAL: Nevada State seal containing the 37 star error.

CONDITION: Bought as Uncirculated. I call it About Uncirculated.

SOURCE: Mehl estate to Dr. Limpert, the forerunner in this pursuit of the seals. His collection was sold by Stack's, New York City, on May 6, 1956.

RARITY: One of the rarest, if not the rarest note in this collection. This is the only note known on Nevada First Charter Period.

the original series with only $897 outstanding in 1915! No notes are known on Austin. The second bank, Reno (#2478), issued only twenty dollar notes of Series 1875 with only $1400 outstanding in 1910.

The First National Bank at Austin was organized on June 23, 1865 but because of troubles stemming from its inaccessibility; the first shipment of notes was very late in arriving and thereby delayed the bank's opening. Austin was located in central Nevada some 550 miles east of San Francisco via the indirect roads and this explains the delays and slow communications. Although organized as noted, it did not open for business until the following November 27th, because the five-, ten-, and twenty-dollar First Charter notes were slow to arrive. The notes were delivered by way of San Francisco. The voyage carrying the notes from Baltimore took more than three months,

the ship having sailed around Cape Horn. Austin became the first national bank to be chartered west of Denver, superseding the First National Bank of Portland by six months. The first national bank in the state of California, The First National Gold Bank of San Francisco (#1741), was not chartered until five years later. "While the seal of the State of Nevada had been prepared shortly after the achievement of statehood in 1864, the seal was not officially approved until February 24, 1866. However, it is thought that the seal appeared on the back of the First Charter notes of the First National Bank of Nevada at Austin as the reworked continental seal for the back of the Nevada First and Second Charter notes was employed on its stationery and bank checks."[5] No note is known on Austin, but if one should ever come to light, I believe it will show the same state seal that is shown on the Reno note.

NOTE #36B:
Please note. This very rare note does not belong to us. Only through the kindness and courtesy of Mr. Robert Medlar, Governor in the A.N.A., am I able to picture this unique note, a brownback of Nevada:

DENOMINATION/ SERIES: Ten Dollars/ Brownback Series 1882
BANK/CHARTER: The First National Bank of Winnemucca, Nevada (#3575), Regional letter "P"

FEDERAL DATA: Serial #A513049A, signed by Rosecrans and Jordan

BANK DATA: Dated October 20, 1886, Plate letter "A," Bank serial #524. Bank operated from 1886 to 1932 and issued only brownbacks Series 1882, but all three Third Charter Series 1902 as well as five, ten, and twenty dollar small-size notes of Type I. Amount of large-size notes outstanding in 1932 was $9,855.

BANK SIGNATURES: Pen signed — F.M. Lee,

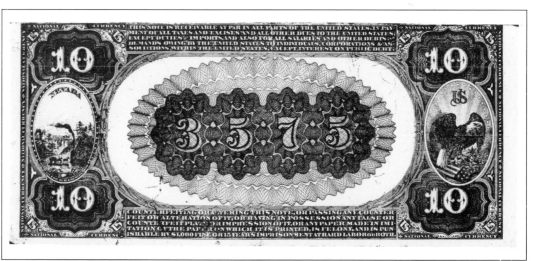

Cashier and Geo. S. Nixon, President
BACK: Charter number (3575)
SEAL: Nevada seal

CONDITION: Fine/Very Fine
SOURCE: Note pictured courtesy of R. Medlar.
RARITY: Extremely rare. Only one known.

119

COMMENTS: The only Nevada First Charter period note known is in this collection and may be the rarest note in the collection. The third bank in the state was Winnemucca (#3575) which operated from 1886 to 1932 and as noted above, was the only Nevada bank to issue brownbacks. There is only one brownback known, so it is just as rare as the First Charter note. NOTE #36B was originally in the Amon Carter, Jr. collection but now belongs to Robert Medlar. Therefore this brownback note is the only note needed to complete this collection of National Bank Notes showing a seal (state).

UPDATE: A recent article by John T. Hickman in *Banknote Reporter*[6] has news of another twenty-dollar First Charter note and includes the chart at right. I have not yet seen this note personally. The note was issued by The First National Bank of Reno, Nevada (#2478).

[5] M. Owen Warns, *The Nevada Sixteen*, (see Bibliography.)
[6] John T. Hickman, "Nevada Banknotes Still Scarce," in *Banknote Reporter,* Vol. XIV, No. 5 May 1986, pps. 19-20.

A Census of Presently Known Notes — May, 1986

$20.	1875	2
10.	1882 Brownback	1
5.	1902 Red Seals	4
10.	1902 Red Seals	7
20.	1902 Red Seals	3
5.	1902 Date-backs	6
10.	1902 Date-backs	8
20.	1902 Date-backs	3
50.	1902 Date-backs	1
5.	1902 Plain-backs	36
10.	1902 Plain-backs	22
20.	1902 Plain-backs	33
50.	1902 Plain-backs	7
100.	1902 Plain-backs	2
	(135 total)	

TO STATE 37:

NEBRASKA

☞

#37 —
NEBRASKA

NAME: Omaha Indian for "flat river"
NICKNAME: The Cornhusker State
ESTABLISHED AS TERRITORY: 1854
ENTERED THE UNION: March 1, 1867
CAPITAL: Lincoln
TERRITORIAL SEAL: Nebraska became a territory in 1854 with its capital at Omaha. The territorial seal shows an unfolded parchment inscribed "CONSTITUTION" with the American flag above (PLATE XIV). At the right is a statesman in a top hat, and at the left is a frontiersman with his rifle. At the top is "Popular Sovereignty," and at the bottom is "Progress." For some still-unknown reason the state seal of Nebraska was never placed on Nebraska state banknotes.

STATE SEAL: The seal of Nebraska was approved on June 15, 1867 and shows a blacksmith with a sledge and anvil in the foreground with shocks of grain and a cabin at the left. In the background is a steamboat on a river and a train headed west near mountain ranges. At the top on a streamer is "Equality Before the Law" and at the bottom is the statehood date, March 1, 1867 (PLATE VII, and inset, above). National Bank Notes of both the First Charter and brownback series display the territorial seal in the left oval on the back.

NOTE #37A:

DENOMINATION/SERIES: Two Dollars/First Charter Original Series
BANK/CHARTER: The Otoe County National Bank Of Nebraska City, Nebraska Territory, (#1417)

FEDERAL DATA: Serial #B113425, signed by Colby and Spinner
BANK DATA: Dated August 15, 1865, Plate letter "A," Bank serial #307. This was the second bank to open in the Territory. It commenced business in 1865 and issued only Originals. Since Nebraska became the 37th state on March 1, 1867, I believe this

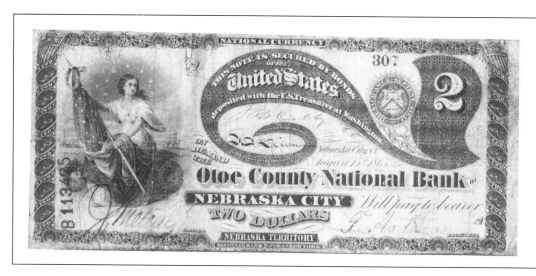

bank then issued First Charter Series 1875 (but perhaps Originals also, before Series 1875), then brownbacks Series 1882, all three Charter Series 1902, then tens and twenties of the small size both Type I and II. Amount outstanding in 1935 was $6,520 in large-size notes.
BANK SIGNATURES: The pen-signed signatures are illegible.
BACK: *Sir Walter Raleigh, 1585*
SEAL: Nebraska territorial seal

CONDITION: All six Nebraska Territory notes known are in similar condition: Good/Very Good
SOURCE: Purchased from Lyn Knight, January, 1979.
RARITY: There are two one-dollar notes known on Omaha and four twos known on the Otoe County National Bank. The bank's name is not shown on the note. We believe Note #37A to be the only two-dollar note to have actually circulated in territorial time.

NOTE #37B:

DENOMINATION/SERIES: Twenty Dollars/Series 1875 First Charter Period

BANK DATA: Dated June 30, 1882, Plate letter "A," Bank serial #3915. This bank opened 1882, one of the very last banks to issue First Charter Series 1875 notes. The next issues were all three Third Charter Series 1902 and tens and twenties of Type I small size. The outstanding in 1935 amounted to $3,770 in large-size notes.

BANK SIGNATURES: J.H. Morehead, Cashier, and John W. Holt, President, pen-signed.

BANK/CHARTER: The First National Bank Of Falls City, Nebraska (#2746)

FEDERAL DATA: Serial #K920463–, signed by Bruce And Gilfillan

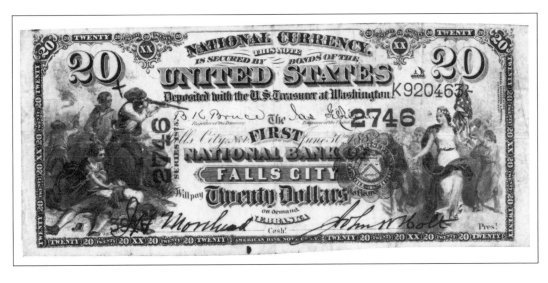

BACK: *Baptism of Pocahontas*

SEAL: Nebraska territorial seal. For some unknown reason the "official" or state seal was never used on banknotes.

CONDITION: Fine

SOURCE: Purchased in Bebee's second auction sale, February 16, 1955.

RARITY: Only ten Nebraska banks issued Original and only nineteen issued Series 1875 as a state, so Nebraska First Charter notes are not common.

NOTE #37C:

DENOMINATION/SERIES: Fifty Dollars/Brownback Series 1882

BANK/CHARTER: The First National Bank Of Tekamah, Nebraska (#4324), Regional letter "W"

FEDERAL DATA: Serial #B611155–, signed by Rosecrans and Huston

BANK DATA: Dated May 28, 1890, Plate letter "A," Bank serial #712. This bank opened in 1890 and went through the end of the National Banking Act (1935) and issued brownbacks and date-backs Series 1882, then date-backs and plain-backs of the Series 1902 as well as tens and twenties of both Types small-size notes. There remained in large-size notes in 1935 the amount of $7,130 out.

BANK SIGNATURES: Pen signatures of C.O. Latta, Cashier, and J.P. Latta, President (probably brothers).

FACE: The left vignette shows Washington Crossing The Delaware,

1776, and on the right-hand side Washington kneeling in prayer at Valley Forge. Above are three female figures representing Victory.

BACK: Large charter number (4324)

SEAL: Nebraska territorial seal. Nebraska is the only state on which only the territorial seal appeared on all bank notes, both territory and state. As stated above, their state seal was never used on national currency.

CONDITION: Extra Fine

SOURCE: Paul Kagin's auction, purchased December 19, 1959.

RARITY: Nebraska brownback notes are not rare. Fifty-dollar notes on any state are scarce.

TO STATE 38:

COLORADO

☞

#38 — COLORADO

NAME: Spanish for "red"
NICKNAME:
The Centennial State
**ESTABLISHED AS
TERRITORY:** 1861
ENTERED THE UNION:

August 1, 1876
CAPITAL: Denver
TERRITORIAL SEAL: The territorial seal of Colorado shows a shield with three mountains and a crossed pick and sledge as a central design. Above is a horizontal fasces and the rising sun. On the crossed bands holding the fasces together are the words "Union and Constitution." Beneath is the motto *Nil Sine Numine* meaning "Nothing without the Lord."
Please see Plate VII
NOTE #38A:

DENOMINATION/SERIES: One Dollar/Original Series of the First Charter Original

STATE SEAL: The state seal of Colorado is similar to the territorial seal. By act of the new legislature the state adopted its then-current territorial seal to become the state seal. Thus with the exception of the official designation showing "State" rather than "Territory" and the date, 1876, in the concentric circle surrounding its seal, Colorado became the only Western territory, and later state, to use the territorial seal as a state seal. It appeared on state National Bank Notes (see inset above).

COMMENTS: Nebraska and Colorado are the only two states which, starting out as a territory, kept the territorial seal on the notes all the way through the National Bank Note issuing period. Nebraska adopted a new state seal which was not used at all on bank notes. But Colorado's

BANK/CHARTER: The Peoples National Bank Of Pueblo, Colorado Territory (#2134 — charter number is not on note)
FEDERAL DATA: Serial #D793952–, signed by Allison and Spinner
BANK DATA: Dated February 20, 1871, Plate letter "A," Bank serial

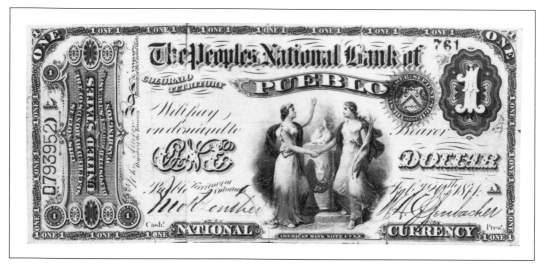

#761. This bank opened in 1874 and closed in 1875 with only $165 out in 1910.
BANK SIGNATURES: In pen, Jno. R. Genther, Cashier, and W.A. Offenbacher, President.
BACK: *Landing of the Pilgrims*
SEAL: Colorado territorial seal
CONDITION: Very Good, but mended on the back with tape.
SOURCE: From the Numismatic Gallery, N.Y.C. (before its move to California), October 20, 1951

RARITY: The territorial bank history began with Charter #1016, Denver, in 1865, and through Charter #2310, Pueblo, a total of thirteen territorial banks issued territorial notes. First Charter notes on Colorado Territory are the most numerous of the territorials available with seals, followed closely by Utah Territory. But this bank has to be rare. There are two or three others known on this bank in choice condition.

territorial seal was also adopted as its state seal and is still in use today. At the Eighth Annual Paper Money Show in Memphis, I talked with Mikel E. Storeim, Colorado dealer and collector, who formed what is probably the foremost Colorado collection known, especially regarding territorial and First Charter state notes. He says there are 51 territorials and thirty First Charter state notes, which proves that I do not know it all. He showed me six First Charter

state notes, including a rare South Pueblo note. Even Steinmetz (whose book data I often use) states, "All First Charter state issues on the eighteen banks that issued them are much scarcer than the territorials." Storeim's number of the known First Charter Period territorial notes must be just about right, for in an informal update shared with me about two years ago by Peter Huntoon, following the publication of his book *Territorials,* 47 notes are listed.

NOTE #38B:

DENOMINATION/SERIES: Five Dollars/First Charter Series 1875
BANK/CHARTER: The National State Bank Of Boulder, Colorado (#2355)

FEDERAL DATA: Serial #Y80711–, signed by Allison and Wyman
BANK DATA: Dated May 25, 1877, Plate letter "C," Bank serial #5718. This bank opened in 1877 and went to the end of the period.

It issued Series 1875 and brownbacks and date-backs (value-backs have a question mark in the records) of the Series of 1882. It also issued plain-backs Series 1902 as well as small-size tens and twenties of Type II. Outstanding large size in 1935 amounted to $2,060.

BANK SIGNATURES:
J.H. Nicholson, Cashier and C.G. Willingham(?), Pres., signed in pen.

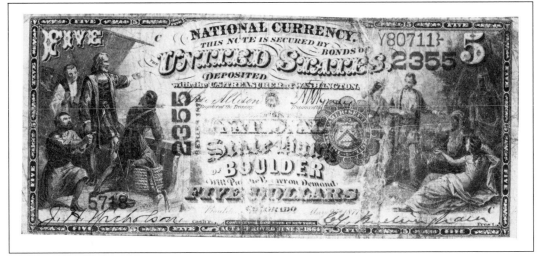

BACK: *Landing of Columbus, 1492*

SEAL: Colorado adopted its territorial seal as its state seal.

CONDITION: Very Good, but needs improving.

SOURCE: My friend Amon Carter gave it to me (at face value, $5.)

RARITY: Although 18 banks operated in the First Charter Period Series 1875 issuing STATE notes, very few are known today, and, like following states that were territories first,

these First Charter state notes are usually rarer than the territorial notes.

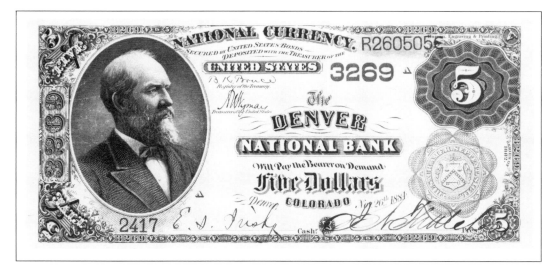

NOTE #38C:

DENOMINATION/SERIES: Five Dollars/Series 1882 Brownback.

BANK/CHARTER: The Denver National Bank, Denver, Colorado (#3269 — no regional letter)

FEDERAL DATA: Serial #R260505–, signed by Bruce and Wyman

BANK DATA: Dated November 26, 1884, Plate letter "A," Bank serial #2417. This bank opened in 1884 and lasted through the life of

the Act. It issued brownbacks, all three Series 1902 and tens and twenties of Type I small-size notes. The amount outstanding in large-size notes in 1935 was $25,067.50.

BANK SIGNATURES: E.S. Irish, Cashier and J.N. Shulekes (?), Vice President, pen signed

BACK: Charter number (3269)

SEAL: Colorado state seal

CONDITION: Bought as Extra Fine but looks Uncirculated to me.

SOURCE: Dr. Limpert's collection sold by Stack's, May 6, 1956

RARITY: Not rare but surely scarce in this nice condition.

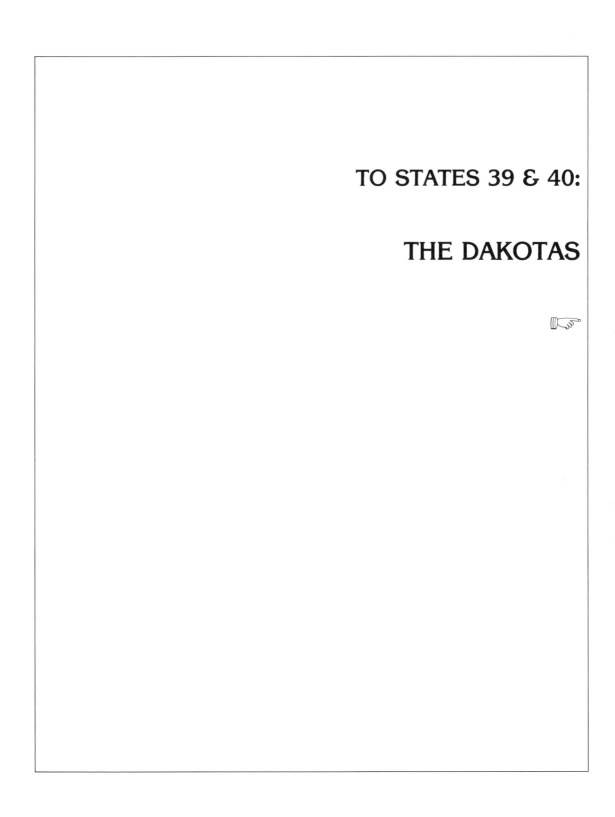

TO STATES 39 & 40:

THE DAKOTAS

DAKOTA TERRITORY

TERRITORIAL SEAL: The seal of Dakota Territory has a large tree with shocks of wheat at its base as a central design. An anvil, sledge, and a plow are at the right. A bow with three crossed arrows are at the left of the tree. Above are thirteen stars and the motto "Liberty and Union, Now and Forever, One and Inseparable" (PLATE VIII). Unlike some territories, all Dakota banknotes show the Dakota territorial seal, both First Charter and brownbacks.

BANKS: The first bank in the territory was Yankton, #2068 (now in South Dakota) in 1872 and was the only bank to issue any Original Series notes. The second bank was Fargo (charter #2377). The first notes were issued in 1878. We presume these territorial banks started issuing notes right away. These dates are the years that the banks started in business. The third bank in Dakota Territory to issue Series 1875 notes (First Charter Period notes surcharged with year 1875) was Deadwood (#2391), now in South Dakota, beginning in 1878. Only Yankton issued any Original First Charter notes. The fourth bank in the territory was Bismark (Charter #2434), started in 1879. The fifth bank was Deadwood (Charter #2461), in business from 1880 to 1894. The sixth bank in the territory of Dakota was Sioux Falls (Charter #2465). This bank operated only from 1880 to 1886 and issued only five-dollar notes, Series 1875. In 1915 the amount outstanding on

NOTE #39A:

DENOMINATION/SERIES: One Dollar/Original Series
BANK/CHARTER: The First National Bank of Yankton, Territory Of Dakota (#2068)

FEDERAL DATA: Serial #D395391–, signed by Allison and Spinner
BANK DATA: Dated December 18, 1872, Plate letter "C," Bank serial #1271. This bank opened in 1872 and went through the entire period.

It issued both Original and Series 1875 First Charter notes. After statehood (South Dakota) this bank then issued brownbacks and date-backs Series 1882, date-backs and plain-backs Series 1902, as well as tens and twenties of Type I small-size Series 1929. Outstanding large size in 1935 amounted to $13,572.50.

BANK SIGNATURES: Pen-signed — C.E. Sanborn, Cashier, and Mearkille Farmer (?), Vice President

BACK: *Landing of the Pilgrims, 1620*

SEAL: This is the Dakota territorial seal. Tree is wrapped like a fasces.

CONDITION: About Uncirculated.

SOURCE: A.E. Bebee, April 20, 1966

RARITY: A rare territorial note. About three ones and one two (I think) are known on this bank. See notes on Dakota Territory.

130

this bank was only $245, 49 five-dollar notes. What with natural wear and tear (attrition) — fires, floods, rats and mice, etc., there couldn't be many of these around! Other banks were:

Seventh — Fargo (Charter #2514)
Eighth — Valley City (Charter #2548)
Ninth — Grand Forks (Charter #2564)
Tenth — Grand Forks (Charter #2570)
Eleventh — Jamestown (Charter #2578)
Twelfth — Jamestown (Charter #2580)
Thirteenth — Mandan (Charter #2585)
Fourteenth — Wahpeton (Charter #2624)

These last eight banks were all in what is now North Dakota.

Fifteenth — Mitchell (now SD) (Charter #2645)
Sixteenth — Valley City (now ND) (Charter #2650)
Seventeenth — Bismark (now ND) (Charter #2677)

The Bismark bank was the last bank in the territory to issue territorial 1875 series notes. This is a total of 17 banks in Dakota Territory, 12 in what is now North Dakota and only five in what is now South Dakota.

NOTE #39B:

DENOMINATION/ SERIES: Five Dollars/Brownback Series 1882

BANK/CHARTER: The Citizens National Bank of Watertown, Territory Of Dakota (#3349)

FEDERAL DATA: Serial #B870374–, signed by Rosecrans and Jordan

BANK DATA: Dated June 8, 1885, Plate letter "A," Bank serial #1. This bank opened in 1885 and closed in 1933 during which time it issued brownbacks

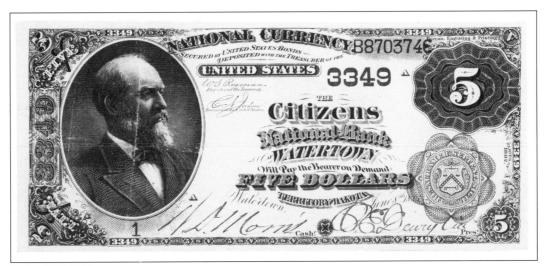

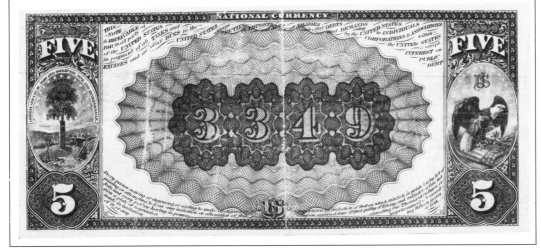

and all three Series 1902, but only fifties and hundreds in small-size Type I. The amount of large-size notes outstanding in 1933 was $10,897.50.

BANK SIGNATURES: H.D. Morris, Cashier and O.E. Dewey, Vice President, pen-signed

BACK: Charter number (3349)

SEAL: Dakota territorial seal

CONDITION: Very Fine/Extra Fine with one crease on the face and two or three on the back.

SOURCE: From Hickman and Waters sale October 1, 1959 (date uncertain)

RARITY: Brownbacks on Dakota Territory are RARE. We know of fewer brownbacks than First Charters, possibly four or five notes. Peter Huntoon records only five brownbacks against sixteen First Charter notes. There are three brownbacks on banks that are now in South Dakota and two that are on banks in North Dakota. The following First Charter notes are known: seven five-dollar, one two-dollar, and one five-dollar notes on Yankton; four five-dollar notes on one Deadwood bank and one more five on the second Deadwood bank; one ten-dollar note on Wahpeton; and one ten-dollar note on Grand Forks. So according to Peter Huntoon's *Territorials*, there are only two First Charter Period notes and two brownback notes known on Dakota Territory on banks now in North Dakota. This compares to a total of fourteen First Charter Period notes and two brownback notes on banks now located in South Dakota.

#39 — NORTH DAKOTA

NAME: Sioux for "allies"
NICKNAME:
The Sioux State
ESTABLISHED AS TERRITORY:

Dakota Territory, 1861.
ENTERED THE UNION: November 2, 1889
CAPITAL: Bismark
STATE SEAL: On November 2, 1889, Dakota Territory became the states of North Dakota and South Dakota. Because, alphabetically, "N" comes before "S," North Dakota became the 39th state and South Dakota became the 40th state. The wags say South Dakotans are still mad

about this. We do know that North Dakota took the Dakota territorial seal, modified it, and it became the seal of North Dakota. They placed in two half circles 42 stars (instead of the territorial thirteen) indicating its entry into the Union, and rearranged or modified other things. Upon checking and counting the number of stars I was amazed to count not 39, but 42, so the actual number of stars must be symbolic rather than actual. I have now learned that 42 was the number of statehood anticipated, and actually did match the number of the states in the Union before the end of 1889, including South Dakota, Montana and Washington.

So the seal of North Dakota was originally the seal of

NOTE #39C:

DENOMINATION/ SERIES: Ten Dollars/ First Charter Series 1875
BANK/CHARTER: The First National Bank Of Grand Forks, North Dakota (#2570)
FEDERAL DATA: Serial #K876980–, signed by Rosecrans and Huston
BANK DATA: Dated June 25, 1890, Plate letter "A," Bank serial #1272. This bank operated from 1881 to 1933. Before statehood this bank issued First Charter Series 1875 and

after statehood it issued Series 1875 then brownbacks and date-backs of Series 1882 and plain-backs Series 1902. Small-size Series 1929 included tens and twenties of Type I and tens only of Type II. In 1933 there remained outstanding on the records $28,865 in large-size notes.
BANK SIGNATURES: S.S. Titus, Cashier and J. Walker Smith, President, pen signed.
BACK: *De Soto Discovering the Mississippi*
SEAL: North Dakota

state seal as adapted from the territorial seal.
CONDITION: Gem Uncirculated. Crisp.
SOURCE: Out of the Mehl estate sold by A. Kosoff, October 10, 1957

RARITY: Rare. Only seven banks issued First Charter notes as a state. How many exist? Probably six or eight.

Dakota Territory. Two differences are that in the state seal there are 42 stars above the central design (as opposed to the territorial seal's 13 — see PLATE VII to compare), and there is an Indian with a spear pursuing a buffalo. Separated by the tree is the date of the state constitution: "Oct. 1st, 1889" (see PLATE XIV). Both First Charter and brownback notes of the state show the seal as described here. The only other difference between this and the territorial seal that I can see is the plow: it is turned the opposite direction.

COMMENTS: The date on NOTE #39C, June 25, 1890, is one of the rather frequent inconsistencies found on National Bank Notes. This bank opened in 1881 and issued Series 1875 notes as a territory. North Dakota became a state on November 2, 1889. But this is also a Series 1875 First Charter note dated less than one year after statehood. We know that the seal changed from territory to state, but, logically this note should have been a brownback Series 1882. This bank did issue brownbacks. Can anyone explain this date?

NOTE #39D:

DENOMINATION/ SERIES: Ten Dollars/Brownback Series 1882

BANK/CHARTER: The Red River Valley National Bank of Fargo, North Dakota (#2514), Regional letter "W"

FEDERAL DATA: Serial #H309340H, signed by Lyons and Roberts

BANK DATA: Dated March 24, 1901 (recharter date), Plate letter "A," Bank serial #804. This bank

operated from 1881 to 1905 and issued Series 1875 as a territory, then as a state issued Series 1875 and 1882 brownbacks. The comments on the bank for note #39C also apply to this bank's earlier issues. The amount outstanding in 1910 was $5,350.

BANK SIGNATURES: Cashier's name faded out, and Robt. Jones, President, signed in pen.

BACK: Charter number (2514)

SEAL: North Dakota state seal

CONDITON: Extra Fine

SOURCE: From the Dr. Limpert Collection sold by Stack's, May 6, 1956

RARITY: Fifty-two banks issued brownbacks in North Dakota as a state, but known notes are still very scarce.

#40 —
SOUTH DAKOTA

NAME: Sioux for "allies"
NICKNAME:
The Coyote State
ESTABLISHED AS
TERRITORY: Dakota
Territory, 1861
ENTERED THE UNION: November 2, 1889
CAPITAL: Pierre
SEAL: South Dakota had to bring in a new seal. It was adopted on October 1, 1889, prior to statehood after losing the territorial seal to North Dakota. It is a beautiful if somewhat busy seal, showing a winding river with a steamboat in the distance, some cattle on the right, and a smelting furnace on the left. A plowman with his team of

horses is in the foreground. At the top is the motto "Under God the People Rule" (PLATE XIV). First Charter and brownback notes use the seal as described. The artist's rendition on bank notes is graphic and shows many details that the "official" seal does not. Again, both North and South Dakota First Charter notes are rare; only three banks in South Dakota issued them. In this collection we show the Mitchell note. Territorial issues of First Charter notes came from five banks, only one of which issued Original Series notes in what is now South Dakota and twelve banks in what is now North Dakota. Twenty-one banks issued territorial brownback notes in what is now North Dakota as compared to 36 in South Dakota.

NOTE #40A:

DENOMINATION/ SERIES: Ten Dollars/First Charter Series 1875.
BANK/CHARTER: The First National Bank of Mitchell, South Dakota (#2645)
FEDERAL DATA: Serial #A932975–, signed by Rosecrans and Huston
BANK DATA: Dated November 2, 1889 (first day of statehood), Plate letter "C," Bank serial #1239. This bank operated from 1882 to

1923 and issued Series 1875 as a territory, then as a state issued First Charter Series 1875 (changed plate to accommodate the date of statehood and the new seal) and all three 1882 Series and plain-backs 1902. There remained outstanding in 1923 the amount of $99,000.
BANK SIGNATURES:
R.F. Simons, "A" Cashier (a small "a" for assistant), and John D. Lander, President, pen-signed.
BACK: *De Soto Discovering the Mississippi.*
SEAL: South Dakota state seal (new)
CONDITION: Extra Fine
SOURCE: Wm. P. Donlon Sale, June, 1971

RARITY: Very rare. Only three banks issued First Charters as a state. We know of only two on the larger Deadwood bank. There are possibly one or two more.

NOTE #40B:

DENOMINATION/ SERIES: Ten Dollars/Brownback Series 1882

BANK/CHARTER: The First National of Flandreau, South Dakota (#5854), Regional letter "W"

FEDERAL DATA: Serial #E280241E, signed by Lyons and Roberts

BANK DATA: Dated May 29, 1901, Plate letter "C," Bank serial #468. This bank operated from 1901 to

1932 and issued all three Series 1882 and plain-backs Series 1902. Also, it issued small-size Type I tens and twenties. The amount of large-size notes in 1932 was $4,990.

BANK SIGNATURES: Jas. T. Bigelow, Cashier, and Thomas Kelly, President, signed in pen.

BACK: Charter number (5854)

SEAL: Seal of South Dakota

CONDITION: Extra Fine

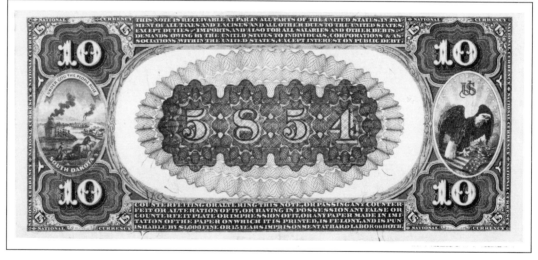

SOURCE: Kagin's auction sale, June 3, 1961

RARITY: South Dakota brownbacks are very scarce.

TO STATE 41:

MONTANA

☞

#41 — MONTANA

NAME: Latin for "mountainous"
NICKNAME: The Treasure State
ESTABLISHED AS TERRITORY: Eastern Montana was part of the Louisiana Purchase; became Montana Territory, 1864.
ENTERED THE UNION: November 8, 1889
CAPITAL: Helena
TERRITORIAL SEAL: Since Montana territorial notes, both First Charter and brownback notes, show no seals, please refer to STATE SEAL description on the next page for information on the Montana territorial seal.

TERRITORIAL NOTES: Six territorial banks issued Original Series notes. They are Helena (charter #1649), Helena (charter #1960 — only in business for one year so did not issue any Series 1875 notes and had only $50 outstanding in 1910), Deer Lodge (charter #1975), Bozeman (charter #2027), Helena (charter #2105), and Missoula (charter #2106). Five of these first six banks also issued Series 1875 territorial notes plus four more for a total of ten banks. After the first bank (#1649) which lasted thirty years, it is interesting to note that the next four lasted seven years or less. Helena (charter #1649) also issued territorial brownback notes. Beginning in 1882, the fourth Helena bank to open for business (charter #2757) issued territorial brownback notes. Along with the first Helena bank (charter

NOTE #41A:

DENOMINATION/SERIES: One Dollar/First Charter Original Series
BANK/CHARTER: The Missoula National Bank, Montana Territory (#2106)

FEDERAL DATA: Serial #D561949–, signed by Allison and Spinner
BANK DATA: Dated June 10, 1873, Plate letter "C," Bank serial #439. This bank operated from 1873 to 1935. During territorial years

this bank issued Original and Series 1875 notes, then as a state it issued all types except value-backs Series 1882 and red seals Series 1902. Large-sized notes in 1935 amounted to $12,305.

BANK SIGNATURES: Ferd. Kennett, Cashier and C.P. Higgins, President, pen signed.

BACK: *Landing of the Pilgrims,* 1620

SEAL: No seal appears on any Montana territorial notes (that I have observed). There

appears a large upright eagle just like the right oval.

CONDITION: Extra Fine plus.

SOURCE: From Hickman and Waters, March 13, 1969

RARITY: Very rare, especially in this condition. There are probably 10 or 12 First Charter territorial notes known. According to Huntoon, there are twenty First Charter notes known on Montana Territory.

#1649), and fourteen other banks, Helena (charter #2757) makes a total of sixteen banks in the territory to issue territorial brownbacks. For more information on the first Helena bank (#1649), see below. For some reason however there were no seals placed on any of the Montana territorial notes (as far as I have observed). Our brownback note of Helena (charter #1649, the oldest bank in the territory, which folded in 1896) is dated March 18, 1886, twenty years after it opened, serial #347, and is probably the worst note, condition-wise, in the collection. After thirty years in business this bank only showed (on treasury records) $3,591 outstanding in 1915. Here again, only five banks issued First Charter notes (Series 1875) after Montana became the 41st state on November 8, 1889. Obviously rarer than the territorial notes is our Miles City note, also from A. Carter (see NOTE #41C).

STATE SEAL: The seal of Montana was approved on March 2, 1893. The seal is based on the territorial seal of 1865 and depicts the Great Falls of the Missouri River at the right, a plow and farming implements in the foreground, forests, and the sun shining over the Rocky Mountains as the background (PLATE VIII). The motto shown is *Oro y Plata,* Spanish meaning "Gold and Silver," indicating mineral wealth. The drawings and "official" seal (see inset) are similar but again the artist's rendition in the bank note seal shows slightly changed features most notable in the flow and falls of the river. For some unknown reason the territorial seal does not appear on any First Charter or brownback (territorial) notes. An identical eagle appears in both ovals. After statehood, the National Bank Notes of both charter periods show the seal as described. The First Charter notes after statehood are rare as only five banks issued them.

NOTE #41B:

DENOMINATION/SERIES: Five Dollars/Brownback Series 1882
BANK/CHARTER: The First National Bank of Helena, Montana Territory (#1649)

FEDERAL DATA: Serial #D667917–, signed by Rosecrans and Jordan
BANK DATA: Dated March 18, 1886, Plate letter "B," Bank serial #347. This was the first bank in the territory and operated from 1866 to 1896. This bank issued Original and Series 1875 First Charter notes as a territory and also brownbacks, then issued brownback notes as a state. The amount on the bank outstanding in 1915 was $3,591.

BANK SIGNATURES: Pen signed, E.W. Hughes, Cashier. The President's name is worn out.

BACK: Charter number (1649)

SEAL: No seal; another eagle at left (same as right)

CONDITION: Good/ Very Good. This is about the worst note in the collection and certainly needs improving.

SOURCE: Purchased from Morey Perlmutter, May 11, 1970

RARITY: Rare. Only sixteen banks issued brownback notes in the territory. How many notes total are known? Possibly eight or ten? Huntoon reports nine.

NOTE #41C:

DENOMINATION/SERIES: Five Dollars/Series 1875 First Charter

BANK/CHARTER: The First National Bank of Miles City, Montana (#2752)

FEDERAL DATA: Serial #Y526359–, signed by Rosecrans and Huston

BANK DATA: Dated November 8, 1889 (first day of statehood), Plate letter "B," Bank serial #4150. This bank operated from 1882 to 1924. It first issued Series 1875 as Montana Territory and then as a state also issued Series 1875 notes. Then it issued all three of the 1902 Series, there remaining at the close in 1924, $150,000.

BANK SIGNATURES: H.B. McVay (?) Cashier and W.B. Jordan, President, pen signed.

BACK: *Landing of Columbus, 1492*
SEAL: The seal of the state of Montana

CONDITION: Call it Fine; soiled and close trimmed.

SOURCE: Traded from Amon G. Carter, Jr. at the A.N.A. convention, 1970, St. Louis

RARITY: Rare. Only five banks in Montana issued First Charter state notes. How many exist now? Five or six perhaps. My partner recently acquired possibly the finest one known, a twenty-dollar note on Butte.

COMMENTS ON NOTE #41D: This reconstructed sheet is a good place to study just how the notes were printed. Notice the serial numbers and plate letters to see how each note is different from any other. Also note the guidelines for the sheet and bureau numbers on top and bottom borders. This we consider a museum item.

NOTE #41D:

DENOMINATION/ SERIES: A reconstructed sheet of 10-10-10-20 Dollar Notes/Brownback Series 1882

BANK/CHARTER: The First National Bank of Great Falls, Montana (#3525 — No regional letter)

FEDERAL DATA: Serial #Z835799–, signed by Rosecrans and Nebeker

BANK DATA: Dated May 29, 1893, Plate letters "A," "B," "C" and "A," Bank serial #3261. This bank opened in 1886 and went to the end issuing brownbacks as a territory. After statehood, it also issued brownbacks, then all three Series 1902 plus tens and twenties of both Types I and II. The amount of large-size notes outstanding in 1935 totaled $5,730 (includes territorials).

140

BANK SIGNATURES:
J.G. Morony, Cashier
and D.J. Hennessy,
Vice President,
signed in pen.

BACK: Charter number
(3525)

SEAL: Montana state
seal (*Oro y plata*)

CONDITION: Bought
as Extra Fine. We
believe the condition is
About Uncirculated.

SOURCE: From
A. Kosoff, California.
(1951)

RARITY: Extremely
rare, as I have never
heard of another sheet
of brownbacks on
Montana. Even with
sixteen territorial banks
and 39 banks issuing
brownback state notes,
Montana singles are still
scarce.

#42 —
WASHINGTON

NAME: After
George Washington
NICKNAME:
The Evergreen State
**ESTABLISHED AS
TERRITORY:** 1853
ENTERED THE UNION: November 11, 1889
CAPITAL: Olympia
TERRITORIAL SEAL: Mr. Elisha P. Ferry, the first state governor (1889-1893), was also the territorial governor (1872-1880). Ferry sent U.S. Treasurer Spinner the seal of Washington Territory which depicts a standing woman

in a hoop-skirt with an anchor at her feet in the foreground. In the background at the right is a settler's cabin and three pine trees. At the left are some buildings and church spires. At the top is *ALKI*, meaning "Bye and Bye," and at the bottom is "1853." For some unknown reason, no seal is shown in the left oval on the back of early National Bank Notes of Washington; that panel has an eagle identical to the eagle in the right oval. Another drawing of the territorial seal has a woman seated, right arm extended, pointing. There is only one Washington territorial First Charter 1875 Series note known and it has no seal. The motto is expressed as *AL-KI*, and there are boats in the harbor.

NOTE #42A:

DENOMINATION/SERIES: Five Dollars/Brownback Series 1882

BANK/CHARTER: The Ellensburgh National Bank, Territory of Washington (#3867)

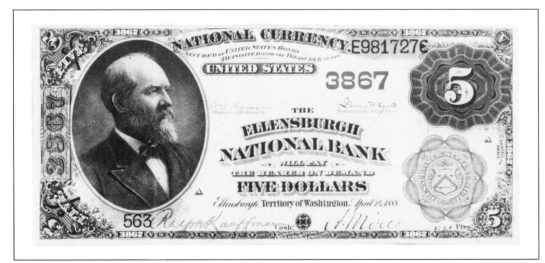

FEDERAL DATA: Serial #E981727, signed by Rosecrans and Hyatt
BANK DATA: Dated April 14, 1888, Bank serial #563, Plate letter "A." This bank operated from 1888 to 1896 and issued only brownbacks, territorial and state. This bank only issued five-dollar notes and was out of business; in 1916 there was only $335 outstanding.
BANK SIGNATURES: Ralph Kauffman, Cashier and A. Mires, "Vice" President

BACK: Large charter number (3867)
SEAL: No seal on note. An eagle is in the left oval.
CONDITION: Very Fine plus.
SOURCE: Purchased by my partner from ROCOA, May, 1974. It had previously belonged to Lyn Knight, Dave Hakes, and Frank Novak who purchased it from a lady in Washington state.
RARITY: Rare, especially in this condition.

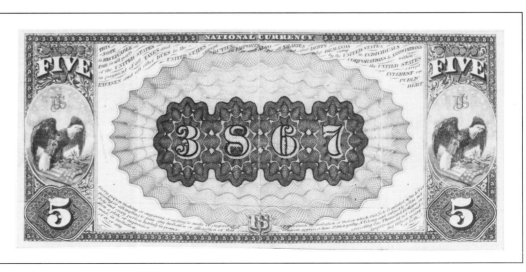

TERRITORIAL NOTES: The only Washington territorial First Charter 1875 Series note known at the present time has no seal. Soon after Washington became a territory in 1853, the territorial seal was adopted, but it was not used on territorial banknotes. In 1878 the First National Bank of Walla Walla, Washington Territory, opened for business under charter #2380. Only one other bank issued territorial notes. Dayton (charter #2520) was only in business from 1881 to 1886 and issued only five-dollar notes (Series 1875) and had only $360 outstanding in 1910! Only one bank issued *state* First Charter (1875 Series) notes, also Walla Walla (charter #2380). These are extremely rare. We believe ours to be the only known Washington State First Charter note. There were 38 territorial banks that issued brownback notes. One would think there would be a good supply, but such is not the case. There are probably 10 to 12 brownback territorial notes known. I can account for only seven, also reported by Huntoon. (See back of this

volume for representations of other Washington territorial seals.)

STATE SEAL: The seal of Washington is said to have been devised in a jewelry store shortly before Washington became a state in 1889 (see PLATE XIV). Using a silver dollar and an ink bottle, a committee member drew concentric circles and printed "The Seal of the State of Washington, 1889" between them. Pasting a postage stamp in the center, he said "The Bust of Washington." With such a state seal, how could there be any differences; only if George's likeness is by a different artist! So far as I know, there is only one First Charter note of Washington state. It has the seal as described.

NOTE #42B:

DENOMINATION/SERIES: Five Dollars/First Charter Series 1875
BANK/CHARTER: The First National Bank Of Walla Walla, Washington (#2380)

FEDERAL DATA: Serial #Y240536–, signed by Rosecrans and Huston
BANK DATA: Dated November 11, 1889 (the first day of statehood), Plate letter "A," Bank serial #20458. This bank opened in 1878 and

went through to the end. The bank issued First Charter Series 1875 notes as a territory. After statehood it issued First Charters Series 1875 then all three Series 1882 and plain-backs Series 1902, but no small size. The amount in 1935 left outstanding was $9,710. NOTE: There is a now-known five-dollar territory note on this same bank, but since it does not show a seal, we will not try to illustrate it for at its asking price of $60,000, it obviously does not belong to us.

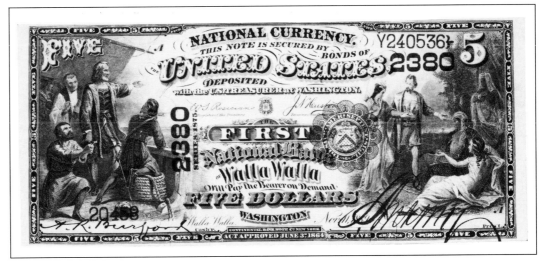

SOURCE: From the Wm. P. Donlon Collection through my friend Wm. "Bill" Anton, Jr., June 30, 1971

RARITY: Must be rare. So far as we know this is the only First Charter note known on the state of Washington.

NOTE #42C:

**DENOMINATION/
SERIES:** One Hundred
Dollars/Brownback
Series 1882

BANK/CHARTER: The
Exchange National
Bank of Spokane,
Washington (#4044),
Regional letter "P"

FACE: Left vignette
shows Commodore
Perry leaving the
Lawrence, his flagship.
Right vignette shows
Liberty seated by fasces,
"The Union: Maintain it."

FEDERAL DATA: Serial
#B605439–, signed by

W.T. Vernon and Chas. H. Treat

BANK DATA: Dated January 16, 1907 (a late date for a brownback), Plate letter "A," Bank serial #17. This bank operated from 1889 to 1929 and issued brownbacks as a territory (for a very short time

evidently, since statehood date is November 11, 1889). The bank then issued brownbacks and date-backs Series 1882, then date-backs and plain-backs Series 1902. The amount outstanding in 1929 was $980,800. This was a large bank.

BANK SIGNATURES:
C.E. MacBroom, Cashier
and Edwin T. Cowan,
signed in pen.

BACK: Charter number
(4044)

SEAL: State seal of
Washington

CONDITION: None
listed at purchase — I
call it Extra Fine.

SOURCE: From Abe
Kosoff in 1969 or 1970

RARITY: Brownback
notes on Washington
state are not rare,
especially Seattle and
Spokane.

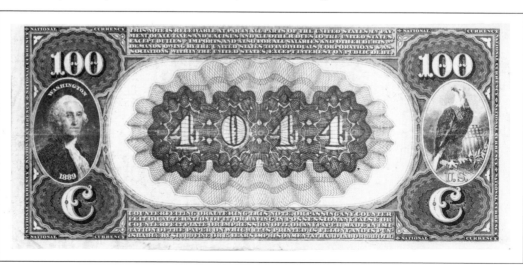

TO STATE 43:

IDAHO

☞

#43 — IDAHO

NAME: Shoshone for "sun coming down the mountain"
NICKNAME: The Gem State
ESTABLISHED AS TERRITORY: 1863
ENTERED THE UNION: July 3, 1890
CAPITAL: Boise

TERRITORIAL SEAL: The territorial seal of Idaho (PLATE VIII) shows a spade-shaped shield with a range of mountains across the top and center. Heading west (from left to right) is a covered wagon with a team of four oxen led by a man on horseback. In the foreground below the covered wagon is a banner proclaiming "The Union" and in the point of the shield is a plow and other farm imple-

ments. Below the shield is the date "1863," the year Idaho became a territory. Stars appear on both sides of the shield going upward following the contour of the shield to the top corners, fading out as they reach the top. The number of stars has no particular significance. Across the entire top of the shield, centered, is a large eagle as a crest. At the top of the seal is "IDAHO." The territorial seal of Idaho is handsome and very significant to me. One reason for this, I suppose, is the extreme rarity of the notes.

NOTE: The "Salve" seal shown here at right actually *preceded* the seal used on First Charter and brownback National Bank Notes, which is similar to the Arms, shown on PLATE VIII. (Also see Appendix for reprints of other early territorial seals.)

NOTE #43A:

DENOMINATION/SERIES: Five Dollars/First Charter Series 1875
BANK/CHARTER: The First National Bank Of Idaho (#1668). At the bottom of the note is written "Boise City, Idaho Territory."
FEDERAL DATA: Serial #N442232–, signed by Allison and Wyman

BANK DATA: Dated April 1, 1867, Plate letter "C," Bank serial #1772. This bank opened in 1867 and went all the way. In fact, this bank is in business and still growing, and a few years ago celebrated their 100th anniversary. In the territorial period it issued Original and Series 1875 First Charter and brownbacks. After statehood it issued

brownbacks again and then all the balance of issues through the small sizes including fifty- and one-hundred dollars of both Types I and II. In 1935 the amount of large size outstanding was $30,480, and this includes the territorial issues.

BANK SIGNATURES: A.G. Redway, "A" (for assistant) Cashier, and John Lesup (?), President, pen signed.

BACK: *Landing of Columbus, 1492*

SEAL: This shows the Idaho territorial seal. Ten years ago when this note was acquired and first seen, this seal looked like a million to me, so excited was I, and it still looks good.

CONDITION: Listed as Very Fine, but I think it is better. It has a couple creases.

SOURCE: ROCOA (Rare Coin Company of America) sale in Peoria, Illinois, May 4, 1974

RARITY: Very rare. There is also an Original $2 "Lazy Two" in this collection.

STATE SEAL: The seal of Idaho (PLATE XV) was approved on March 14, 1891 and was based on the seal of the territory. A central shield shows mountain ranges and the rising sun in the distance and a farmer plowing. An elk's head appears as a crest over the shield. Above the elk's head is the motto *Esto Perpetua* meaning "It is Forever." At the right side of the shield is a miner with his pick, and on the left is Justice as represented by a woman with scales and a liberty-pole. Beneath the shield is a sheaf of wheat and two cornucopias. Two drawings I have and the "official" seal of Idaho are all similar; I can find no differences in the seal as it appears on brownback notes. No First Charter state notes were issued. All Idaho notes are rare since only seventeen banks issued Series 1882 brownbacks.

HISTORICAL NOTES: Idaho became a territory in 1863 and "... on March 11, 1867 the First National Bank of Idaho, Boise City, I.T. was authorized to commence the Business of Banking." (See reprint from the *Idaho Statesman,* Saturday AM, April 27, 1867.) Because they had already adopted a seal for the territory, this seal was placed on territorial bank notes. "Boise City," as it was called for

many years was the only bank in the territory to issue First Charter Period notes, both Original and Series 1875. (See BANK DATA [note #43A, below] for charter #1668, second oldest bank in the west, after Omaha.) There followed seven more banks in Idaho Territory that issued brownback notes (of which only two are known, one of which is in this collection.) In fact, three out of the four known notes of the entire territory are in this collection, an Original Series "Lazy Two," a Series 1875 five-dollar note, and one brownback (see pictures of notes.) Of course both First Charter notes are on Charter #1668. There is a five-dollar brownback on Pocatello, Idaho Territory in this collection and in another collection, a Serial #1 brownback (a ten) on Lewiston, Idaho Territory. The state seal was adopted in 1891, a year after statehood, and bears little resemblance to the territorial seal. There were no First Charter notes of the state, only brownbacks.

NOTE #43B:

DENOMINATION/SERIES: Five Dollars/Series 1882 Brownback

BANK/CHARTER: The First National Bank of Pocatello, Territory Of Idaho (#4023)

FEDERAL DATA: Serial #K84595–, signed by Rosecrans and Hyatt

BANK DATA: Dated May 3, 1889, Plate letter "B," Bank serial #663. This bank operated from 1889 to 1928 and issued territorial brownback notes. Then, after statehood, it issued brownbacks and date-backs of Series 1882 also date-backs and plain-backs of the 1902 Series. The amount outstanding in 1925 was $12,300 (includes territorials.)

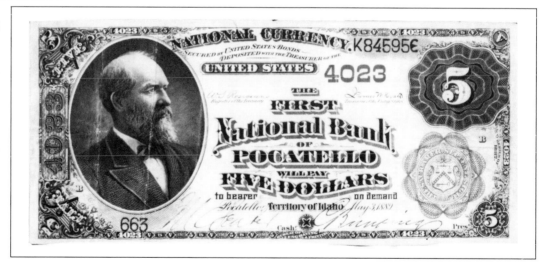

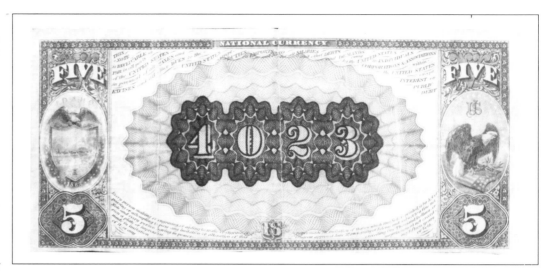

NOTE #43C:

DENOMINATION/SERIES: Ten Dollars/Series 1882 Brownback

BANK/CHARTER: The Idaho National Bank of Lewiston, Idaho (#5600 — no regional letter)

FEDERAL DATA: Serial #X760360–, signed by Lyons and Roberts

BANK DATA: Dated October 3, 1900, Plate letter "B," Bank serial #83. This bank operated only four years, 1900 to 1904, and issued only brownback notes of Series 1882. As of the year 1910 the balance outstanding on the records amounted to $640.

BANK SIGNATURES: F.M. Hinkly, Cashier, and G.W. Thompson, "V" President, signed in pen

BACK: Charter number (5600)

SEAL: State seal of Idaho, very different from the territorial seal.

CONDITION: About Very Fine

SOURCE: In 1961 I had accumulated at least one First Charter or one brownback note of every state and the District of Columbia except Idaho. I knew that Bill Donlon had a brownback. He did not want to sell it, so I knew I would have to be reckless to make him listen. So I offered him $1000 (a large sum in that time). The only stipulation was that he also included a Delaware brownback that I also needed. He shipped them to me quick, special delivery to my front door.

RARITY: Rare. Less than twelve are thought to exist.

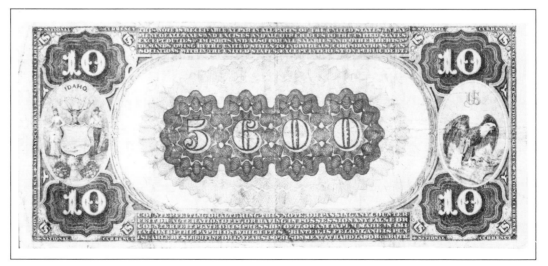

148

TO STATE 44:

WYOMING

☞

#44 — WYOMING

NAME: Delaware Indian for "end of the plains"
NICKNAME: The Equality State
ESTABLISHED AS TERRITORY: Became Wyoming Territory in 1868.
ENTERED THE UNION: July 10, 1890
CAPITAL: Cheyenne
TERRITORIAL SEAL: Wyoming became a territory in 1869. Wyoming is unusual in that all First Charter state notes and early state brownbacks show the territorial seal.

The territorial notes show no seal. Dr. Limpert's description of the territorial seal is as follows: "... shows a central shield with a train in mountainous country at top and an arm with sword, lower right, and a plow and implements in lower left. Above the shield is *Cedant Arma Togae* meaning 'Let Arms Yield to Gowns' or, 'Let Military Might Yield to Civil Authority.' " (As mentioned in the article accompanying the color plates, there is an error in Wyoming's motto there.) I would offer some additional descriptive words: the Latin motto is above the shield with "1890" just below the top center. In the top half of the shield are mountains and a train headed west (to the left). In the lower right quarter

NOTE #44A:

DENOMINATION/SERIES: Five Dollars/First Charter Series 1875
BANK/CHARTER: The Wyoming National Bank of Laramie City, Wyoming Territory (#2110)
FEDERAL DATA: Serial #H193623–, signed by Allison and Wyman

BANK DATA: Dated June 10, 1873, Plate letter "D," Bank serial #1578. This bank operated from 1873 to 1895 and issued both Original and Series 1875 First Charter notes. After becoming Wyoming state in 1890, it also issued Series 1875 First Charters and brownbacks Series 1882. The total outstanding in 1910 amounted to

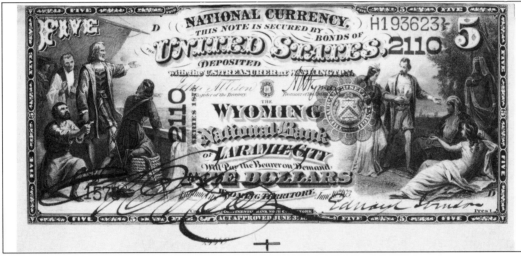

$1,300. At this bank's origin its territorial issues included 1000 "Lazy Twos" and 3000 ones. This is a total of 1000 sheets, or $5000 in face value.
BANK SIGNATURES: C.O. Root (vanity signature), Cashier, and Edward Ivinson, President, pen-signed.
BACK: *Landing of Columbus, 1492*
SEAL: No seal. An eagle appears in the left oval exactly as in the right oval.
CONDITION: Uncirculated. Cut close

and even into the border slightly on the face. The back is better.
SOURCE: Purchased from Hickman and Oakes auction sale.
RARITY: Very rare. Aside from this cut sheet of four fives, there are a two and a couple of ones (I think) on this bank plus a very rare twenty on Cheyenne out of Amon Carter's collection. Possibly one or two more exist for a total of eight or nine. Huntoon lists nine First Charter notes and one brownback on Wyoming Territory.

is an arm with a sword upraised and in the lower left quarter is a plow with a shovel and pick crossed in front of the plow with a shepherd's crook slanting left across the lower section of the plow handles. The word "Wyoming" appears underneath the shield (similar to PLATE VIII, but most like territorial seal on state banknotes — see picture of NOTE #44C.)

Reprinted in the appendix are three different drawings of the territorial seal. Two of the three show the words "Territory of Wyoming" at the top and "Great Seal" at the bottom. The other drawing leaves out the word "of" and shows a shield with a broad bottom rather than a pointed bottom. One of these drawings also has a fasces emblem in the top of the shield with a rather large elk's head as a crest.

(NOTE: Wyoming contains the headwaters of three of the country's largest river systems. The Bighorn flows north to join the Columbia; the North Platte runs east to merge with the Missouri/Mississippi complex; and the Green River flows south to become the Colorado.) Though no seal was shown on the territorial notes (also true for Oregon, Montana and Washington territories), we show black-and-white representations of their early seals for interest. Other versions of Wyoming's territorial seals, and others as well, appear in the Appendix.

NOTE #44B:

DENOMINATION/SERIES: Ten Dollars/Series 1882 Brownback
BANK/CHARTER: The First National Bank of Rawlins, Territory Of Wyoming (#4320)

FEDERAL DATA: Serial #E253225–, signed by Rosecrans and Huston
BANK DATA: Dated May 26, 1890, Plate letter "C," Bank serial #1. This bank opened in 1890, before statehood, and went to full term.

First, it issued brownbacks as a territory and then as a state issued brownbacks and date-backs Series 1882 then date-backs and plain-backs of the Series 1902. In small size it issued all three denominations of both types. In 1935, there remained $4,540 in large size outstanding.
BANK SIGNATURES: J.C. David, Cashier, and I.C. Miller, "V" President, pen-signed.
BACK: Charter number (4320)

SEAL: No seal, same as last note, #44A
CONDITION: Fine; there are some folds.
SOURCE: From Wm. Anton, Jr. through his father, who was an avid collector who advertised for rare nationals.
RARITY: Extremely rare. Although seven banks issued territorial notes, so far as is known this is the only brownback territorial note to have survived.

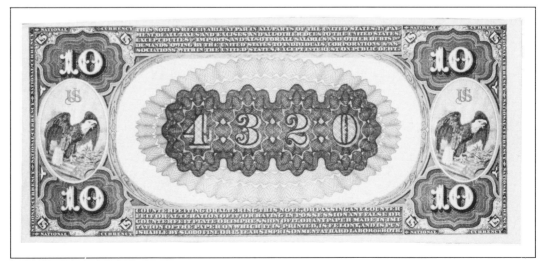

TERRITORIAL BANKS: Beginning in 1871 and running through the first half of 1882 there were only four banks to operate and issue First Charter notes in Wyoming Territory. Due to a rare sheet of four five-dollar notes on Laramie City (#2110), there are known today among collectors eight to ten different notes. These four banks issued no brownback territorial notes. The next seven banks to open in the territory issued brownback notes as a territory, but for some reason, only one note is known today (Rawlins, #4320.) Three of these seven banks had a very small circulation of notes.

STATE SEAL: Limpert's description of the Wyoming state seal says that it was adopted in 1893, three years after statehood (See PLATE XV.) It has a woman on a pedestal holding a banner in her right hand. The banner is inscribed with the words "Equal Rights." On the right is a pillar and a lamp with a miner or oil seeker with pick standing beside the pedestal. On the left is another pillar and a cattleman with a lariat. My own notes include the additional information: on the right pillar, the word "mines" is at the figure's shoulder and the word "oil" is at the level of his knee. On the left pillar the word "livestock" is above and "grain" is below. Also under the pedestal there is a small shield. An eagle is located on the base of the pedestal and is standing on the shield. The top section of the shield shows a five-pointed star with Roman numerals on each side of the top point of the star; "XL" on the left and "IV" on the right. This is shown on one drawing and in the seal on brownback notes. On the other drawing and the "official" seal the arabic numerals "44" are on the star itself — small items,

but included here for the sake of completeness. Below the shield and on either side are the two dates, 1869 and 1890, the first signifying the organization of the Territory of Wyoming and the latter, the date of statehood. Idaho, and especially Wyoming, pushed for women's suffrage, so a woman stands on a pedestal. Susan B. Anthony, a leader in the suffrage movement which gave women the right to vote, was from Wyoming. There is, here again, little in common between the state and the territorial seals of Wyoming.

COMMENTS ON NOTE #44D: State First Charter notes on the Stock Grower's of Cheyenne are not rare and show the date of statehood on the face of the notes. Many years ago Dr. Limpert reported that a brownback note of Wyoming state with the territorial seal had been reported to him. It belonged to Tom Mason of Cheyenne (now deceased). Of course it is rare — there can't be many out there, even though seven banks' brownback notes used this first seal until 1893.

We now have in this collection a very rare ten-dollar brownback on The Albany County National Bank of Laramie City, Wyoming, Charter #3615. This note shows the first or territorial seal because the state seal was not adopted until 1893, some three years after statehood. The reason we are not showing this note is because of its condition; it is only classed as Good but the seal is definitely the territorial seal.

NOTE #44C:

DENOMINATION/SERIES: Five Dollars/First Charter Series 1875
BANK/CHARTER: The Stock Growers National Bank of Cheyenne, Wyoming (#2652)

FEDERAL DATA: Serial #Y130931–, signed by Rosecrans and Huston
BANK DATA: Dated July 10, 1890 (first day of statehood), Plate letter "C," Bank serial #7828. This bank opened in 1882 and went full term.

The bank first issued Series 1875 territorial notes, then as a state also issued Series 1875 First Charter notes, then all three Second Charter Series 1882 as well as plain-backs of the 1902 Series. The bank issued no small-size notes. Outstanding in 1935 was $4,422.50 (includes territorial notes).

BANK SIGNATURES: (?), Cashier and Haman G. Hay, President (vanity signature), pen-signed.

BACK: *Landing of Columbus, 1492*

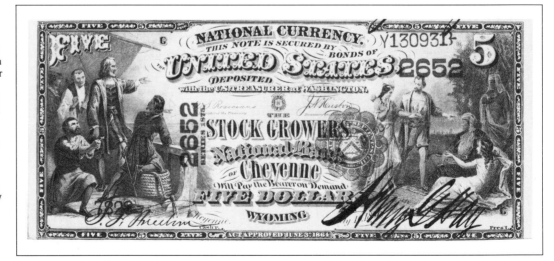

SEAL: This shows the territorial seal for the reason that the state seal was not adopted until 1893, nearly four years after statehood.

CONDITION: Choice. Very Fine.

SOURCE: From Limpert Collection sold by Stack's, May 6, 1956

RARITY: Must be considered rare even though several of this bank's notes are around. Two other banks issued First Charter notes as did this bank, but they are rare as I have never heard of

any of these. This bank had a great title and a western theme, so possibly as many as a dozen were saved.

NOTE #44D:

DENOMINATION/ SERIES: Twenty Dollars/Brownback Series 1882

BANK/CHARTER: The First National Bank Of Laramie, Wyoming (#4989), Regional letter "W"

FEDERAL DATA: Serial #T617175T, signed by Tillman and Morgan

BANK DATA: Dated March 15, 1895, Plate letter "A," Bank serial #3255. This bank opened in 1895 and

went the full term. It issued brownbacks and date-backs Series 1882; date-backs and plain-backs of the 1902 Series, as well as tens and twenties of both Type I and II, small size. Large-sized notes that remained outstanding in 1935 amounted to $5,250.

BANK SIGNATURES: Signed in pen by B.C. Jones, Cashier, and G. Mark Ivinson, President

BACK: Charter number (4989)

SEAL: Wyoming state seal

CONDITION: About Uncirculated.

SOURCE: Purchased from Morey Perlmutter, Watertown, Mass. (Boston), December 2, 1970

RARITY: Very scarce. Eighteen banks issued brownbacks as a state, and possibly two or three banks' notes showed the territorial seal (very rare). There may be three or four dozen surviving state brownbacks.

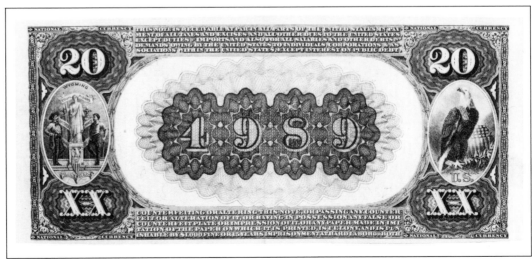

#45 — UTAH

NAME: Navajo for "upper"
NICKNAME: The Beehive State
ESTABLISHED AS TERRITORY: 1850
ENTERED THE UNION: January 4, 1896
CAPITAL: Salt Lake City

TERRITORIAL SEAL: The principal object on the Utah territorial seal (see PLATE VIII) is the large beehive sitting on its base, showing a small hole at the bottom center of the hive, with bees streaming out, up, and around the hive. On the left rear appear several sego lilies. At the top is written "Sept. 9th" and at the bottom in Roman numerals is the date 1850 (MDCCCL).

STATE SEAL: The state seal of Utah (PLATE XV) was approved on April 3, 1896, shortly after statehood, and is based on the territorial seal, first used in 1850. A central shield has a large beehive with sego lilies (the state flower) on either side with some bees flying around. The word "Industry" appears above and "1847," the year the Mormons arrived in Utah, is below. An American flag is draped on each side of the shield and the American eagle is the crest above it. Two drawings in my possession and the "official" seal are all similar.

COMMENTS: Twelve banks issued brownback state notes and all are scarce. But only two banks, Ogden and Provo (a small bank) issued First Charter state notes and only one of these notes is known. My partner just recently acquired from the Amon Carter estate one I believe to be very rare — unique, as far as I know. This was one of two notes I've had my eye on for several years, the other being the Winnemucca brownback. This is the last note acquired for our collection and, save only one note with a seal,

NOTE #45A:

DENOMINATION/SERIES: One Dollar/First Charter Original Series.

BANK/CHARTER: The Miner's National Bank of Salt Lake, Utah Territory (#1646 — not shown on the note)
FEDERAL DATA: Serial #B146841, signed by Colby and Spinner

BANK DATA: Dated May 1, 1866, Plate letter "C," Bank serial #1479. This bank only operated from 1866 to 1869, and issued only Original notes. There was outstanding in 1910 only $686.

BANK SIGNATURES: Jno. Shin (?), Cashier, and J.H. Kiskadden, President, signed in pen.

BACK: *Landing of the Pilgrims, 1620*

SEAL: Territorial seal of Utah

CONDITION: Very Fine. I say Extra Fine,

but it has rounded corners, especially the top right.

SOURCE: Hickman and Oakes auction, September 20, 1978; originally from the Carter collection

RARITY: Rare. This is one of the great notes in this collection. This is the first bank in the territory and, as far as I know, the only note on this bank in existence. Aside from all this, it is the only note of Utah to read "Great Salt Lake."

makes our collection of United States and territories complete as to seals. It is fully complete in regards to brownback territorial notes showing no seals. The note I'm referring to is the choice Ogden twenty-dollar First Charter note which is the only one known. This state note goes to prove what I said earlier, that is, the <u>state</u>-issued notes are much rarer than the territorial notes. After four Salt Lake City banks issued Original First Charter Period notes, the last two of these banks plus Ogden and Provo City also issued Series 1875 First Charter Period territorial notes. One of these, The Deseret (the best known), and eleven more banks issued brownback territorial notes which I believe to be rarer than the First Charter Period notes. Two dates appear on the brownback state seals: 1896 — the date of statehood, and, near the top, 1847 — the date the Mormons settled Utah and the "Bountiful Valley." Utah First Charter territorial notes are second only to Colorado Territory in the number of territorial First Charter notes known. But First Charter notes on Utah Territory, other than on The Deseret, are rare indeed. Note the picture of an Original on the first bank in the territory, The Miner's National Bank of <u>Great</u> Salt Lake City (#1646). This is the only bank note to say "Great." There is one of these in our collection.

NOTE #45B:

DENOMINATION/SERIES: Five Dollars/Series 1882 Brownback

BANK/CHARTER: The First National Bank Of Park City, Territory Of Utah (#4564)
FEDERAL DATA: Serial #W179478–, signed by Rosecrans and Nebeker

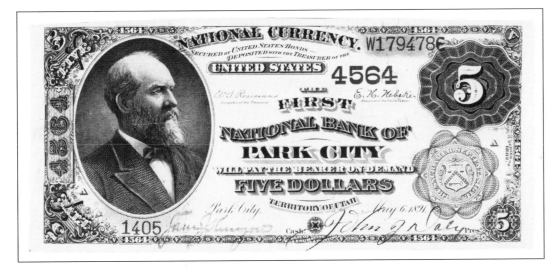

BANK DATA: Dated May 6, 1891, Plate letter "A," Bank serial #1405. This bank operated from 1891 through 1935. The bank issued brownback series, then after statehood issued brownbacks, date-backs Series 1882, then date-backs and plain-backs Series 1902, issuing no small-size notes. The amount outstanding in 1935 was $2,725.

BANK SIGNATURES: Sam J. Kenyon, Cashier, and John J. Daly, President, signed in pen.

BACK: Charter number (4564)

SEAL: Utah territorial seal

CONDITION: Uncirculated

SOURCE: Bob Medlar was kind enough to let me have this note; we did some trading.

RARITY: Rare. Although twelve banks issued territorial brownback notes, they seem to be rarer than the First Charters. Peter Huntoon lists eighteen First Charter notes and only six brownbacks.

NOTE #45C:

DENOMINATION/SERIES: Twenty Dollars/Series 1875 First Charter
BANK/CHARTER: The First National Bank Of Ogden, Utah (#2597)

FEDERAL DATA: Serial #K722814, signed by Tillman and Morgan
BANK DATA: Dated January 6, 1896 (date of statehood January 4, 1896), Plate letter "A," Bank serial #1366. This bank issued Series

1875 First Charter as a territory when it opened in 1881. As Utah State it issued Series 1875 First Charter notes, also. It also issued all three issues of 1882 and Series 1902, Third Charter Period plain-backs, as well as small tens and twenties of both types. Outstanding large-size in 1935 was $26,110, territorials included.

BANK SIGNATURES:
(?) Cashier, and Thomas D. Dee, "V" President

BACK: *Baptism of Pocahontas*

SEAL: Seal of Utah Territory with large beehive

CONDITION: About Uncirculated

SOURCE: Out of the Amon Carter Collection through Lyn Knight, 1983.

RARITY: Extremely rare. This is the only First Charter state note with the Utah territorial seal known. On the face, lower center, is "State of Utah."

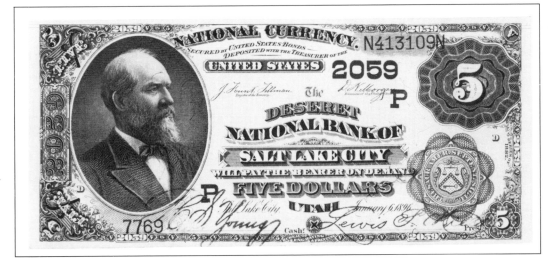

NOTE #45D:

DENOMINATION/ SERIES: Five Dollars/Series 1882 Brownback

BANK/CHARTER: The Deseret National Bank Of Salt Lake City, Utah (#2059), Regional letter "P"

FEDERAL DATA: Serial #N413109N, signed by Tillman and Morgan

BANK DATA: Dated January 6, 1896 (two days after statehood), Plate letter "D," Bank serial #7769. This is a large bank which opened in 1872 and

went full term. It began by issuing Original and Series 1875 First Charter territorial notes and, after Utah became a state, it released some of all issues starting with brownbacks, except value-backs (1882), red seals (1902), and type II tens and twenties. The amount of

large-sized notes still out in 1935 was $47,285.

BANK SIGNATURES: Signed in pen, C.S. Young, Cashier (Brigham Young's son), and Lewis L. Mills, President (Young's son-in-law)

BACK: Charter number (2059)

SEAL: State seal of Utah. Notice how they have taken the territorial seal and added to and embellished it.

CONDITION: Extra Fine

SOURCE: Purchased from Wm. A. Philpott, Jr. Dallas, TX

RARITY: Far from common since only twelve banks issued brownback notes on the state.

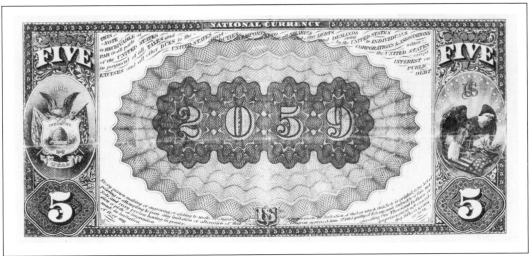

#46 —
OKLAHOMA

NAME: Choctaw for "red people"
NICKNAME: The Sooner State
ESTABLISHED AS TERRITORY: Part of the Louisiana Territory, Oklahoma became Indian Territory in 1830. It became Oklahoma Territory in 1890, with Gutherie as its capital.
ENTERED THE UNION: November 16, 1907
CAPITAL: Oklahoma City
HISTORICAL NOTES: The western portion of the Louisiana Purchase was considered "Indian Territory." From Indiana, Illinois, Wisconsin, and the Southeastern United States, members of a dozen tribes were brought to "Indian Territory" by the U.S. Government. Literally uprooted, this displacement was called "The Trail of Tears" and is a shameful page in United States history. In 1830 Congress formally established Indian Territory and the history of Oklahoma is largely the history of the American Indian. Broken promises and broken treaties resulted in the Indians' being constantly herded into the Indian Territory in the thought (in that day and time) that this was a permanent place for the Indians. But the white man's greed cheated the Indians out of most of this legacy. On April 22, 1889, the first "run" of settlers pushed the Indians out of their established territory again. In 1890, Oklahoma became a territory with Gutherie as capital. On November 16, 1907,

NOTE #46A:

DENOMINATION/SERIES: Twenty Dollars/Brownback Series 1882.

BANK/CHARTER: The First National Bank Of Tulsa, Indian Territory (#5171), Regional letter "W"
FEDERAL DATA: Serial #T651103T, signed by Lyons and Roberts

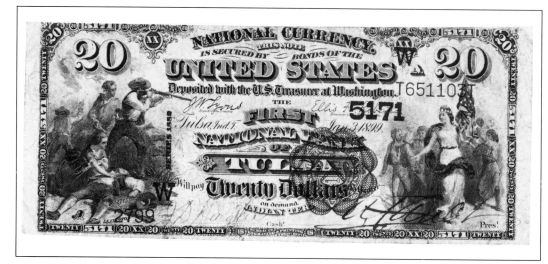

BANK DATA: Dated January 3, 1899, Plate letter "A," Bank serial #2799. This bank operated 1899 to 1933 and issued brownback notes then, as Oklahoma state, it issued all three Series of 1882 notes (brownbacks included) then plain-backs Series 1902. In small size, it issued only fifties and hundreds in type I. The amount of large size (plus territorial notes) out in 1935 was $24,537.50.

BANK SIGNATURES: J.D. Hagler, Cashier, and A. Faust, President

BACK: Charter number (5171)

SEAL: No seal, another eagle as right oval

CONDITION: About Fine but soiled.

SOURCE: Traded this from Amon Carter.

RARITY: Not rare

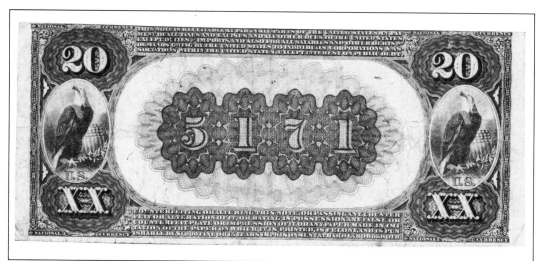

Oklahoma and the Indian Territories entered the Union as the forty-sixth state.

SEAL: In 1906 Oklahoma's state seal was designed (see PLATE XV). This design features a large five-pointed star with one ray pointed straight up. The center of the star shows the central device of the Oklahoma territorial seal, a wreath. Around the inner top of the wreath is the motto *Labor Omnia Vincit* meaning "Labor conquers all things." Below is an Indian and a white man, clasping hands, making a treaty, and Justice represented as blindfolded with scales. The top point of the star shows the symbol of the ancient Chickasaw Nation: an Indian warrior with bow and shield. The upper right point is the symbol of the ancient seal of the Choctaw Nation: a tomahawk, bow, and three crossed arrows. The lower right point shows the symbol of the ancient seal of the Seminole Nation: a village of houses and a factory by a lake with an Indan paddling his canoe. The lower left ray points to the symbol of the ancient seal of the Creek Nation: a sheaf of wheat and a plow. The upper left ray indicates the symbol of the ancient seal of the Cherokee Nation: a seven-pointed star partly surrounded by a wreath of oak leaves. Between each ray are five groups of nine stars for a total of 45 stars; the large star itself becomes the forty-sixth, and represents the new state of Oklahoma. My two drawings and the "official" seal are all similar. There are no seals on Indian Territory, Oklahoma Territory or Oklahoma state notes. No First Charter notes were issued, but many brownbacks were, all of which

NOTE #46B:

DENOMINATION/SERIES: Five Dollars/Brownback Series 1882
BANK/CHARTER: The Stillwater National Bank, Stillwater, Territory Of Oklahoma (#5347), Regional letter "W"

FEDERAL DATA: Serial #R530983R, signed by Lyons and Roberts
BANK DATA: Dated April 24, 1900, Plate letter "A," Bank serial #1340. This bank opened in 1900 and went all the way, issuing

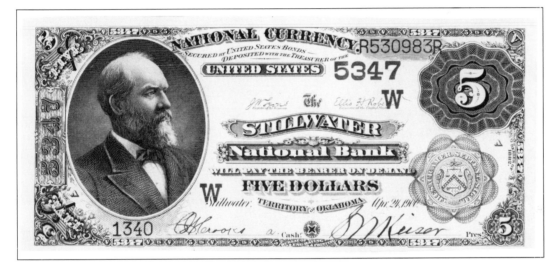

brownback territorial notes such as this one, then as a state continued with date-backs and value-backs Series 1882 and plain-backs of 1902 and small-size fives of both types. Total amount of large size out in 1935 was $1,610.
BANK SIGNATURES: C.W. Crooks, Cashier, and S.N. Kiser, President, signed in pen.
BACK: Charter number (5347)
SEAL: None, from here on.

CONDITION: Gem Crisp Uncirculated. New, like money in the bank.
SOURCE: Purchased from Paul Kagin
RARITY: No Oklahoma Territory brownback notes are rare, but the condition of this note is unusually choice.

have an identical eagle in the left and right ovals. All territorial notes are brownbacks <u>only</u> through 1901, then red seals until the end of the period. I believe that Oklahoma state brownbacks are rarer than either Indian Territory or Oklahoma Territory notes.

NOTE #46C:

DENOMINATION/ SERIES: Ten Dollars/ Brownback Series 1882

BANK/CHARTER: The State National Bank of Oklahoma City, Oklahoma (#4862), Regional letter "W"

FEDERAL DATA: Serial #N322603N, signed by Rosecrans and Nebeker

BANK DATA: Dated February 11, 1893, Plate letter "C," Bank serial #2179. This bank opened in 1893 and went to term issuing

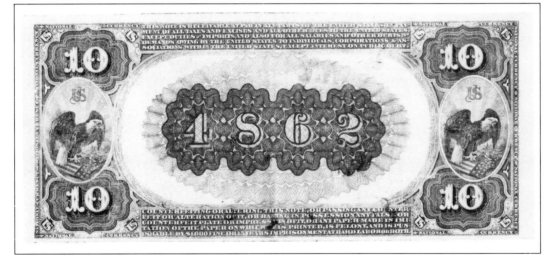

brownbacks as a territory and then, as a state, brownbacks and date-backs Series 1882. It then issued date-backs and plain-backs of 1902 and most small-size issues. In 1935 the amount of large size outstanding was $31,750.

BANK SIGNATURES: Pen signed, but cannot be certain of either one.

BACK: Charter number (4862)

SEAL: No state seal placed on notes.

CONDITION: Very Fine

SOURCE: Purchased from Paul Kagin, October 17, 1972

RARITY: Not rare, but we believe the state issues are scarcer than the territorial notes.

TO STATE 47:

NEW MEXICO

☞

#47 —
NEW MEXICO

NAME: Spanish name for the area
NICKNAME: The Land of Enchantment
ESTABLISHED AS TERRITORY: September 9, 1850
ENTERED THE UNION: January 6, 1912
CAPITAL: Santa Fe
SEAL: The seal of the State of New Mexico (See PLATE VIII) was approved on March 13, 1913. The only change from the territorial seal to the state seal was the changing of the word "territory" to "state." The seal shows a large American eagle with arrows in its talons, shielding a smaller Mexican eagle with a serpent in its beak and a cactus in its talons. Below the eagles is a streamer with the motto *Crescit Eundo*, meaning "It grows as it goes." No seals appear on National Bank Notes of either charter period. Legend has it that Montezuma was born at Pecos Pueblo, New Mexico, and mounted an eagle which flew south. He was followed by his people. The eagle finally landed on a cactus and siezed a snake with its beak; this place became the capital of the Aztec Empire, the present Mexico City, Mexico. New Mexico Territory notes are not common and, indeed, the First Charter notes are rare, there being only six banks to issue them. The first two of these six banks also issued Original Series notes. Our note is on The Second National Bank of New Mexico at Santa Fe, signed by the Spiegelberg brothers.

NOTE #47A:

DENOMINATION/SERIES: One Dollar/Original Series First Charter

BANK/CHARTER: The Second National Bank Of New Mexico At Santa Fe, Territory Of New Mexico (#2024 — number not on note)
FEDERAL DATA: Serial #D548020–, signed by Allison and Spinner

BANK DATA: Dated April 15, 1873, Plate letter "C," Bank serial #85. This bank operated from 1872 to 1892 and issued only Originals and Series 1875 First Charters and had a balance outstanding in 1910 of $2,337.
BANK SIGNATURES: Willi Spiegelberg, Cashier, and L. Spiegelberg, President, signed in pen.
BACK: *Landing of the Pilgrims, 1620.*

SEAL: No seal, another standing eagle.
CONDITION: About Fine
SOURCE: From Hickman and Waters March 13, 1969
RARITY: Rare. Only two banks in the territory issued Original Series. The next four issued Series 1875. How many out there? About two dozen total First Charter Period notes. Peter Huntoon records 24: eleven Original Series and thirteen Series 1875.

COMMENT ON NOTE #47B: No seals appear on National Bank Notes of New Mexico. All New Mexico National Bank Notes of the First Charter Period and brownback series are, of course, territorial, for New Mexico came into the Union too late for these two issues to show any seal. Charter #1750 was the First National Bank of Santa Fe, the oldest bank in the territory (and the Southwest). This bank issued Original and Series 1875 as well as brownbacks. Charter #2024 (also Santa Fe) issued both Original and First Charter notes. Four other banks issued Series 1875 First Charter Period notes. Eighteen banks issued brownback notes.

NOTE #47B:

**DENOMINATION/
SERIES:** Five
Dollars/Series 1882
Brownback

BANK/CHARTER: The
First National Bank Of
Raton, Territory of New
Mexico, (#4734),
Regional letter "W"

FEDERAL DATA: Serial
#K717157K, signed by
Rosecrans and Nebeker

BANK DATA: Dated
April 26, 1892, Plate
letter "C," Bank serial
#2077. This bank
operated from 1892 to

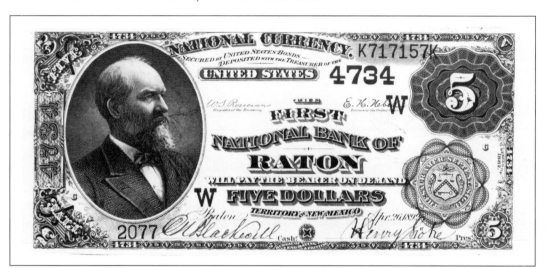

1926 and issued
brownbacks and
date-backs Series 1882
as a territory. After
statehood this bank also
issued date-backs and
plain-backs of 1902.
The amount outstanding
in 1926 was $96,900
(total of all issues).

BANK SIGNATURES:
C.N. Blackwell, Cashier,
and Henry Gohe,
Presient, signed by
hand.

BACK: Charter number
(4734)

SEAL: No seal. Same
"squat" eagle.

CONDITION: About Uncirculated
SOURCE: Purchased from Morey Perlmutter, May 18, 1970.

RARITY: Brownback notes on New Mexico are rare; perhaps two dozen exist. Huntoon records 27 brownbacks on New Mexico Territory.

#48 — ARIZONA

NAME: Papago
for "little spring"
NICKNAME:
The Grand Canyon State
**ESTABLISHED AS
TERRITORY:**
February 24, 1863
ENTERED THE UNION:

February 14, 1912
CAPITAL: Phoenix
SEAL: One of the points of interest about Arizona is that it has changed the location of its capital so many times. The capital was Prescott from 1863 until 1867; Tuscon from 1867 to 1877; Prescott was again the capital from 1877 to 1889; and Phoenix has been the capital since 1889. The seal of Arizona (see PLATE XVI) is based on the territorial seal. The seal shows a background of mountains with a rising sun. At the right side below the mountains is a reservoir and dam with irrigated fields, orchards, and grazing cattle below it. At the left below the mountains is a quartz mill and a miner with pick and shovel. At the top inside the shield is the Latin motto *Ditat Deus* meaning "God enriches." Limpert says that the seal is based on the territorial seal which is shown (page 13) on the Governor's letterhead in Limpert's book, *United States National Bank Notes Old Series*. This seal, dated 1863, shows mainly a peak and the miner with pick and shovel as the dominant features, and includes the motto described

NOTE #48A:

DENOMINATION/SERIES: Five Dollars/Series 1875 First Charter

BANK/CHARTER: The First National Bank of Tucson, Territory of Arizona (#2639)

FEDERAL DATA: Serial #U626418–, signed by Bruce and Gilfillan

BANK DATA: Dated March 1, 1882, Plate letter "A," Bank serial #1013. First bank in the territory. Opened in 1882 and closed in 1885. Issued only five-dollar notes and only Series 1875. There remained in 1910 only $335 outstanding; of the 67 five-dollar bills out, only three are known.

BANK SIGNATURES: B.M. Jacobs, Cashier, and P.R. Tully, President, pen-signed.

BACK: *Landing of Columbus, 1492*
SEAL: No seal on notes.
CONDITION: Extra Fine. Top right corner is off and it is cut close at the top.
SOURCE: Purchased from Bill Anton, Jr., February 3, 1977. See The Tucson Story in Chapter 4 of this book.
RARITY: Rare, as only three are known.

above. Arizona attained statehood in 1912, long after the issue of Original Series and brownback notes, this seal does not appear on United States paper money. This does not explain why the territorial seal was not used on the First Charter Series 1875 nor the Second Charter Series 1882 brownbacks. This is another of the mysteries concerning National Bank Notes.

Only one bank issued Series 1875 First Charter notes: Tucson (#2639), which was in business from 1882 to 1885. This bank had $335 outstanding in 1910, which consisted of 67 five-dollar notes. Only three of these are known. Only nine banks issued territorial brownback

notes. All are rare. State issues are as rare as the territorial notes until after1910, but no brownbacks were issued on the state of Arizona. There were only three banks that issued date-backs (Series 1882), and two banks that issued value-back notes (Series 1882), but the third issue of 1902 plain-backs, the last issue of the old large-size notes, are a little more common.

NOTE #48B:

DENOMINATION/SERIES: Twenty Dollars/Brownback Series 1882
BANK/CHARTER: The Consolidated National Bank of Tucson, Territory of Arizona (#4287), Reginal letter "P"
FEDERAL DATA: Serial #N196886N, signed by Rosecrans and Huston
BANK DATA: Dated April 15, 1890, Plate letter "A," Bank serial

#1164. Opened in 1890 and went to term. As a territory it issued brownbacks and date-backs Series 1882 and date-backs of 1902. Arizona became a state on February 14, 1912, then as a state issued date-backs, plain-backs Series 1902, and small-size five-, ten- and twenty-dollar notes of both types. The amount of large size out in 1935 was $7,310.

BANK SIGNATURES: Pen-signed, O.W. Feeney, Cashier, but the

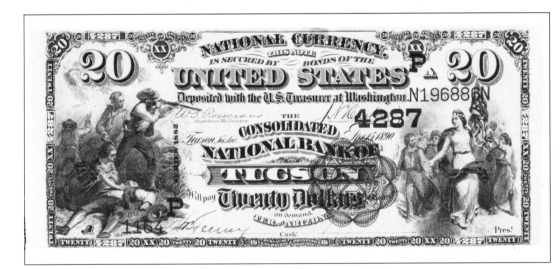

president's signature has faded and looks like a stamped signature. Practically all National Bank Notes of these periods (First Charter and brownbacks) were signed individually, by hand. Later, as populations and banks grew, this task became burdensome. Around 1890 some larger banks began to use stamped signatures, and frequently the inks used proved to be less permanent than those on notes signed by hand. Later still, the

signatures were engraved on the plates.
BACK: Charter number (4287)
SEAL: No seal on Arizona notes
CONDITION: Extra Fine/About Uncirculated
SOURCE: Bought from M. Perlmutter, May 18, 1970
RARITY: Arizona brownbacks are rare. All are territorial notes and only nine banks issued brownback notes. Peter Huntoon records only six brownbacks of Arizona Territory.

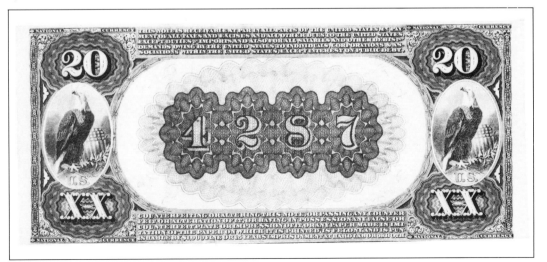

#49 — ALASKA

NAME: Aleut for "great land"
NICKNAME: Land of the Midnight Sun
ESTABLISHED AS TERRITORY: 1912
ENTERED THE UNION: January 3, 1959
CAPITAL: Juneau

SEAL: The seal of Alaska (see PLATE XVI) was approved on April 8, 1960 and is the result of the evolution of two or three seals. In 1884 Congress provided for a civil government for Alaska and the first governor on his own initiative designed and had made a seal for the District of Alaska. The seal was used until 1910 when Governor Walter E. Clark said that the seal placed too much emphasis on icebergs, northern lights, and native people. He had a draftsman in Juneau draw a rough draft of a new seal which incorporated the original features plus symbols for mining, agriculture, fisheries, fur seal rookeries, and a railroad. The design was approved by the Acting Attorney General of the United States. A "more refined" drawing was made by an unknown person in the Department of the Interior, and the new seal was ready for use in early 1911. After Alaska's status was changed from that of a district to

NOTE #49:

DENOMINATION/SERIES: Five Dollars/Third Charter Red Seal Series 1902
BANK/CHARTER: First National Bank of Fairbanks, District of Alaska (#7718), Regional letter "P"

FEDERAL DATA: Serial #D209117–, signed by Lyons and Roberts
BANK DATA: Dated March 1, 1905, Plate letter "A" (but it is rather faint under the vertical charter number) Bank serial #1058. This bank

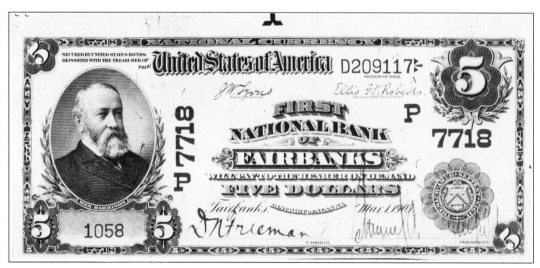

operated from 1905 to 1935 and issued all three series of the Third Charter Period 1902. The amount of large-size notes outstanding in 1935 was $5,880.

BANK SIGNATURES: D.N. Freeman, Cashier, and Samuel A. (last name illegible). It is not certain that these are pen signatures.

FACE: The left vignette is a portrait of President Benjamin Harrison and on the right side is a red scalloped treasury seal — this is why we call these "red seals."

BACK: In center, *Landing of the Pilgrims.* National currency has a plain open back. Notice the center guide marks on the top margin.

CONDITION: Uncirculated.

SOURCE: Purchased from Hickman and Waters, April 12, 1969

RARITY: All Alaska notes are rare, however, there are several sheets of these, some of which were cut up a few years ago. The number of cut sheets is unknown.

a territory in 1912, the new designation was substituted on the seal. The seal is 2⅛ inches in diameter. As one can see by the drawing of the present-day seal there have been several changes and refinements. Obviously some things had to be deleted, but not much.

COMMENTS: NOTE #49 is the only Alaska note we have. Only one bank in Alaska issued brownback notes, Juneau (Charter #5117), and none are known to collectors. It is extremely unlikely that any seal is shown on the notes, if any exist. There was only $930 outstanding in 1935. The bank also issued date-backs, of which one is known, a twenty in a territorial collection, also the earliest known Alaska note.

Alaska was designated a district on May 17, 1884, a territory on August 24, 1912, and a state on January 3, 1959. National Bank Notes of Alaska carried no seals, for the design of the back was changed with this issue. The earlier note says "Territory of Alaska." The red seals say "District of Alaska" and later issues say neither territory nor district. The lack of a designation on Alaska nationals is one of those exceptions to all the rules.

YEARS OF ISSUE
OF CHARTER NUMBERS

Charter Numbers	Assigned During Year	Number of Banks Chartered	Charter Numbers	Assigned During Year	Number of Banks Chartered
1–179	1863	179	5241–5662	1900	422
180–682	1864	503	5663–6074	1901	412
683–1626	1865	944	6075–6566	1902	492
1627–1665	1866	39	6567–7081	1903	514
1666–1675	1867	10	7082–7541	1904	460
1676–1688	1868	13	7542–8027	1905	486
1689–1696	1869	8	8028–8489	1906	462
1697–1759	1870	63	8490–8979	1907	490
1760–1912	1871	153	8980–9302	1908	323
1913–2073	1872	161	9303–9622	1909	320
2074–2131	1873	58	9623–9913	1910	291
2132–2214	1874	83	9914–10119	1911	206
2215–2315	1875	101	10120–10305	1912	186
2316–2344	1876	29	10306–10472	1913	167
2345–2375	1877	31	10473–10672	1914	200
2376–2405	1878	30	10673–10810	1915	138
2406–2445	1879	40	10811–10932	1916	122
2446–2498	1880	53	10933–11126	1917	194
2499–2606	1881	108	11127–11282	1918	156
2607–2849	1882	243	11283–11570	1919	288
2850–3101	1883	252	11571–11903	1920	333
3102–3281	1884	180	11904–12082	1921	179
3282–3427	1885	146	12083–12287	1922	205
3428–3612	1886	184	12288–12481	1923	194
3613–3832	1887	220	12482–12615	1924	134
3833–3954	1888	122	12616–12866	1925	251
3955–4190	1889	236	12867–13022	1926	156
4191–4494	1890	304	13023–13159	1927	137
4495–4673	1891	179	13160–13269	1928	110
4674–4832	1892	159	13270–13412	1929	143
4833–4934	1893	102	13413–13516	1930	104
4935–4983	1894	49	13517–13586	1931	70
4984–5029	1895	46	13587–13654	1932	68
5030–5054	1896	25	13655–13920	1933	266
5055–5108	1897	54	13921–14317	1934	397
5109–5165	1898	57	14318–14348*	1935	31
5166–5240	1899	75			

*Banks were chartered up to this number, however banks with numbers higher than 14320 (Liberty National Bank & Trust Co. of Louisville, Ky.) did not issue any notes.

The above chart is from Arthur Friedberg's *Paper Money of the United States,* Coin and Currency Institute, Inc., 1978.

#50 — HAWAII

NAME: Hawaiian for "homeland"

NICKNAME: The Aloha State

ESTABLISHED AS TERRITORY: 1900, though it was established as the Republic of Hawaii in 1894 and was annexed by the United States in 1898.

ENTERED THE UNION: August 21, 1959

CAPITAL: Honolulu

SEAL: The great seal (see PLATE XVI) was officially designated by Act 272 of the 1859 Territorial Legislature and is based on the territorial seal. It is circular and between the outer lines are the words "State of Hawaii" at the bottom and *Ua mau ke ea o ka aina i ka pono,* meaning, "The life of the land is perpetuated in righteousness." The year 1959 just within the circle signifies the date the state government was organized. The heraldic shield in the center has a figure of King Kamehameha I on the left side of the shield and the Goddess of Liberty, holding the Hawaiian flag on the right side. Below the shield is the Phoenix surrounded by two small taro leaves, banana foliage and sprays of maidenhair fern. With color added, the seal becomes the state coat of arms.

The coat of arms of the kingdom was adopted in May, 1845. As originally designed, it was quartered with the stripes of the national banner in the first and fourth quarters and the puloulou or tabu ball and stick in the second and third. At the center of the large shield is a small shield which shows the ancient triangular flag of Hawaiian chiefs with two spears crossed. Both the puloulou and the flag on crossed spears were used to indicate tabu and a place of refuge. Over this central design was a crown. On each side was the figure of a chief in feather cloak and helmet. The one on the left, Kamanawa, is bearing a spear; the one on the right is Kameeiamoku, a Kahili. These figures, facing inwards, are believed to represent the warrior twins who supported King Kamehameha I in his endeavors to unite the islands. Below was the motto of the Kingdom, *Ua mau ke ea o ka aina i ka pono,* meaning "The life of the land is perpetuated in righteousness." Later representations show a feathered cape as a background. During the period of King Kalakaua several changes were made. The two figures were faced outwards rather than inwards. A Maltese cross was added over the crown, and the cross of an undetermined order is below the motto. The feather cape became an ermine cape, and a second crown was added over the entire coat of arms. These changes also appear in the coat of arms used by both King Kalakaua and Queen Liliuokalani on official palace invitations and on the 1883 coins. There is no evidence that these changes were ever officially approved.

COMMENTS: NOTES #50B and 50C illustrate the last two types of the Second Charter Period National Bank Notes.

Hawaii became a territory on April 30, 1900. That same year Honolulu (Charter #5550) and one other bank, Wailuku (Charter #5994) issued brownbacks, but I have never seen or heard of a brownback from the latter bank. Some fourteen brownback notes are known on Honolulu (#5550). Of course, no seals appear on Hawaii brownback notes.

We think that we can safely say that no seal of any kind was placed on any note beginning with Oklahoma. The only one with any degree of uncertainity is Juneau, Alaska (#5117), because it is still unknown to our field.

NOTE #50A:

DENOMINATION/ SERIES: Five Dollars/Brownback Series 1882

BANK/CHARTER: The First National Bank of Hawaii at Honolulu, Territory of Hawaii (#5550), Regional letter "P"

FEDERAL DATA: Serial #K30622K, signed by Lyons and Roberts

BANK DATA: Dated July 25, 1900, Plate letter "D," Bank serial #3007. This bank

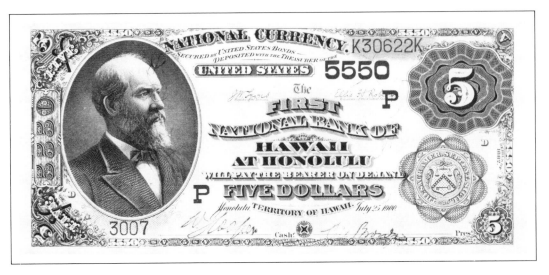

opened in 1900 and went to term. It issued all three Series 1882 and plain-backs of the 1902 Series as well as fives and tens, fifties and hundreds of both type I and II of the small-size notes. The amount of large size outstanding in 1935 was $28,770.

#50A BANK SIGNATURES: W.G. Cooper, Cashier, and Cecil Brown, President, signed in pen.

BACK: Charter number (5550)

SEAL: No seal.

#50B BANK DATA:
Dated July 25, 1900, Plate letter "K " (third plate), Bank serial #23201. Same bank as above.

BANK SIGNATURES:
Stamped signatures of (?) Peck, Cashier, and Cecil (?) Wood, President

BACK: In the center are the dates, written as follows: 1882 X 1908. The X represents a small, rather

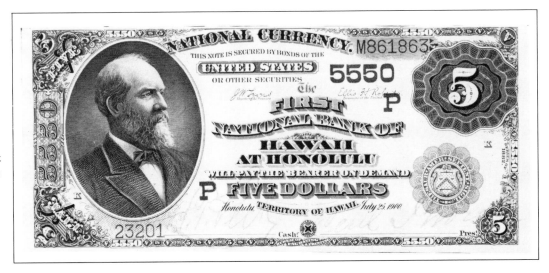

NOTE #50C:

DENOMINATION/SERIES: Five Dollars/Series 1882 Value-back

#50C BANK/CHARTER: The First National Bank of Hawaii at Honolulu, Territory of Hawaii (#5550), Regional letter "P"

United States Capitol in right. This same double-oval design appears on the date-backs as well. This is a value-back, representing the third part of the Second Charter Period, Series 1882.

#50A CONDITION: Uncirculated.

SOURCE: Purchased from L.S. Werner, N.Y.C., October 6, 1958

RARITY: Although this is a large bank, brownbacks on Hawaii are rare. Peter Huntoon records only fourteen in his first tabulation. Our note and several others will bring the number of brownback notes on Hawaii to about twenty. All are on the same bank (#5550).

NOTE #50B:

DENOMINATION/SERIES: Five Dollars/Series 1882 Date-back

BANK/CHARTER: The First National Bank of Hawaii at Honolulu, Territory of Hawaii (#5550), Regional letter "P"

#50B FEDERAL DATA: Serial #M861863–, signatures are the same as on the note above: Lyons and Roberts.

ornately-drawn x-shaped design. This we call a "date-back," as these are the dates of the second part of the Second Charter Period.

#50B SEAL: None

CONDITION: About Uncirculated, cut close on top.

SOURCE: (Record is incomplete.)

RARITY: Scarce

#50C FEDERAL DATA: Serial #T838947–, same signatures (Lyons and Roberts)

BANK DATA: Same date, Plate letter "I," Bank serial #50560. The

rest of the bank information applies as above.

BANK SIGNATURES: Stamped and faded out

BACK: Five Dollars spelled out in center, Washington in left oval and

#50C SEAL: None

CONDITION: Extra Fine, but cut deep into the border on both sides (top edge).

SOURCE: From The Numismatic Gallery, Abe Kosoff, California; Auxiliary sale (when all remaining lots were marked one grade lower in order to sell them), October 20, 1951

RARITY: Normally the value-backs are the rarest of all the different series of National Bank Notes.

DISTRICT OF COLUMBIA

NAME: Washington
NICKNAME: The Nation's Capital
NATION'S CAPITAL (OFFICIALLY):
December 1, 1800

SEAL: The seal of the District of Columbia was adopted in 1871 (PLATE XVI) and depicts a statue of Washington on a pedestal with a figure of Justice in the foreground and the Capitol in the right background. George Washington is holding a standing fasces emblem with his left hand and a sword, point to ground, in his right hand. In the lower left is an American eagle with the United States shield on its breast, three arrows in his left talon and laurel branches in

its right talon. In the center at the bottom is the date "1871" surrounded by a wreath. Justice is holding a laurel wreath in her right hand and in her left is a tablet or book that says "Constitution." At the bottom on either side of the date on banners are *Justitia* and *Omnibus* meaning "Justice for All." The first seal of the District of Columbia (similar to arms on PLATE VIII, but most like the first seal used on banknotes) shows Columbia seated with pole and liberty cap in her right hand and with a scroll or parchment, slightly rolled, in her left. This figure is seated to the left of a rather large plaque depicting the bust of George Washington. There is nothing at the bottom (see banknotes) as on the previously described seal. On the right in the background is a picture of the Capitol Building in the District of

DISTRICT OF COLUMBIA #1

DENOMINATION/SERIES: Ten Dollars/Original Series 1875 First Charter
BANK/CHARTER: The Farmers And Mechanics National Bank of Georgetown, District of Columbia (#1928)

FEDERAL DATA: Serial #D63819–, signed by Allison and Spinner

BANK DATA: Dated February 15, 1872, Plate letter "B," Bank serial #5828. This bank operated from 1872 to 1928 and issued large-size notes only: both Original and Series 1875, brownbacks and

date-backs of Series 1882, also date-backs and plain-backs of the Third Charter Period Series 1902. There remained outstanding in 1928 the amount of $83,960.

BANK SIGNATURES: Pen-signed M. Laird, Jr., Cashier, and H.M. Sweeney, President

BACK: *De Soto Discovering the Mississippi*

SEAL: This is the first seal of the district, with Washington's head on a plaque.

CONDITION:
Extra Fine

SOURCE: Purchased at auction from the Numismatic Gallery, Beverly Hills, California, October 20, 1951

RARITY: District of Columbia First Charter notes are scarce. Nine banks issued Original Series and the first four failed, then two new banks joined the others to make only seven to issue Series 1875 First Charter notes. So there could not be very many of these notes out there.

Columbia.

From the beginning of the building of the United States Capitol to its completion there were a total of nine architects who worked on it. Dr. William Thornton (1793-1802) (my maternal family name is Thornton) proposed a saucer-like dome. His talented design won over his competitors. The third architect, Benjamin Latrobe (1803-17) decided to raise Dr. Thornton's dome on a polygonal drum. Finally Charles Bullfinch had it built using a wood frame and copper sheathing. He increased its size but deemed it still not enough to dominate the enlarged Senate and House wings. In 1851 Congress voted to replace Bullfinch's dome with the American Baroque dome we see today. This was finished by Thomas U. Walter (1851-1865) with help from

two of his friends. So the polygonal dome was the one there when Abraham Lincoln delivered his inaugural address and is the one which appears on the early seal described above. The present dome is cast iron, affirming Lincoln's desire that it be a symbol to give the people courage to see the war effort to a successful conclusion.

Here, as usual, the differences between the two seals appear on the brownback series notes. None of the District of Columbia notes are rare. Thirty-one banks issued notes in the District of Columbia, two of which were in Georgetown (surrounded by the City of Washington). Nine banks issued Origial Series and the last five of these and two others issued Series 1875 notes. Thirteen banks issued brownback notes. I have not observed enough brownback

DISTRICT OF COLUMBIA #2

DENOMINATION/ SERIES: Ten Dollars/Series 1882 Brownback

BANK/CHARTER: The National Metropolitan Bank of Washington, District of Columbia (#1069)

FEDERAL DATA: Serial #E658464–, signed by Bruce and Wyman

BANK DATA: Dated March 25, 1885, Plate letter "A," Bank serial #1. This bank opened in

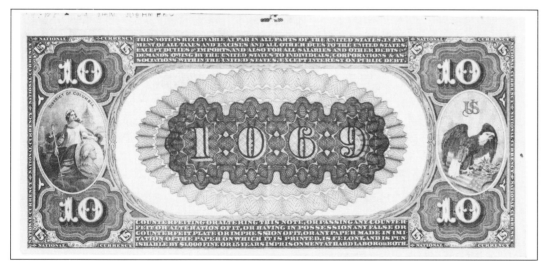

1865 and went the distance, issuing Original and Series 1875 First Charters. It then issued brownbacks Series 1882, all three issues of the Third Charter Period of 1902 and small-size tens and twenties of type I. The large-size notes outstanding in 1935 amounted to $40,313.

BANK SIGNATURES: Geo. H.B. White, Cashier, and J.M. Thompson, President

BACK: Charter number (1069)

SEAL: First seal of the district — same seal as on the last note, with the polygonally-shaped wooden dome which our Capitol wore when Abraham Lincoln was inaugurated as the sixteenth President of the United States)

CONDITION: Crisp Uncirculated

SOURCE: Purchased from L.S. Werner, New York, N.Y., August 30, 1961

RARITY: District brownbacks are scarce. Only thirteen banks issued brownbacks, and these are divided into first and second seals. John Hickman has recorded 25 brownback notes with the first seal and 38 with the second (or present) seal.

notes to hazard a guess as to which seal is the scarcer one on the notes. The total number of known notes from the District of Columbia is very small in comparison to notes from the more populous cities.

Here is another "Description of the Official Seal of the District of Columbia" as given in a government pamphlet with a drawing of the seal: "The background shows the Virginia shore with the Potomac River flowing between Virginia and the City of Washington. The statue on the pedestal represents George Washington and the female figure represents Justice blinded, with a wreath in her right hand and a tablet in her left hand on which the word 'Constitution' appears in three lines of four letters each. To the right of the female figure is the Capitol of the United

States and to the left is an eagle, a sheaf of wheat and agricultural products. In the left background is the rising sun. Beneath the figures is a wreath with the figures 1871 and on a scroll underneath are the words *Justitia Omnibus.* The District of Columbia has no colors which belong to the seal." In the Federal Building, where the affairs of the district are worked, they were using gold seals and red seals, but the "official" seal which they gave me at the executive office and autographed by Martin K. Shaller, Executive Secretary, is impressed on a letterhead and is plain (white). Another is impressed on a plain index card. The seal is now "dated" for the district no longer contains extensive farm lands.

DISTRICT OF COLUMBIA #3

DENOMINATION/ SERIES: Ten Dollars/Brownback Series 1882

BANK/CHARTER: The Farmers and Mechanics National Bank of Georgetown, District of Columbia (#1928)

FEDERAL DATA: Serial #U289037–, signed by Rosecrans and Nebeker

BANK DATA: Dated January 16, 1892, Plate letter "B," Bank serial #12111. Remainder of data is the same as for

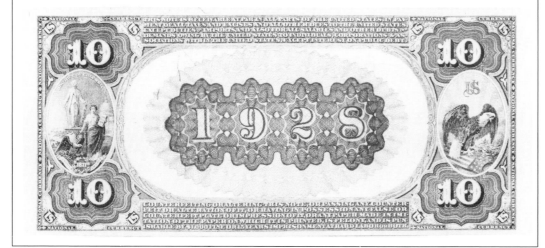

the District of Columbia #1 note.

BANK SIGNATURES: E.P. Berry, Cashier, and S. Thomas Brown, President, pen-signed.

BACK: Charter number (1928)

SEAL: This is the second seal of the district.

CONDITION: Uncirculated.

SOURCE: Purchased from the Overton Coin Company, September 16, 1954

RARITY: Same as above.

CHAPTER SEVEN
PROMOTING THE HOBBY

Realizing the need to perpetuate our field of endeavor, I would like to speak to this subject. Our hobby can only stay alive and grow as we encourage others to become interested. And this goes double for our children and all young people. Whether it is stamps, coins, paper money ("syngraphics"), antiques or art, or any other field of collecting, all will be lost unless we can generate an interest in our favorite pursuits to those coming after us.

It will be only by eduction that this goal will be attained — by showing, with pride, the joy of ownership; by sowing the seeds of desire for, and pleasure in the beauty of design, artistry, color and craftsmanship in the execution of these evidences of our past: the romance and the history of our stamps, coins and paper money. These bits of our background are part of every individual who works for a livelihood or the betterment of life. Through them, we may trace our accomplishments in the making of our beloved country and the development of our heritage.

These reasons for encouraging the young collector also apply to the investor today. Whatever your view of collecting as investment, pro or con, the investor forms a "pool" or a "holding pen," if you will. Ultimately it is the collector who will have a chance to purchase these same treasures, albeit belatedly and with some regret of the inflationary chain of transactions. The situation is rather like our living, (assets and earnings) — in reverse — "going by Washington." Like for growing plants, animals, vegetables, fruits or flowers, there is a disease, fungus or parasite, it seems, to each of our chosen paths.

But no matter how prevalent these "negatives" may be, with pluck and industry on our part, the "positives" will ultimately win out. We will overcome all backward tendencies if we will boost our "first loves" with more and better exhibits and clubs to promote our treasures through love of our heritage and history.

Let us help our hobby grow as a pleasurable pursuit, enjoying every moment of it by sharing it with others. We will join them on this romantic and fascinating trip through our history, at the same time sharing our valuable and hard-learned experience with staying ahead of inflation.

CHAPTER EIGHT
CONCLUSION

Having procrastinated several years in the writing of this book, I am now happy that I did hold off publishing the book, for several reasons. As of the beginning of 1986 most of the territorial and state issues of the National Bank Note First Charter Period and brownbacks have now become known to collectors and specialists in the field. Although notes of the territories remain the ultimate in collecting nationals, towns, cities, states and areas, especially a collector's home state or state of origin remain the most popular mode of collecting these pieces of history.

Yet to be found is the Mississippi First Charter note — three banks issued them, but thus far, these have eluded collectors. Only one bank in Alaska issued brownbacks, at the outset, but those also remain undiscovered. The term "unique" is dangerous when applied to any collectibles, but I know of only one of the following: Nevada (state) only one First Charter and one brownback note known. Only one brownback note is known on Wyoming Territory. Only one Washington Territory First Charter and one First Charter on Washington state are known at the present. I know of only two First Charter notes on Idaho Territory and two brownback notes. Only three First Charter notes are known on the entire states of Florida, Arkansas and Arizona (Territory).

In general, early banknotes of the South and West are very scarce to rare and more difficult to find in nice condition. There are only five First Charter notes known on Nebraska Territory: two ones and three twos, none of which are in fine condition.

Then we must consider the rare state notes, due to the short time span elapsing between territorial status and statehood. In addition, there is the fact that a few states upon reaching statehood dallied too long before adopting their state seals. Wyoming waited between three and four years — 1890 to 1893. Idaho's statehood was on July 3, 1890, but their seal was not adopted until March 14, 1891. Utah's statehood was on January 4, 1896, and their seal followed later, on April 3, 1896. These facts, et. al, create the possibility of territorial seals on state banknotes. This is borne out by (a) the twenty-dollar First Charter note on Ogden, #2059, and possibly #2641, Provo City, which also issued First Charter state notes, and (b) the fact that these also show the territorial seal.

For brownback notes, Idaho had seven banks that issued brownback state notes, possibly prior to statehood, and these or some of these may show territorial seals, as opposed to Utah and Wyoming, mentioned just above. Thus far I know of no Idaho state notes which show the territorial seal.

Wyoming, on the other hand, having a time lapse of three to four years' span between statehood and adoption of the state seal, has the best chance of more brownback notes' showing the territorial seal like our Albany County National Bank of Laramie City (#3615). We know the not-too-rare First Charter notes on Wyoming state — #2652, The Stock Growers National Bank of Cheyenne, which shows the territorial seal — How many of these? Perhaps a dozen and a half to two dozen. More than likely, the two banks immediately preceding the Stock Growers, #2110 and #2518, both on Laramie City, both issued First Charter Series 1875 notes, and these also show the territorial seal, as does the Stock Growers. Among the first eight banks that issued brownback notes as a state, these could all show the territorial seal, and the last five of these eight are very likely to. Beginning with #3299, Buffalo, #3416 Cheyenne, #3556 Douglas, #3615 Laramie City (the only one of these that we *know* of), as well as #3920 Rock Springs, I personally believe all FIVE of these brownback banknotes will show the territorial seal, as does #3615 Laramie City.

So, in conclusion, we know that all the rare notes have not surfaced, and that until these are actually discovered this intriguing pursuit will remain completely unresolved. Unfortunately, the bureau's proof impressions (now held by the Smithsonian) of sheets issued to each bank are inconclusive, because very few back impressions exist.

Several things must now be borne in mind. The study of the "Seals On National Bank Notes" is entirely dependent on the number of rare notes known. I am speaking here about the differences in the seals, not so much of the lack of seals. It is hard to find a reason why certain territories' notes showed no seal, even though most had seals. Some of the cases were Montana Territory (both First and Second Charter Period brownbacks), Wyoming Territory (both charter periods), Washington Territory (both periods), Oklahoma and Indian Territories (brownbacks), and Oklahoma state. New Mexico and Arizona Territories, which issued both charter period notes also did not show seals. Alaska Territory, with only one bank issuing a brownback note which is still unknown, probably did not display a seal. Even Hawaii, with only two banks issuing brownbacks, showed no seal. Perhaps a major reason was that the seal was not on hand at the bureau in time to cut into the steel engraving plates. In any case, apparently a policy change beginning with Oklahoma Territory dictated the deletion of all seals from the notes from then on.

In general, then, we must say that the only way to be sure what seal (or if a seal) was used and when, is to actually examine the notes. The best way to do this is to acquire the note, which I have attempted to do. The second best way is to study a photograph of the note, which I am attempting to provide to the serious student. With the recent acquisition of two very rare notes, the Ogden, Utah First Charter state note with the Utah territorial seal, and the Wyoming state brownback, Albany County National Bank of Laramie showing the territorial seal, I thought I had it made. I thought that all of the unknowns had come to light. But with additional research and cross-referencing for this book, I am just about certain that there are more exceptions to be found.

A few years ago, in looking through some of Amon Carter's collection, I discovered two exceptions to the customary use of the same eagles in the right and left ovals where no seal was used. Both were on First Charter notes. The first is a one-dollar Original Series on the First National Bank of Helena, Montana Territory (Charter #1649, Bank serial #2777, Plate letter "C.") A standing eagle is on the right side and in the left oval is the "squat" eagle. The second exception is a ten-dollar First Charter Series 1875 note on the First National Bank of Albuquerque, Territory of New Mexico, Charter #2614, Bank serial #6209, Plate letter "C," with the right oval showing the "squat" eagle and the left oval showing an upright or standing eagle. So we know that all the notes printed from these two plates were like these two. After seeing the first note, the Helena (the bank opened in 1866, an early date for a territorial without a seal), I thought that the bureau just grabbed any eagle which was readily available. But the second note, Albuquerque, shoots down that theory. Then, at the 1985 Paper Money Show in Memphis I saw a third First Charter Period note with different eagles. This note is a rare twenty-dollar First Charter Series 1875 note on Cheyenne, Wyoming Territory, charter #1800, from the estate of Amon Carter, Jr. It shows the normal upright eagle in the right oval, and the squat eagle in the left oval. However, I have never seen a change in eagles on any brownback note.

Regarding the territorial seal found on Wyoming and Utah state notes, very possibly the notes on other banks following in Wyoming and Utah, (as well as on Boise City [#1668], Idaho state) also show the territorial seals. After this bank's rechartering in 1887, another three or more years elapsed before the new state seal was approved in 1891. The Smithsonian has now acquired all plates and records from the Bureau of Engraving and Printing, so it is a matter of public record as to the appearance of many of these issues. My short November (1985) visit did not allow time to satisfy my curiosity concerning the brownback issues of state notes between statehood dates and adoption of the state seals. On the unknown First Charter territorial notes that showed no seal, I would expect that about 99% of them show matching eagles.

I understand there are about twenty boxes, file folder size, 8½" x 12" or larger, approximately two inches deep, filled with plate impressions of brownbacks of numerous banks. These are sheet impressions of four notes each. But I was told they are all face plate impressions. Thus it will be difficult to learn which seal appeared on a particular bank's notes. This being true, the only positive way of knowing which seal actually appeared on a specific note is to examine the note itself.

As a student I am very anxious to see more of these early notes, especially of Idaho, Wyoming, and Utah. This writer would like to hear from anyone with information of any other notes showing any other seals or differences in the seals. Please help — it will be greatly appreciated.

In hindsight now I am very glad that this book was postponed long enough to almost complete the collection, as well as to find, secure and reproduce for the book the exceptional and beautiful color work of the *State Arms of the Union*.

We know there are more enlightening discoveries out there to encourage "syngraphists" as well as to challenge many future numismatists.

Dewitt G. Prather, Publisher
1623 Lansdale Drive — Charlotte, N.C. 28205
Phone (704) 537-3962

HISTORY IN YOUR HAND

by John T. Hickman

"This bill looks strange," the merchant said,
"I'd somehow got it in my head
That all my bills had seals of green
And so I don't believe I've seen
A bill like this; the seal is brown,
And here's a name — a distant town.
It even has a different look;
I'm wondering now if I've been took."
"Don't worry, friend, that money's good,
It always was, and well it should.
Our country's bonds, then backed by gold,
When gold was cheaper, when it sold
An ounce for twenty bucks or so,
And other prices too, were low,
Backed up those notes, one hundred per,
You couldn't lose, not ever, Sir."
It started many years ago,
A Civil War, with days of woe,
Had stretched our money out of reach,
And so our problem was to teach
Our people and our bankers all
To use new money, and to call
For NATIONAL BANKS throughout the land.
The old type bank notes then were banned
And bright new Nationals proud with art
Circulated through the mart.
Each was the same, but different, too.
They all had names that even you
Would recognize; our own bank here
Got its own notes like others near.
They circulated far and wide
And spread the word of local pride.
To fuel the commerce of the nation
From Big Stone Gap to White House Station,
From Ballston Spa to Tonapah,
From Birmingham to Beaver Dam,
From Rising Sun to Six Mile Run,
From Callaway to Buzzards Bay,
They coursed like blood through human veins,
Down city streets and country lanes,
In our pockets, purses, tills
They settled up our peoples' bills.
At Kinderhook, they bought a book;

At Newport News, they paid for shoes.
A house in Memphis paid their Queens
With notes from banks in New Orleans.
An abstract fee was paid in Nampa
With notes a drummer brought from Tampa.
A Tulsa cowpoke locked in jail
Used Kansas notes to pay his bail.
They circulated up and down
The countryside, until we found
A better way, or so we thought,
To stretch our money when it bought
Too many goods in times of stress
And put the country in duress.
A Central Bank is what we need!
A place to finance and to lead,
The way to proper fiscal class!
We all salute you Carter Glass.
You gave us money quite elastic,
Even at a cost most drastic.
And so, the Fed Reserve was born
And too, in time our banks were shorn
Of all their bonds and all their notes
Used to finance wars and boats.
Gone are gold seals, brown and blue,
Soon the red seals will be too.
Numbers now instead of names,
Hard for some to learn new games;
And now that green seals are the most,
Please permit this final toast:
Here's to metals, ores and jewels,
Coal, and oil and other fuels
Here's to Farmers, Merchants, Traders,
Butchers, Drovers, Wagon laders
Here's to Citizen, Central, City
Atlas, Aetna, titles witty
Here's to local names and faces,
Mountains, streams and other places,
Battlefields, and Forts and townsites,
Broken dreams and other dam sites,
Whaling ships and Shoe and Leather,
Indian names and changing weather,
Here's to NAMES all o'er this land —
Here's to history in your hand.

(Reprinted by permission)

BIBLIOGRAPHY

Anton, William T., Jr., and Perlmutter, Morey. *The Celebrated Albert A. Grinnell Collection of United States Paper Currency: Catalogued by Barney Bluestone*. 1971.

Bureau of Engraving & Printing, c. 1900. Composite of State and Territorial Seals.

Florida, Secretary of State George Firestone. "History of the Great Seal."

Friedberg, Arthur L., and Friedberg, Ira S. *Paper Money of the United States*. 9th rev. ed. New York: Krause Publications, The Coin and Currency Institute, Inc., 1978.

Hawaii, Hawaii State Library System booklet, June, 1970.

Hickman, John T. "Nevada Banknotes Still Most Elusive." *Bank Note Reporter,* 14 (May 1986): pp. 1, 19-20.

Huntoon, Peter W. *Territorials: A Guide To U.S. Territorial National Bank Notes*. Washington, D.C.: The Society of Paper Money Collectors, Inc., 1980.

Idaho, Secretary of State. 1941-1942 report on the Seal of Idaho Territory.

Limpert, Dr. Frank A. *United States National Bank Notes: Original Series: First and Second Charter Periods*. Royal Oak, Michigan: 1953.

Maryland, Secretary of State. Maryland State pamphlet on heraldry, coats of arms, state seal.

Polito, Robert V., and Robert M. Ramsey. *National Banks of the United States: 1863-1935*. 1st ed. Lancaster, Pennsylvania: Steinmetz Coins & Currency, Inc., 1977.

Saylor, F.H. "Oregon Without A Seal of State." *Oregon Native Son,* 5, (1899) pp. 23-7, courtesy of Oregon State Library.

Shankle, George Earlie, Ph.d. *State Names, Flags, Seals, Songs, Birds, Flowers, and other Symbols*. 1st ed. New York: The H.W.Wilson Company, 1934.

Warns, M. Owen. *The Nevada "Sixteen": National Banks and Their Mining Camps*. Washington, D.C.: The Society of Paper Money Collectors, Inc., 1974.

Wilson, Vincent, Jr. *The Book of the States*. 2d rev. ed. Brookeville, Maryland: American History Research Associates, Inc., 1972.

Washington, Secretary of State Earl Coe, "AL-KI" seal, recorded May 1st, 1854 by C.H. Mason, Secretary Washington Territory.

Washington, State Library. Early Washington Territorial seals.

Wyoming, Secretary of State Thyra Thomson. Historical references on early Wyoming seals.

APPENDIX:

Additional Information on States, Seals and Symbols
and their History

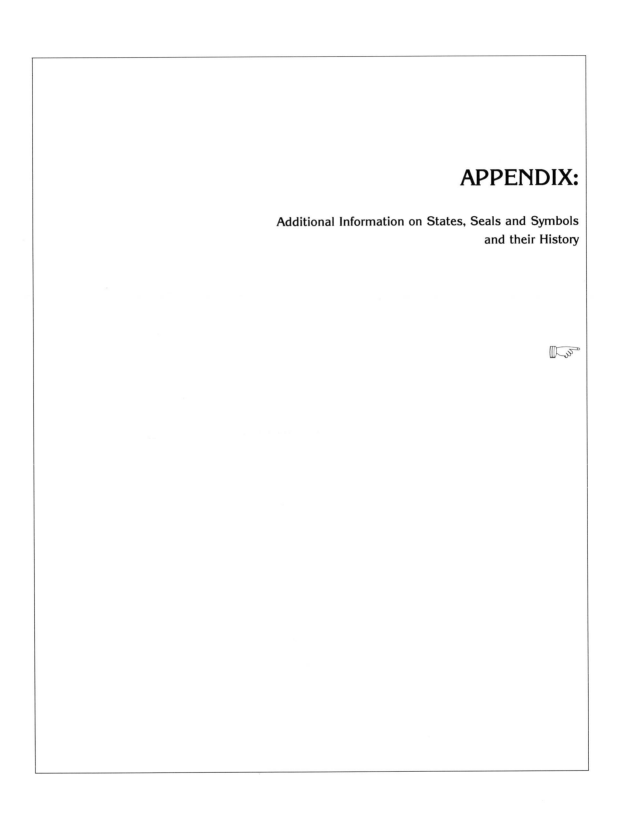

FLORIDA:

History of the Great Seal

The Territory of Florida had a seal which may be described as follows: An American eagle with outspread wings resting on a bed of clouds occupies the center of a circular field. In the right talon of the eagle are three arrows, in the left an olive branch. Above the eagle is a semi-circle of thirteen stars. Around the outer circle is the legend, "The Territory of Florida." The diameter of the seal is two inches.

The Seal of the Territory of Florida

This seal was used as the seal of the state for more than a year after Florida's admission to the Union in 1845. The Constitution of 1838, under which Florida was admitted, provided (*Art. III., sec.* 21), "There shall be a seal of the State which shall be kept by the Governor, and used by him officially, with such device as the Governor first elected may direct, and the present seal of the Territory, shall be the seal of the State, until otherwise directed by the General Assembly."

The only action in regard to the seal taken by the General Assembly in 1845, or by any subsequent legislature until 1868, was to give the Secretary of State custody of the "great seal" and to make it the seal of his office. (*Acts,* 1845, ch. 1, secs. 2, 4). The Secretary of State retained custody of the seal under this act until 1868, since which year he has been designed in the Constitution as "custodian of the Great Seal of the State" (*Constitution of* 1868, *Art.* VII., *sec.* 2; *Constitution of* 1885, *Art.* IV., *sec.* 21).

Governor William D. Moseley evidently exercised his constitutional prerogative as the Governor first elected, and ordered a new seal made, for late in December, 1846, the first Great Seal of the State of Florida was delivered to the Secretary of State. The actual designer of the seal, whether Moseley or some person appointed by him, is not known, nor is a contemporary description of it available. The following description is from impressions

on official documents.

An outline map of Florida occupies the top and right of a circular field. On an island in the lower left are one large and three small palm trees and an oak tree, under which sits a female figure with one hand outstretched to the Gulf of Mexico and the other holding a pike upon which rests a liberty cap. About her are casks and boxes and a variety of flowering shrubs. On the water are four ships — a

Florida's First State Seal

three-masted square rigger under full sail, another under jibs and topsails, a schooner, and a fishing smack. The legend around the outer rim is "State of Florida — In God is Our Trust." The diameter of the seal is two and three-fourths inches.

This seal was in use as late as 1861 and probably until supplanted by the present seal of Florida in 1868. The Constitution of 1861 simply stated (*Art.* III, *sec.* 12), "There shall be a seal of the State, which shall be kept by the Governor, and used by him officially," while the Constitution of 1865 provided (*Art.* III, *sec.* 13), "The State Seal last heretofore used, (until altered by the General Assembly,) shall continue to be the Great Seal of the State, and shall be kept by the Governor for the time being, and used by him officially." It does not appear that the General Assembly took any action on the subject.

The Constitution of 1868 (*Art.* 16, *sec.* 20) gave the following directive: "The Legislature shall, at the first session, adopt a seal for the State, and such seal shall be the size of the American silver dollar, but said seal shall not again be changed after its adoption by the Legislature." In compliance with this mandate, the Legislature of 1868 adopted a joint resolution, approved by Governor Harrison Reed on August 6, which provided: "That a Seal of the size of the American silver dollar having in the centre thereof a view of the sun's rays over a highland in the distance, a cocoa tree, a steamboat on water, and an Indian female scattering flowers in the foreground, encircled by the words, 'Great Seal of the State of Florida: In God We Trust,' be and the same is hereby adopted as the Great Seal of the State of Florida."

The Constitution of 1885, under which Florida still operates, retained the seal of 1868 in the following words (*Art.* XVI, *sec.* 12), "The present Seal of the State shall be and remains the Seal of the State of Florida."

The Seal of Today

Reprinted from State of Florida pamphlet.

OREGON:

Oregon Without a Seal of State

No. 1.

No. 2.

The caption to this article may be looked upon as one not worthy of belief; still, investigation in the premises will convince doubters that the statement is true.

Oregon has had three kinds of government from 1843 to the present time: provisional, territorial and state. During the life of each a seal was used, and under the last two forms acts were passed descriptive of the official seal. It will be the purpose of this article to briefly outline the evolution of the seal and its descriptions. In doing so, dates cannot be given at all times, as documentary evidence of action is lacking; evidence of use, however, will substantiate assertions made.

There is no record obtainable showing that the provisional government ever prescribed the form of or adopted an official seal by any act of its legislature. Those who trust to memory, and others writing upon the subject, state that Hamilton Campbell made in 1846 what is known as the "salmon seal" (No. 1), which was used by Governor Abernethy as an official seal until it was superseded by a territorial one. This seal contained two objects, wheat and salmon, which have since made famous the word above them. Before its use began, it is said that Colonel Joe Meek, the sheriff of the commonwealth, made the service of official documents *impressive* by accompanying their delivery with words something like "d—, d—, dashes!" Be this true or false, the older pioneers will admit that it is not an unlikely statement, for a recall to mind of many incidents in the colonel's career will be evidence that such was at times just his style of expression.

On August 14, 1848, the act creating Oregon a territory was passed, and the author of the bill therefor, Judge J. Quinn Thornton, who was in Washington in the interests of the provisional government, had a territorial seal made (No. 2), which he sent to Governor Lane in 1849, but he declined to accept it. In 1850, Mr. Thornton tendered it to Governor Gaines, and it was by him adopted and afterwards used as the seal of the territory. The territorial legislature did not, however, consider the matter until January 18, 1854, when by act it was made the seal of the territory. Its description is as follows:

"In the center, a shield, two compartments. Lower compartment — in the foreground, a plow; in the

distance mountains. In the upper compartment — a ship under full sail. The crest, a beaver. The sinister supporter — an Indian with bow and arrows, and a mantle of skins over his shoulder. The dexter supporter, an eagle, with wings displayed. The motto — *alis volat propriis* — "I fly with my own wings". Field of the lower compartment, argent; of the upper blue."

The seal was made and was in use for several years before this description became a law, and no doubt its impression was before those who framed the act. But a glance at No. 2, which is a good fac-simile of the seal adopted as stated, does not show a dividing line on the shield which makes two compartments therein, nor does the description specify in what manner the division is to be made. The perspective would indicate as much, though, and it is presumed that the division was left to the sense of imagination. It was directed that it "be deposited and recorded in the office of the secretary, to remain a public record," but, so far as can be ascertained, this was never done. In the description no provision is made for a legend; the seal bears — "Seal of the Territory of Oregon." Subsequently an attempt at facsimile making of

No. 3.

the territorial seal was made (No. 3), for imprint upon matter printed "by authority." If the reader will notice, this attempt falls far short of near approach in the reproduction of the original design, and that the plow is left out altogether. A study of the territorial seal will show progressive ideas as well as an inclination to retrograde. The motto is a sentiment most true, for Oregon has flown so far by her own wings to prominence noticeable, and can wing her way to heights which only the great can reach, if her people will give heed to the upbuilding of the many and varied industries which can be conducted with profit within its borders. No objection can be made to the beaver, as it commemorates our earliest home industry, the coining of beaver money; nor to the ship, a prospective of the forest of masts that come to our harbors for articles of export; nor to the mountains, as the beauties of the snow-capped sentinels on every hand are unsurpassed for grandeur in the world. But the warrior, pictured as if he had on a pair of gun boots, a creature so much in evidence for treachery, cruelty and murder, to say the

No. 4.

least, could be improved upon by substitution of more fitting object. Leave the eagle as it is, put the sheaves of wheat where the redskin stands, and paint a royal chinook over the plow, and the seal would be a more appropriate one for a state seal than our present one.

By 1857 the husbandman among the pioneers had been crowded out in the management of affairs of state by an influx of politicians, and the mistakes in seal-making were much greater than during territorial infancy. The prophetic vision of the real builders of Oregon was largely disregarded, and supplanted by party creeds and desire to boast over departing force of other power, and the seal of state is an index of the ideas of the newer element.

In 1856 congress passed an enabling act, by virtue of which a constitutional convention was held in 1857. This convention adopted a seal of state to be as follows:

"An escutcheon, supported by thirty-three stars, and divided by an ordinary, with the inscription, 'The Union.' In chief, — mountains, — an elk with branching antlers, a wagon, the Pacific ocean, on which a British man-of-war departing, an American steamer arriving. The second, — quartering with a sheaf, plow, and pick-axe. Crest, — the American eagle. Legend, — State of Oregon."

No. 5.

It was further provided by the laws that "The secretary shall be required to procure the seal described in the preceding section, and draw his warrant on the treasurer therefor."

The act of 1856, the convention of 1857, and the election and inauguration of state officials in 1858, sadly

mixed affairs, for Oregon was not admitted to statehood until February 14, 1859, and until June 2 of the latter year the territorial seal was used.

At this time a seal was received which has since been used as the seal of the state. In this pretended seal will be found the faults enumerated in illustration No. 8. Before the receipt of this seal, and almost immediately following the convention of 1857, a fac-simile of the seal was procured (No. 4). It was enclosed in a shield outline, has 36 stars instead of 33, an extra sheaf and a rake thrown in, as well as a date, 1857. Soon after this a second (No. 5) was obtained. It shows 35 stars, together with the extras of its predecessor. About the same time two others, one (No. 6), and the other twice its size, were secured. These show 38 stars and retain the extras of former ones.

After the state was admitted, some one discovered a mistake in the fac-similes in hand, and ordered two other fac-similes, with the date, 1859, on them. One of them (No. 7) has the faults of No. 5, the other is the same as No. 6, except the change in date. These did not supplant former ones, only an addition to the collection.

Some years elapsed and one of our state printers was turning the pages of Webster's dictionary, and found therein half-tone engravings of the impressions of the seals of the various states, Oregon's being among them. It did not look familiar to him, and he went to the office of the secretary of state, got an impression of the supposed seal of state, found such different from his fac-similes in hand, and ordered a new one (No. 8) made. In this the eagle looks in the opposite direction; has "Seal of the" prefixed to the legend, "State of Oregon"; 32 stars instead of 33; a setting sun which almost crowds out the entering steamer and the date, 1859. Make the prefix read "The seal of the," and it is a fair copy of the seal in the office of the secretary. This fac-simile did not do away with the older ones, for today all of them are being used as the state seal on documents printed "by authority." Any one

No. 6.

holding a commission as a notary, etc., will find the 38-star 1857 fac-simile displayed in the head lines, and when compared with the impression below, will find that they are not alike. The supreme court seal shows the escutcheon and objects therein of No. 8, but is supported by only 31 stars, 14 on one side and 17 on the other. The seal of the adjutant-general has 10 stars on one side and 11 on the other, 21 in all; the wagon and elk are left out, and the setting sun is extra conspicuous. The seals used by other officials have not been seen, but it is more than likely that their make-up will swell the list of carelessness in the execution of the seal of state as it should be.

On the title page of what is commonly termed "Deady's Code" can be seen another fac-simile. It is the same in form as No. 6, except as to date, which is left off, and as to the territorial motto which appears over it. Compare this fac-simile with the description of the state seal, found on page 496 of such book, and note differences.

No. 7.

On the east and west wings of the state capitol, equally faulty fac-similes are placed, and the stone which Oregon contributed toward the building of the monument erected at the national capitol, in memory of Washington, is not as it should be, in commemoration of a man "who never told a lie." On this slab is found an emblem purporting to be a facsimile of our seal of state. It has in the upper compartment the extra setting sun of No. 8, and in the lower the extra sheaf and rake of No. 6, and the escutcheon is supported by only 30 stars. The next time an Oregonian tells the story of the "hatchet" he ought to be struck with one.

In Bancroft's history of Oregon can be found an imprint of what is said to be a fac-simile of our state seal. The author might well be ashamed of it, not only because of the work of execution, but for the mistakes. It has the extra to the legend; not enough stars, and the objects within the escutcheon are a mixture of all the faults found in the fac-similes heretofore described. It has been said that such history contains many inaccuracies. This is one. The charter plates, which the Grand Cabin issues to subordinate Cabins, have in the display heading the 38-star 1857 fac-simile of the larger size, and may be so used because it is a part of our pioneer history. Our great daily adopted in its infancy a part of the fac-simile of the 1857 seal, and on all the bronze-lock attachments on the doors in its grand building it can be found. These fixtures were made in the East, and it was a cold day at the time

of casting, for summer's sheaf is wanting, and snow shovel takes the place of pick-axe.

In the last fac-simile (No. 9) will be found all that the law provides for the seal of state. Compare it with No. 8, which is a fair copy of the one in the office of the secretary of state, and draw your own conclusions.

The act which describes the seal says that it "shall be," etc., and the instructions to the secretary, in relation to the securing of a state seal, are just as mandatory. A something else does not, cannot carry out such mandate. Article V, section 18, of the constitution says: "All

No. 8.

commissions shall issue in the name of the state, shall be signed by the governor, sealed with the seal of the state, and attested by the secretary of state."

No. 9.

We have no state seal and never had one, only a pretended one. What are you going to do about it? We would respectfully suggest that a state seal be secured which will meet all requirements of the law in relation thereto. It would not be amiss if a new act was passed providing that the state seal should have objects thereon indicative of the days of the "prairie schooner," coupled with the pioneer's vision of what Oregon is and can become; and that all past efforts, together with fac-similes shown, be turned over to keepers of historical relics and placed in the curio department.

F.H.S.

SOURCE: OREGON NATIVE SON
Volume V, Number 1, May 1899-Apr. 1900
Courtesy of Oregon State Library

186

WASHINGTON:

The territorial seal shown on page 143 of this book is a reproduction of the first impression of the Washington territorial seal as recorded by Charles H. Mason, Territorial Secretary, which is now on file in the office of the Secretary of State in Olympia, published by Secretary of State Earl Coe. It is described as follows:

Lt. J.K. Duntan of Governor Stevens' surveying expedition proposed the design, which includes a log cabin and an immigrant wagon with a fir forest in the background on one side, and on the other, "a sheet of water" being traversed by a steamer and sailing vessel, a city in perspective, with the Goddess of Hope and an anchor in the center. The female figure is pointing upward, indicating the word *AL-KI*, meaning "Bye and Bye," now the state motto of Washington.

THE DESIGN was selected from half a dozen pencil sketches made by Jack E. Moody, illustrator for the Department of State in Olympia. In preparing commemorative material for distribution by the department he discovered several versions of the territorial seal existed, owing to lack of facilities for accurate reproduction in the 1850's. As different artists copied the first one, reproduced exact size at the top, the Goddess of Hope's figure changed in posture, face and degree of plumpness. Lieut. J. K. Duncan of Gov. Isaac Stevens' survey party made the original, filed May 1, 1854 by Territorial Secretary Charles H. Mason. The middle seal appeared in 1857 in a book written by James G. Swan when he was Stevens' private secretary in Washington, D. C. The lower one was published in Edmond L. Meany's history of the state.

Information made available by the Washington State Library, Olympia, Washington.

IDAHO:

The Seal of Idaho Territory

No official record remains of the adoption of the first Idaho seal in 1863. Silas D. Cochran, clerk in the office of Secretary Daniels, told Donaldson, author of "Idaho of Yesterday" that he drew the design, admittedly patterned after the seal of the State of Oregon. It is described as follows:

"An eagle with outspread wings holding the point of a shield in its beak; a rising sun in the center point beneath the eagle and over a chain of mountains. Men were working in the ravines; through the fields below ran a stream, over which an immigrant train was passing. Stars of a number equal to the number of states were placed around the rim. At the bottom of the shield were the words, 'The Union'; around the border 'Seal of the Territory of Idaho'; and at the bottom the date 1863." (Bancroft)

In 1866 the Governor was Caleb Lyon who claimed to have designed the seal of the State of California. It was he, doubtless, who inspired the House to adopt a resolution, which was approved January 11, 1866, requesting the governor "to design, adopt, and engrave an appropriate seal for the Territory of Idaho, as the one now in use is a very imperfect imitation of the Oregon seal." The Governor's description of his handiwork follows:

"The Coat of Arms of Idaho
Shield
"A view of the Shoshone River, with the mountains of Owyhee at the left and a distant view of the mountains of Bannack on the right, with a new moon in the sky and a steamer on the river."

Supporters
"Liberty with her sword at the right, and Peace with her palm branches on the left."

Crest
"An elk's head to the neck with full antlers."

Motto
"Salva. 'Welcome to the miner'. 'Welcome to the farmer'. 'Welcome to the merchant'."

Governor Lyon's drawing of the "coat of arms" is not known to be in Idaho, but the seal based upon it has quite a history. It was manufactured in San Francisco and was intended to be available for Secretary Howlett to use in attesting the laws and journals of the fourth session. The secretary, however, was not satisfied with the seal and sent it back to the maker for correction, as appears in the letter which Howlett wrote to Secretary Seward when transmitting the legislative proceedings of that session to Washington for approval and payment of cost of publication. He wrote:

"Sir: I have the honor to transmit by today's mail to your address one copy each laws and journals of the fourth session of our Territorial legislature, which would have been transmitted sooner, but not having a copy of the old seal to print from (Gilson the absconder had doubtless left it in San Francisco), and as the third session of our legislative assembly had adopted a new seal, I sent the design by Marshall Alvord to be engraved and returned immediately together with copies ("cuts") for printing, which were a long time in reaching us, and when received were found to be incorrect, consequently had to be returned to San Francisco for correction. But to prevent further delay in getting out the laws I had space left and have impressed them (by hand) with the old seal". (No doubt only a few copies; the copy now in the law library has no seal.)

Whether the seal was faithful to Lyon's design or not it possessed extraordinary features. Studied without reference to Lyon's description it appears as follows:

A shield bearing in the distance a range of snowy mountains with a deep gap from which a river proceeds widening into the foreground; over the mountains a half moon and also, in close juxtaposition, a sun, making the scene one of light; on the river a steamboat. Above the shield the head and antler of an elk with extremely long white face and with scrolls on either side of the face; on each side of the shield a woman wearing a cap, the one of the left in shortened dress and with a wisp of grain in her right hand and a spear, which rests in fasces, in her left. Below the shield the Latin word "Salve," and encircling the whole, the words "Seal of the Territory of Idaho," with a six-point star at the bottom separating the first and last words of the phrase.

Several objects which look like heavenly bodies but which may be mere blemishes on the engraving appear scattered over the design as a whole. The female figure on the left we learn from Governor Lyon's description represents Peace, the object in her hand being really a palm branch; the one on the right represents Liberty.

It would seem that little, if any, change was made when Secretary Howlett returned the seal to San Francisco for correction. Edward J. Curtis, Secretary from 1869 to 1878, used the seal for the laws of four sessions and then, in 1877, reverted to the 1863 seal. One wonders if this could have been the result of the political disorder of the time. Governor Brayman and Curtis did not get along well together. The latter finally lost his job through the stubborn efforts of the old governor. May it not have happened that in the struggle the governor aided and abetted a raid to steal the seal in order to discommode his hated neighbor by depriving him of the chief symbol of his office? However this may be a seal does not appear to have been lying around the Secretary's office, for Sidebotham, who succeeded Curtis, did not use any seal to attest the laws of 1879.

When the next legislative assembly met Idaho had another secretary, T. F. Singiser, who either could not locate or did not like the seal with the horse's head adorned with antlers and the moon shining by day. On the 1881 laws he used a seal, which we shall call the "new" seal, exhibiting the following modifications of the seal used from 1869 to 1875:

1. The lettering is changed.
2. The elk's face is lifted and darkened.
3. The women are redesigned, their caps removed, and they are given a meadow to stand in.
4. The scrolls are completely refashioned.
5. The picture in the shield is revised by eliminating the boat on the river and the sun in the sky. The moon's position is shifted and the sky and landscape are darkened to be consistent with night. Mountains and river are changed.

Even here at last, however, the seal could not rest secure. Singiser himself in 1883 employed the bald-faced-horse-with-antlers seal. Secretary "Alphabetical" Pride in 1885 preferred the new seal, while E. J. Curtis, who was again Secretary for the remainder of the territorial period, played fair with everybody by using the earlier version in 1887 and the new one in 1889.

Further research is needed to disclose the reason for the unending battle of the seals. But may it not be symbolic of the contrariness which has characterized so much of Idaho's political history? We have a tradition of independence and our representatives have often been among the insurgents of Washington. In the territorial period our delegates were on the minority side in the House of Representatives during sixteen out of the twenty seven years. They were of the same political party as the Presidents only three years and four months of that time. Throughout statehood our senators and representatives have often opposed the policies of the Presidents. Idaho presents a good claim to be the original range of the "Sons of the Wild Jackass."

From 26th Biennial Report of Secretary of State of Idaho, 1941-1942.

WYOMING:

Seals of the Territory of Wyoming
1869-1890

The first Seal of Wyoming Territory was designed by Wyoming's first Governor, John A. Campbell, who issued a proclamation on May 19, 1869, ordering its adoption. This seal, as seen at the left, was used until another was adopted by the 1869 Legislative Assembly.

The Proclamation described the seal as follows:

Proclamation Providing for a Territorial Seal

A mountain with locomotive and train of cars crossing over its summit. Near the summit a spring of water, from which flow(s) two streams, one to the east, and one to the west. In foreground at base of the mountain, a shovel and pick-ax, shepherd's crook and a plow, grouped, — all engraved on a shield running from left to right. On each side and underneath the shield, the motto "Let us have Peace." Over the mountain the figures "1868." Crest, an elks head surmounting fasces. The whole surrounded by a double circle, with the words, "Wyoming Territory," "Great Seal."

Ordered that the above be the Great Seal of Wyoming Territory, until another is adopted by the Legislature.

The diameter of the Seal, from the outer circle, was two and three-quarter inches.

The Seal adopted by the Legislative Assembly, December 9, 1869, was, with some minor changes, in accordance with a design submitted by Governor Campbell.

The Legislative Act described the seal as follows:

That the Seal of the Territory of Wyoming shall be of the following design, namely: A Norman shield, on the

upper half of which is emblazoned a mountain scene, with a railroad train, the sun appearing above the horizon, the figures "1868" below the middle point of the top of the shield. On the first quarter below, on a white ground, a plow, a pick, a shovel, and a shepherd's crook; on the next quarter, namely: the lower point of the shield, on a red ground, an arm up-holding a drawn sword; the shield to be surmounted by the inscription, "Cedant Arma Toga,"[a] and the entire design surrounded by the words, "Territory of Wyoming, great seal."

On March 10, 1882, the Legislative Assembly amended the 1869 Act correcting the error in the Latin quotation from "Cedant Arma Toga" to "Cedant Arma Togae," also the year 1868 was changed to 1869. These were the only changes by law, but when struck the Norman shield was embellished as seen in the accompanying print. This seal was used until the First State Legislature adopted a new seal for the State.

With the admission of the State into the Union, our lawmakers saw fit for Wyoming to adopt a State Seal, to differ from the Territorial Seal.

On January 10, 1891, the first State Legislature passed

---

[a]"Let arms yield to the gown, or, Let military authority give way to civil power."

The diameter for the 1869 seal, from outer circle, was two and three-quarter inches; the 1882 seal was two and one-half inches.

*Judging from the criticisms in the Cheyenne Daily Sun March 5, 1891, the new State Seal was not very popular. Twelve designs were submitted to the First State Legislature. The one selected was designed by Mr. Buechner, Representative from Laramie County. The selected seal which left the House with the enrolled act for the Governor to sign never reached him; this seal was substituted while on its way to the Governor's office. The seal was struck and turned over to the Secretary of State about March 1, 1891; the fact that this was not the selected design was then discovered, for the woman in the selected seal wore a flowing robe, while the woman in the substituted seal was in the nude — see seal next page. Mr. Buechner investigated the matter, and on March 8, 1891, found the original design, which was quite different from the one which had been submitted. It is doubtful this seal was ever used, as it is evident from official papers in the vault of the Secretary of State, the Territorial seal was used until the Second State Legislature, 1893, convened and provided for a new State Seal.

an act providing for a State Seal.*

An Act providing for the Great Seal of the State of Wyoming, and describing the same.

SECTION 1. There shall be a great seal of the State of Wyoming, which shall be of the following design, namely: A circle two and one-fourth inches in diameter, upon the half of which is emblazoned a landscape, representing in the centre, a valley, through which flows a stream, upon the banks of which cattle are grazing and a man plowing; to the right of said valley, an oil derrick, and tank; to the left of said valley, a range of mountains, upon the slope of which said mountains is represented mining works. Said landscape is surrounded by a ribbon scroll reaching from both sides of said landscape up to the top centre of said landscape, upon which rests a platform upon the outer edge of which is engraved the words, "Equal Rights." Upon said platform stands the figure of a woman, with right arm uplifted, pointing to a five pointed star, within which are engraved the figures "44". From the said uplifted arm hangs a broken chain. To the left of said platform are engraved the figures, "1869". To the right of said platform are engraved the figures, "1890." Entirely surrounding the said circle is a plain band three-eighth of an inch in breadth upon the upper half of which are engraved the words, "Great Seal," and upon the lower half, the words, "State of Wyoming" is letters three-sixteenth of an inch high. A fac-simile of the above described seal is here represented, and is hereby made a part of this act.

Sec. 2. All acts and parts of acts in conflict with this act are hereby repealed.

Sec. 3. This shall take effect and be in force from and after its passage.

The first State Seal, the act for which was passed January 10, 1891, having met with so much disapproval was doomed to be discarded. The Second State Legislature On February 8, 1893 passed an Act providing for a new State Seal, which is shown above.

An Act providing for the Great Seal of the State of Wyoming, and describing the same.

SECTION 1. There shall be a great seal of the State of Wyoming, which shall be of the following design, viz.: A circle two and one-fourth inches in diameter, on the outer rim or edge of which shall be engraven the words "Great Seal of the State of Wyoming", and the design shall conform substantially to the following description: A pedestal showing on the front thereof an eagle resting upon a shield, said shield to have engraven thereon a star and the figures "44", being the number of Wyoming in the order of admission to statehood. Standing upon the pedestal shall be a draped figure of a woman, modeled after the statute of the "Victory of the Louvre," from whose wrists shall hang links of a broken chain, and holding in right hand a staff, from the top of which shall float a banner with the words, "Equal Rights," thereon, all suggesting the political position of woman in this State. On either side of the pedestal, and standing at the base thereof, shall be male figures typifying the livestock and mining industries of Wyoming. Behind the pedestal, and in the background, shall be two pillars, each supporting a lighted lamp, signifying the light of knowledge. Around each pillar shall be a scroll with the following words thereon: On the right of the central figure the words "Live Stock" and "Grain", and on the left the words "Mines" and "Oil". At the base of the pedestal, and in front shall appear the figures "1869-1890," the former date signifying the organization of the Territory of Wyoming, and the latter the date of its admission to statehood. A fac-simile of the above described seal is here represented, and is hereby made a part of this act.

Sec. 2. All acts and parts of acts in conflict with this act are hereby repealed.

Sec. 3. This act shall take effect and be in force from and after its passage.

APPROVED February 8, 1893.

The 1921 Legislature amended the Act of 1893 which provided for and defined a new State Seal. The only changes incurred by this amendment is the size of the Seal, the diameter to the inner circle was reduced from two and one-fourth inches to one and one-half inches.

SOURCE: WYOMING BLUE BOOK
Edited by Virginia Trenholm
in three volumes.
(Wyoming State Archives, Historical and Museums Dept. 1974)
This page is from Volume II.

ARIZONA:

The seal below, a reproduction of the first territorial seal of Arizona, is from the Spinner Collection of Seals, as shown in the book by Dr. Frank Alvin Limpert, *United States National Bank Notes, Original Series, First and Second Charter Periods,* 1st ed., Royal Oak, Michigan, 1953.

Dr. Limpert comments that Spinner would have his daughter write letters to state and territorial governors requesting official seals, which were more than likely used then as models for the design of the backs of National Bank Notes.

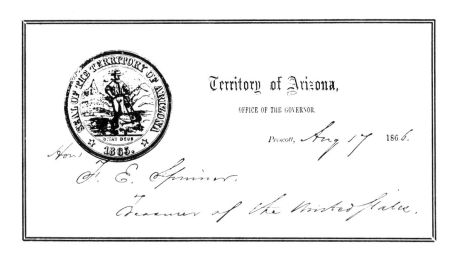

The reproduction at left is an example of a feat of modern camera technology plus the work of a highly-skilled photographic craftsman. The original is an embossed impression of the third territorial seal, the seal which was actually used officially in Arizona around 1900. The seal is impressed on a yellow piece of paper, and no ink is in the seal area at all. We are proud to display this beautiful representation of a beautiful seal.

HAWAII:

State Seal

The Great Seal was officially designated by Act 272 of the 1959 Territorial Legislature and is based on the Territorial Seal. It is circular and between the outer lines are the words: "State of Hawaii Ua mau ke ea o ka aina i ka pono". The year 1959 just within the circle signifies the date the State government was organized. The heraldic shield in the center has a figure of King Kamehameha I on the right side and the Goddess of Liberty, holding the Hawaiian flag, on the left side. Below the shield is the Phoenix surrounded by taro leaves, banana foliage and sprays of maidenhair fern. With color added, the seal becomes the STATE coat of arms.

Seal, Territory and Republic

The Great Seal of the Territory of Hawaii was the same as the seal of the State except that it had "Territory of Hawaii" at the top, and the year "1900" signifying the year the Territorial Government was officially organized, within the circle. The seal of the Republic had "Republic of Hawaii" at the top and "MDCCCXCIV" within the circle. The year 1894 signified the date the Republic was established.

Coat of Arms and Seal, Kingdom of Hawaii

The coat of arms of the Kingdom was adopted in May 1845. As originally designed, it was quartered, with the stripes of the national banner in the first and fourth quarters, and the puloulou or tabu ball and stick in the second and third. At the center was the ancient triangular flag of Hawaiian chiefs, with two spears crossed. Both the puloulou and the flag on crossed spears were used to indicate tabu and a place of refuge. Over this central design was a crown. On each side was the figure of a chief in feather cloak and helmet, the one on the left, Kamanawa, bearing a spear; the one on the right, Kameeiamoku, a kahili. These figures, facing inwards, are believed to

represent the warrior twins who supported King Kamehameha I in his endeavors to unite the islands. Below was the motto of the Kingdom, "Ua mau ke ea o ka aina i ka pono". Later representations show a feather cape as a background. During the period of King Kalakaua several changes were made. The two figures were faced out rather than in. A Maltese cross was added over the crown, and the cross of an undetermined order below the motto. The feather cape became an ermine cape, and a second crown was added over all. There is no evidence that these changes were ever officially approved. However, they appear in the coat of arms used by both King Kalakaua and Queen Liliuokalani on official Palace invitations and on the 1883 coins.

State Motto

"Ua mau ke ea o ka aina i ka pono". This motto was given to the Kingdom by King Kamehameha III at the time sovereignty and the flag was restored by the British in 1843. It was made the official motto of the State of Hawaii by Joint Resolution 4, 30th Territorial Legislature, May 1, 1959. The official translation is "The life of the land is perpetuated in righteousness".

State Bird

The Nene or Hawaiian Goose (Branta sandvicensis) was adopted as the bird emblematic of the Territory of Hawaii by House Concurrent Resolution 52, 29th Territorial Legislature, May 7, 1957. It continues as the official bird of the State of Hawaii since actions of the Territorial Legislature continue in force until superseded by a State law.

Reprinted from Hawaii State Library System booklet, June, 1970.

STATE	ENTERED UNION Date	No.	CAPITAL	AREA Sq. Mi.	Rank	POPULATION 1980	Rank	FLOWER	BIRD	TREE
Alabama	12/14/1819	22	Montgomery	51,609	29	3,444,165	21	Camellia	Yellowhammer	Southern Pine
Alaska	1/ 3/1959	49	Juneau	586,400	1	302,173	50	Forget-me-not	Willow Ptarmigan	Sitka Spruce
Arizona	2/14/1912	48	Phoenix	113,909	6	1,772,482	33	Saguaro	Cactus Wren	Paloverde
Arkansas	6/15/1836	25	Little Rock	53,104	27	2,286,419	32	Apple Blossom	Mockingbird	Pine
California	9/ 9/1850	31	Sacramento	158,693	3	23,668,562	1	California Poppy	Valley Quail	Redwood
Colorado	8/ 1/1876	38	Denver	104,247	8	2,889,964	30	Columbine	Lark Bunting	Colorado Blue Spruce
Connecticut	1/ 9/1788	5	Hartford	5,009	48	3,107,576	24	Mountain Laurel	American Robin	White Oak
Delaware	12/ 7/1787	1	Dover	2,057	49	594,338	46	Peach Blossom	Blue Hen Chicken	American Holly
Florida	3/ 3/1845	27	Tallahassee	58,560	22	9,746,421	9	Orange Blossom	Mockingbird	Sabal Palm
Georgia	1/ 2/1788	4	Atlanta	58,876	21	5,463,087	15	Cherokee Rose	Brown Thrasher	Live Oak
Hawaii	8/21/1959	50	Honolulu	6,424	47	964,691	40	Hibiscus	Hawaiian Goose	Kukui
Idaho	7/ 3/1890	43	Boise	83,557	13	944,038	42	Lewis Mock Orange	Mountain Bluebird	Western White Pine
Illinois	12/ 3/1818	21	Springfield	56,400	24	11,427,414	5	Native Violet	Cardinal	Bur Oak
Indiana	12/11/1816	19	Indianapolis	36,291	38	5,490,260	11	Peony	Cardinal	Tulip
Iowa	12/28/1846	29	Des Moines	56,290	25	2,913,808	25	Wild Rose	Eastern Goldfinch	Oak
Kansas	1/29/1861	34	Topeka	82,264	14	2,364,236	28	Sunflower	Western Meadow Lark	Cottonwood
Kentucky	6/ 1/1792	15	Frankfort	40,395	37	3,660,257	23	Goldenrod	Cardinal	Tuliptree
Louisiana	4/30/1812	18	Baton Rouge	48,523	31	4,206,098	20	Southern Magnolia	Eastern Brown Pelican	Bald Cypress
Maine	3/15/1820	23	Augusta	33,215	39	1,125,030	38	Pine Cone	Chickadee	Eastern White Pine
Maryland	4/28/1788	7	Annapolis	10,577	42	4,216,941	18	Black-Eyed Susan	Baltimore Oriole	White Oak
Massachusetts	2/ 6/1788	6	Boston	8,257	45	5,737,081	10	Mayflower	Chickadee	American Elm
Michigan	1/26/1837	26	Lansing	58,216	23	9,262,070	7	Apple Blossom	Robin	White Pine
Minnesota	5/11/1858	32	St. Paul	84,068	12	4,075,970	19	Showy Lady's-slipper	Loon	Red Pine
Mississippi	12/10/1817	20	Jackson	47,716	32	2,520,631	29	Magnolia	Mockingbird	Magnolia
Missouri	8/10/1821	24	Jefferson City	69,686	19	4,916,759	13	Hawthorn	Eastern Bluebird	Dogwood

Reprinted by permission. Information presented on pp. 108-11, *The Book of the States* by Vincent Wilson, Jr. The American History Research Associates, Inc., 1972. Days and months of entry to the Union and District of Columbia data, as well as update of census figures and rankings are additions of the author.

STATE	ENTERED UNION Date	ENTERED UNION No.	CAPITAL	AREA Sq. Mi.	AREA Rank	POPULATION 1980	POPULATION Rank	FLOWER	BIRD	TREE
Montana	11/ 8/1889	41	Helena	147,138	4	786,690	43	Bitterroot	Western Meadow Lark	Ponderosa Pine
Nebraska	3/ 1/1867	37	Lincoln	77,227	15	1,569,825	35	Goldenrod	Western Meadow Lark	American Elm
Nevada	10/31/1864	36	Carson City	110,540	7	799,184	47	Sagebrush	Mountain Bluebird	Single-Leaf Pinon
New Hampshire	6/21/1788	9	Concord	9,034	44	920,610	41	Common Lilac	Purple Finch	White Birch
New Jersey	12/18/1787	11	Trenton	8,219	46	7,365,011	8	Purple Violet	Eastern Goldfinch	Red Oak
New Mexico	1/ 6/1912	47	Santa Fe	121,666	5	1,303,445	37	Yucca	Road Runner	Pinon
New York	7/26/1788	11	Albany	49,576	30	17,558,072	2	Rose	Bluebird	Sugar Maple
North Carolina	11/21/1789	12	Raleigh	52,712	28	5,881,813	12	Dogwood	Cardinal	Pine
North Dakota	11/ 2/1889	39	Bismarck	70,665	17	652,717	45	Wild Prairie Rose	Western Meadow Lark	American Elm
Ohio	3/ 1/1803	17	Columbus	41,222	35	10,797,624	6	Scarlet Carnation	Cardinal	Ohio Buckeye
Oklahoma	11/16/1907	46	Oklahoma City	69,919	18	3,025,495	27	Mistletoe	Scissor-tailed Flycatcher	Redbud
Oregon	2/14/1859	33	Salem	96,981	10	2,633,149	31	Oregon Grape	Western Meadow Lark	Douglas Fir
Pennsylvania	12/12/1787	2	Harrisburg	45,333	33	11,864,751	3	Mountain Laurel	Ruffed Grouse	Eastern Hemlock
Rhode Island	5/29/1790	13	Providence	1,214	50	947,154	39	Violet	Rhode Island Red	Red Maple
South Carolina	5/23/1788	8	Columbia	31,055	40	3,122,814	26	Yellow Jessamine	Carolina Wren	Cabbage Palm
South Dakota	11/ 2/1889	40	Pierre	77,047	16	690,768	44	American Pasque	Ringnecked Pheasant	Black Hills Spruce
Tennessee	6/ 1/1796	16	Nashville	42,244	34	4,591,120	17	Iris	Mockingbird	Tulip Poplar
Texas	12/29/1845	28	Austin	267,339	2	14,227,574	4	Bluebonnet	Mockingbird	Pecan
Utah	1/ 4/1896	45	Salt Lake City	84,916	11	1,461,037	36	Sego Lily	California Gull	Blue Spruce
Vermont	3/ 4/1791	14	Montpelier	9,609	43	511,456	48	Red Clover	Hermit Thrush	Sugar Maple
Virginia	6/25/1788	10	Richmond	40,815	36	5,346,797	14	Flowering Dogwood	Cardinal	Flowering Dogwood
Washington	11/11/1889	42	Olympia	68,192	20	4,132,204	22	Coast Rhododendron	American Goldfinch	Western Hemlock
West Virginia	6/20/1863	35	Charleston	24,181	41	1,950,258	34	Rosebay Rhododendron	Cardinal	Sugar Maple
Wisconsin	5/29/1848	30	Madison	56,154	26	4,705,642	16	Butterfly Violet	Robin	Sugar Maple
Wyoming	7/10/1890	44	Cheyenne	97,914	9	469,557	49	Wyoming Paint Brush	Western Meadow Lark	Plains Cottonwood
District of Columbia	12/ 1/1800	*	* * *	* * *	*	638,432	*	* * *	* * *	* * *

Reprinted by permission. Information presented on pp. 108-11, *The Book of the States* by Vincent Wilson, Jr. The American History Research Associates, Inc., 1972.

NOTES

NOTES

NOTES